Jörn Rüsen, Henner Laass (eds.)
Humanism in Intercultural Perspective

CW00384212

Being Human: Caught in the Web of Cultures
Humanism in the Age of Globalization   Volume I

Editorial

Globalization demands for setting up new cultural orientations. Different traditions and forms of life struggle for recognition throughout the world and have to meet the necessity of values and norms with universal validity. Similarities and differences in understanding the world have to be analyzed and recognized which requires a new reflection on what it means to be a human being concerning its anthropological universality, but also its diverseness and changeability.

The books of the series **Being Human: Caught in the Web of Cultures – Humanism in the Age of Globalization** are committed to a new Humanism, which not only highlights humaneness in its cultural and historical varieties but also presents it as a transculturally valid principle of human interaction in all cultural life-forms.

The series is edited by Jörn Rüsen (Essen), Chun-chieh Huang (Taipei), Oliver Kozlarek (Mexico City) and Jürgen Straub (Bochum), Assistant Editor: Henner Laass (Essen).

Advisory board:
Peter Burke (Cambridge), Chen Qineng (Beijing), Georg Essen (Nijmegen), Ming-huei Lee (Taipei), Surendra Munshi (Calcutta), Erhard Reckwitz (Essen), Masayuki Sato (Yamanashi), Helwig Schmidt-Glintzer (Wolfenbüttel), Zhang Longxi (Hong Kong)

JÖRN RÜSEN, HENNER LAASS (EDS.)

Humanism in Intercultural Perspective

Experiences and Expectations

[transcript]

In Cooperation with the Institute for Advanced Study in the Humanities, Essen, the Institute for Advanced Studies in Humanities and Social Sciences, National Taiwan University, the Faculty of Humanities of the University Duisburg/Essen

Printed with support of the Stiftung für Kulturwissenschaften (Essen).

Humanism in the Era of Globalization – An Intercultural Dialogue
on Humanity, Culture, and Value
sponsored by Stiftung Mercator

**Bibliographic information published by
the Deutsche Nationalbibliothek**
The Deutsche Nationalbibliothek lists this publication in the Deutsche Nationalbibliografie; detailed bibliographic data are available in the Internet at http://dnb.d-nb.de

Cover layout: Kordula Röckenhaus, Bielefeld
Proofread by: Shari Gilbertsen
Typeset by: Mark-Sebastian Schneider, Bielefeld
Printed by: Majuskel Medienproduktion GmbH, Wetzlar
ISBN 978-3-8376-1344-5

Distributed in North America by

Transaction Publishers
New Brunswick (U.S.A.) and London (U.K.)
Transaction Publishers   Tel.: (732) 445-2280
Rutgers University   Fax: (732) 445-3138
35 Berrue Circle   for orders (U.S. only):
Piscataway, NJ 08854   toll free 888-999-6778

Content

Part III: Religious Dimensions

Part IV: Perspectives of Interpretation

Part V: Towards the Future

Foreword

JÖRN RÜSEN

This book is based on the presentations and discussions of a conference on "Humanism in the Era of Globalization, an Intercultural Dialogue on Culture, Humanity, and Values," which took place from July 6th till 8th 2006 in Essen. The conference was the ceremonial opening of an international research project with the same title as the conference. This project is run by the Institute of Advanced Study in the Humanities (Kulturwissenschaftliches Institut - KWI) in Essen (Germany) in close cooperation with the neighbouring universities of Bochum, Dortmund, and Duisburg-Essen. It is sponsored by the Stiftung Mercator, Essen.

As the head of the project I would like to express my gratitude to different persons and institutions. First of all I would like to thank Rüdiger Frohn, chair of the board of the Stiftung Mercator, for his interest in our work, his constructive criticism and generous advice. With his rich experience in politics and his interest in basic questions of cultural orientation and its practical realization he has stimulated the work of the project from its very beginning. Additionally, the insistence of the Stiftung Mercator to cooperate with the three Ruhr-Universities, has lead to new ways of cooperation across institutional borders and has set a paradigm of the further work of the KWI.

Without the support of the crew of the KWI in Essen the project would not have effectively run. A special thank goes to Norbert Jegelka, its chief administrator, for his competence in planning and management. I am grateful to Irmtraud Seebold and Martin Gieselmann for their engagement in managing the project. Together with Norbert Jegelka they civilized my anti-burocratic attitudes and academic anarchism. They mastered the difficulties of bringing together and integrating a group of very different researchers and of giving their common work an effective form. Furthermore, they prepared and realized the very different activities of the project like conferences, workshops, a post-graduate school, visiting scholars, cooperation with schools and institutes of political education etc.

I would like to express my thanks to the contributors for their texts and their willingness to follow my quests for shaping them into the framework of this book. I am grateful to Henner Laass who as my assistant editor contributed to this book with of lot of conducive criticisms and ideas, Angelika Wulff for her intensive work on the manuscripts and to Shari Gilbertsen for her inestimable help in correcting the language of the papers. Special thanks are owed to the Stiftung für Kulturwissenschaft (Essen) for their appreciation of the work of the humanism-project and their decision to support the publication of the book.

Finally, I would like to thank my partners all over the world who joined my enthusiasm for a new humanism and gave it the necessary openness and flexibility: Chen Qineng and Jiang Peng from the Chinese Academy of the Social Sciences in Beijing, Huang Chun-Chieh from the Institute of Advanced Study in the Humanities and Social Sciences at the National Taiwan University in Taipei, Bernhard Lategan from the Stellenbosch Institute for Advanced Study in South Africa, Surendra Munshi and Ranjan Ghosh from India, Masayuki Sato from Japan, Johann Tempelhoff from South Africa, Oliver Kozlarek from Mexico, and many others.

I hope that with the engagement of its many co-operators the project will substantially contribute to an intercultural communication, – not only on the level of academic discourse – which will confirm and develop the validity of human dignity across and within different traditions and life forms all over the world.

Essen, July 2009   *Jörn Rüsen*

Introduction.

Humanism in the Era of Globalization: Ideas on a New Cultural Orientation

Jörn Rüsen

> The purpose of study is nothing but humanity. Humanity is the virtue by which Heaven participates in us.
>
> *Cui Shu*[1]

1. A New Kind of Humanism is Necessary

One of the most important intellectual tasks of the present is the development of a new kind of humanism. Current global conflicts in politics, economics, culture and religion call out strongly for defining and strengthening a global culture of values and humanity. Fundamentalism and terrorism, as well as hunger, poverty and misery in many parts of the world provide quite sufficient evidence for the necessity of this. The absence of equilibrium in world economic structures, the insufficient will to implement the principles of good governance on the part of many of the world's regimes plus powerful societal tensions, require new and better responses to the call for a new order; but they also necessitate the constructive dialogical and intercultural establishment of a value system before this order can be accepted as either new, or indeed for that matter, constructive. It is equally necessary to evolve an understanding of humankind in the era of globalization which, while inclusive of all civilizations, will at the same time emphasize their particularity and diversity. This understanding should impart normative elements of cultural orientation to all arenas of intercultural encounter and communication. Since we as human beings share a common nature and as this nature includes the mental formations of culture – giving sense and

---

1 | Cui Shu: Lun Yu Yu Shuo. Quoted in German by Quirin 1994: 389.

meaning to human life – and because this self- awareness ("humanness") includes the normative elements of our lives as they are practiced, there is a chance to come to an agreement on such a comprehensive view of cultural orientation without sacrificing either our identities or alterities.

All cultural traditions include humanistic elements. "Humanistic" simply means that the fact of being a human being ascribes to every one of us a worthiness in relationship both to others and to the self. But these traditional elements are not sufficient to the challenges involved in grafting valid universal norms onto the globalization process; for even if they have a universalistic dimension their validity is pre-eminently limited to the dimension of that culture within which these particular norms have been developed. At the very least, people of other cultures with different traditions would hesitate to accept them within a global value system without critical reflexion.

After the traumatic events of the 20ᵗʰ century, traditional European humanism, with its obvious ethnocentric features had to undergo fundamental criticism as revealed in the light of post-modernism and post-colonialism. In the West it has mostly been replaced by a form of cultural relativism that fails to solve the urgent problems of intercultural communication which have become evident since the September 11 incident.

In the face of the challenge posed by globalization, the cultural orientation of the present is faced with two distinctive options: one would be (and is fast becoming) a clash of civilizations; the other could be the development of a new trans-cultural ethos of mutual recognition based on the shared norms of a dialogue aimed at mutual understanding.

In western civilization humanism has always been a central issue within the humanities; but having lost a considerable amount of credibility in the wake of the intense self-critiquing undertaken on the part of western post-modern and post-colonial theorists, it now plays only an insignificant role if one does not entertain the idea of a return to such a style of non-viable traditionalism in the future. This situation is highly problematic, as there are pressing requirements calling for newly viable concepts of what it means to be human. And only by way of the humanities and social sciences, and the hope that their rational arguments will lead to a general agreement, can such concepts be developed.

2. The Role of a New Humanism in the Clash of Civilizations

The present intercultural debate is marked by a concept of civilization that is closely related to separate cultural traditions and places world civilizations in merely superficial relationships with one another; and being regarded by the followers of Spengler and Toynbee to be independent and autonomous constructions of human world concepts and the orientation of human action. Their concepts of Man are characterized by differences which can't be synthesized into unity.

All world civilizations have developed universalistic concepts of humankind, i.e. concepts that claim to be valid for all people. These however, reveal culturally specific traits and are thereby different. On the level of conceptual discourse, the relation between different world civilizations can be defined as a contest of universalistic concepts of humanity – these concepts often being arrayed against each other: The way in which non-European nations in particular (China, India, Japan, Africa, parts of Latin America) are gaining a new-found self-confidence to enter into the intellectual trends that globalization represents, is a clear move against the historically dominant West. There is also a tendency on the part of these societies to define and highlight themselves against the West in cultural terms, a tendency which is encouraged by the dominant currents throughout western intellectual discourse: The West is engaging in an on-going painful self-critique in which it is divesting itself of its own traditional universalistic humanism and is instead cultivating a form of cultural relativism that has abandoned these outmoded universalistic standards of humanity.

This surrendering by the West goes along with the relativization of those insights within the humanities claiming to be of universal validity; and it goes along with their losing the function of giving orientation to society. Together with the anti-western attitude of many non-European countries in their identity building process, both tendencies create a tense atmosphere. There is still no general concept of communication that different cultural traditions and claims for the recognition of one's own cultural identity can resort to.

Can differences of interrelationship be recognized on the basis of a new concept of humanity? The global situation of intercultural discourse calls for a culture where these differences can be recognized. The tendency towards fundamentalism in world religions more than sufficiently proves this need.

In their basically oppositional development, forms of cultural identity have developed concepts of humanity that go beyond ethnic, national, or even cultural limits. Instead of using this universalism against each other, it would be more sensible to integrate it into a general concept of humanity where cultural differences are conceptualized as internal differentiations of a universal idea of humankind. In theory, the clash of civilizations in the sense of a clash of different cultural identities would thus be overcome and new forms of discursive understanding would be made possible.

Such a project is not realized through minor academic debates but needs to be drafted, tried out and convincingly developed over a long process of critical dialogue between representatives of different civilizations.

3. New Humanism and Global Economics[2]

It is often held that cultural convergence is a major factor of globalization. To those who believe in this line of reasoning it is a forgone conclusion that certain institutions such as capital markets are organized according to best practice and thus prevail in the global competition due to their advanced efficiency and growth. A well-known example is intellectual property rights. Under the guidance of the WTO there is a worldwide process of formalized homogenization under way which has resulted in conflicts. Countries such as China are forced to take action against their own internal culturally divergent attitudes towards intellectual property rights. But it is still an open question as to whether or not such a convergence is in fact a necessity. As developments in the software industry in recent years have shown, intellectual property rights might become irrelevant in the light of technological advances overtaking this industry. The open source paradigm then becomes a cultural factor per se that changes the criteria for cultural divergence and convergence. Technology as a product of human culture becomes a factor of cultural divergence in the realm of national economies.

This is but one example showing that the evolution of market forces need and constantly creates diversity. On the level of national economies there is also no discernible convergence in connection to a certain institutional standard: Although Scandinavian countries hold top positions on the World Competitiveness Index, they are not found among the countries with highly liberalized markets; China, a socialist state, has an economic system that relies on Manchester Capitalism. At the same time the cultural foundation underpinning any national economic system becomes more and more transparent. The USA as an "institutional benchmark" witnesses cultural conflicts for which Christian revivalism has become a major driving force. And on the level of business there are to be found ongoing processes of comparable complexity: More and more globally active corporations realize that the shifting cultural sands on which their regional units are built do not generate only problems, but rather can be seen as a source of creativity. New disciplines such as "diversity management" are bringing this multiplicity to the level of the individual.

These historical changes sum up the quandary faced by those who would integrate humanism into economic policy. It is obvious that the market is not a means to fulfill its own ends but rather receives its objectives from forces acting from outside. However, more often than not economic factors place restrictions on the freedom of people to choose their aims. This is why a debate on humanism as it pertains to national economies is inevitable at this point. In addition humanisms' role in the global marketplace transcends the old ideological conflicts such as that between capitalism and socialism. It is a fact that the dynamics of ("free market") capitalism has contributed to the

2 | I am grateful to Prof. Carsten Herrmann-Pillath for his support in applying the idea of a new humanism to economics.

prosperity of ever increasing numbers of people. Nevertheless the questions on the "why" and "what for" of that prosperity have to be raised. Even many economists today believe that the deeper roots of economic dynamics are to be found outside the market itself. Key concepts such as social capital point at the cultural bedrock of economic systems – though culture itself is not an economic commodity. Instead, culture gains strength by being disseminated through becoming a "public commodity" that transcends privately owned interests. Humanism and its leavening role in the world's economies mark a continuing exploration of the characteristics and risks of free market capitalism.

The driving force behind modern economic policy stems from a historic change: that of a "moral economy" into market economics; the rules of the market having become superior to the principles of social responsibility. In the language of the Communist Manifesto this tendency is put into these words:

The bourgeoisie, wherever it has got the upper hand, has put an end to all feudal, patriarchal, idyllic relations. It has pitilessly torn asunder the motley feudal ties that bound man to his "natural superiors," and has left no other nexus between people than naked self-interest, than callous "cash payment." It has drowned out the most heavenly ecstasies of religious fervour, of chivalrous enthusiasm, of philistine sentimentalism, in the icy water of egotistical calculation. It has resolved personal worth into exchange value, and in place of the numberless indefeasible chartered freedoms, has set up that single, unconscionable freedom – Free Trade.[3]

Modern capitalism can be understood as an amoral economic system. Today one can observe a re-moralization: On the level of macro-economics we can observe the world-wide efforts to frame a market economy into sets of political and social rules which might tame its dynamics for the benefit of the majority of the worlds' population. Economic policies have always been politically and socially contextualized; but in the globalization process have transgressed all national borders, and it seems that there is no alternative trans-national influence conciliatory to the meta-economic needs of the people whose lives are radically conditioned by the forces of the market. But there is a growing awareness that an economic system which follows exclusively its own rules can become self destructive, and according to this criticism a world-wide effort has emerged to overcome this "market fundamentalism" (George Soros) in favour of a "capitalism with a human face."[4] On the level of business administration the growing importance of "corporate social responsibility" as a factor of practical activity corresponds to this tendency. Following from

---

3 | http://www.anu.edu.au/polsci/marx/classics/manifesto.html [24.08.2007]; the German text in: Marx/Engels 1972: 464 ff.

4 | The "Global Marshall Plan Initiative" is a paradigmatic example. Cf. Radermacher 2004.

this, humanism can become a cultural factor which might open up new perspectives of economic practice within the globalization process.

4. The New Humanism and Religion

Religion has always played an important role in the processes of the construction of human cultural identities. Today religion seems to be a worrisome obstacle to the development of a value system universal enough to have any cross-cultural relevance. Religious fundamentalism aggressively opposes any attempt to establish a universalistic humanism as a leading principle of understanding cultural diversity, since the humanist outlook very often goes along with a secular way of life. But even beyond this opposition between religion and secularism, religion remains a problem of intercultural communication. At the very moment when religious belief combines with universal truth-claims it negates all other belief systems as untrue, thus invalidating any differing religious views as to the nature of truth. The only solution seems to be to overcome the specific and peculiar forms of religious zealotry in favour of a common universalistic morality or system of ethics (Küng 1995). But religion cannot be reduced to or even dissolved into morality. It remains, alongside its own logic, within the domain of cultural orientation. Does this logic inevitably lead to exclusion and negation: Might it not, on the strength of universalistic truth claims, reconsider its own position? If this type of universalism achieves a humanistic quality, it may change its relationship to other universalisms; from that of exclusiveness to a universal inclusiveness.

5. The Challenges Posed by Dehumanization

The most radical challenge to a new humanism is the traumatic historical experience of crimes against humanity. These crimes have disfigured the features of human history with many large, cancerous dark spots, radically questioning any humanistic notions of history fashionable with modern historical thinking since the Enlightenment and its follower Historicism and with the many forms of "new history" in the 20th and 21st century. There are a lot of moral arguments in favour of creating a new humanism in order to solve the problem of intercultural communication within the modern globalized agenda. But how valid is morality if it does not correspond to history? If the impression of inhumanity prevails, is humanism only a utopian vision, unable to address the real problems of human existence? The Holocaust is a paradigm for this challenging inhumanity, representative in its most radical formulation. The answer must come in the form of a "new" humanism which interweaves anthropological insights into the fragility and fallibility of human life with the development of new categories of historical interpretation while also stressing the impact that suffering has on human potential and development and changing traditional historical interpretive criteria into much more open-ended ones (see Rüsen 2008b: 191-200).

Finally, another challenge to humanism must be stressed: the growing power of concepts of naturalism in current intellectual life. By speaking of "humanity" as a principle of human self-understanding and as a guideline for human life-in-practice, humanism emphasizes the cultural qualities of civilized people as essentially different from being in a state of nature, let alone from all other species in the visible world. Herder expressed this trans-natural "nature" of humankind by addressing his fellow men as *Freigelassene der Schöpfung* (released slaves of the creation) (Herder 2002, vol. III/1: 135). This has to be understood as man liberated from the *limitations* of nature, from the submission to the constraints of living by its laws. Man has brought about another order of existence with new laws, namely the laws of reason and morality, the commitment to which defines the humanity of humans. Different from all other natural beings which were thrown into a pre-determined order of existence, human beings have created this order themselves, facilitated by their competence in generating the sense-making interpretive criteria of their lives for themselves. Realizing this competency in the multiplicity of culture, human life has to be understood as a process of cultivating one's own unique character. Humanity is itself a process by which self-empowerment goes beyond all natural limits and leads us into the world of culture – since culture is the opposite of nature. It is constituted by a set of values and norms which have to be ascribed to every single member of the human race. This set of values has changed in the course of time, but some common features nevertheless can be enumerated: The idea of equality, the entitlement to basic rights, social cohesion as a consequence of the fragility of human life, and the general moral rule that these values and norms which a person or social group feels entitled to or committed to should be valid for each and every other person and social group as well.

It is this emphasis on a normative concept of the "cultural nature of man" which puts humanism in stark contrast and opposition to all movements aimed toward "naturalizing" human nature. For the sense-making world of humans, the term "naturalism" is exclusively defined with reference to the biological attributes of the human race. Today humanism is challenged by powerfully argued biological theories aimed at understanding human behaviour through reference to the genetic conditions of human life and by the physical structuring of the human brain.

In this respect humanism can be acknowledged as, and actually presents itself as, a critique of all such theories of human nature (cf. Sturma 2006). Instead it lays claim to the non-deterministic nature of the human person in so far as this pertains to the arenas of life-practice and social relationship, where all participants become referents to their cultural orientations. By this reference they can understand each other and give reasons for what they are doing, suffering, and for failure. Humanism makes human life comprehensible by referring to (subjective) reasons for what people do and not to (objective) causes of their doing. Humanism emphasizes human subjectivity as a constitutive element for rendering intelligible the world of human experience, whereas naturalism stresses only the biologically determined aspects of human life, which have a more external relationship to human subjectivity. Humanism will always argue for the values, norms and constraints of human culture, which can never be replaced by a one-sided application of scientific knowledge. Humanism insists on the principal difference between cultural knowledge humans always use in giving their lives meaning and significance on the one hand, and the logic of scientific knowledge and its rational explanation by referring to causal laws.

6. Further Steps

This book is the first attempt to present such a worldwide humanism which can inspire the different fields of human activities and social practices, encompassing different traditions and world views and at the same time giving place for these differences in the common processes of globalization. It is impossible to address all the above mentioned issues within the scope of any single article, but the field in general is brought more into focus. The first part seeks to thematize the present situation by referring to different cultural traditions and their roles in shaping world views within which the different cultures have to face their common destiny, the challenge of globalization. Two non-European voices present humanism as an answer to this challenge using their different and unique perspectives. But within these different perspectives a common tendency is visible: At one glance, Euro-centric dominance in shaping humanist thought has been relegated to the back shelves; but at the same time its influence on the task of shaping a new humanism beyond a strict hegemony of one tradition over all others can still be respected and enhanced by the rich voices of humanists from many geo-historical traditions.

The second part presents a variety of cultures by thematizing the Chinese, the Indian, the African, the Islamic and the western traditions and their present-day-importance for intercultural communication. There exist, of course, more humanisms in other traditions and in cultural orientations in different places of the world. They can be addressed as potentials of humanizing the world, or they can be observed as still effective in many ways. This book does not pretend to present the range of humanisms in history and to day, but it gives an impression of its variety. The many forms of humanism are a precondition for a fruitful future-directed intercultural communication on basic values of cultural orientation. It gives hope for the emergence of a word-wide discourse, but, at the same time, it indicates the lot of work still to be done in order to bring about a new humanism which transgresses all cultural differences and opens up new spaces for acknowledging them.

The third part picks up the challenge of the religious tensions of today. The three Abrahamitic religions were addressed: Judaism, Christianity, and Islam. All of them have their own humanistic elements and anti-human dangers. The constellation of contributions lends an image which presents religion as an essential element of future-directed, and at the same time, necessarily self-critical analysis for the development of these humanist dialogues. Religious differences have the power to divide human kind into conflicting parties. But religion itself has always been a power of transgressing the borders of division of people as well. It has united the people beyond their ethnic, national and cultural differences without ignoring them. It is this power in the depths of the human mind where religious beliefs move the lives of the people, which is necessary for the strength of a new humanism in the intercultural communication of today.

The fourth part is dedicated to three approaches to humanism: the issue of gender in shaping humanism, the importance of literature, and social conditions of cultural life. Nobody can deny that the normative character of being a human being has been realized in highly different chances and degrees. One of the most important goes along the line of gender difference. This difference is historically changing, of course, and especially so in the process of modernization. It would be a simplistic view to diagnose a growing equality; but if humanism is aware of the importance of gender the criteria of equality should be applied in a critical way against the different traditions and for a future perspective of change and alteration.

Last, but at all least, literature is presented as an important cultural medium without which humanism will lose the empowering force of the human imagination. Without the imaginative forces of the human mind the new humanism in concern can't be articulated and realized. Humanism should be considered as a moving cultural force in political, economic and social life. But its sense-generating power has to go beyond the limits of this "reality" into the realms of imagination, fantasy and fiction. It will not escape the constraints of practical life, but empower the human mind to go beyond it and to make it more humane.

The idea of humanism must always to be put into social contexts in order to make it plausible and give it its place in real life. Looking at the issue of human values only in the field of culture, i.e. in the processes of human sense generation, will miss it. Humanism has to be understood and further developed as a mental and spiritual element within the constraints and burdens of concrete social life. Here is the place where its solidity and soundness are being tried and tested.

At the end, three outlooks are presented which address the future of humanism. This future is a matter of organizing and critically reflecting intercultural communication as the special field of cultural activities all over the word. It is a matter of thematizing cultural difference under the auspices of the unity of mankind come and it is a matter of experiences and strategies of practical life, especially in the field of politics.

Taking all parts of the book together, it presents conditions and chances to meet the cultural challenges of globalisation and to give answers that may open a door to a new vision of what it means to be a human being and to a way of life, in which the idea of human dignity is moving the minds of the people.

Part I: The Challenge of Globalization

Humanism in a Global World

DIPESH CHAKRABARTY

1.

As we leave the shores of the 20th century to move into the uncharted waters of the twenty-first, we look behind to take our bearings for the future. Is there a way of summing up our immediate past? Is there any one problem that defines the 20th century? Of course, a century is a long span of time marked by many different developments. Yet certain problems sometimes come to the fore. We can think of the European eighteenth century as a global period that saw Holland, France and Britain replace Spain and Portugal as founders of modern empires, and as a period of Enlightenment that upheld powerfully an abstract idea of the human equality. It was also, ironically, a period that overlooked the problem of slavery and the question of discrimination against women. The 19th century – some very important critics (among whom we have to count Nietzsche) notwithstanding – concluded on a high note of progress, leaving to the peoples of less industrialized and colonized nations the legacies of Marxism and liberalism as the two greatest gifts of European political thought. How would one see the global history of the 20th century? From what developments of the 20th century shall we derive our resources to deal with the future?

There could no doubt be more than one answer to this question. Let me begin with one that we have already been given, for this is an answer that bears significantly on the theme of this essay: Humanism in an age of globalization.[1] "The problem of the 20th century", wrote the great African-America thinker W. E. B. Du Bois peering into the future just as the century began, "is the problem of the color-line" (Du Bois 1989 [1903]: 13). He was prescient in saying this. Du Bois' color line ran right through the colonial divide in the first fifty or sixty years (or longer in case of South Africa) of the century and through the lives of those whose ancestors had lived through

---

1 | The author is grateful to Professor Jörn Rüsen for the original invitation to present this paper at a conference he organized in Essen in 2006 and to discussions with both Professor Rüsen and other participants in the seminar.

Atlantic systems of slavery. In Du Bois' words, the color-line concerned "the relation of the darker to the lighter races of men in Asia and Africa, in America and the islands of the sea" (Du Bois 1989 [1903]: 13). The same line also divided the indigenous peoples from their white settler-colonial rulers and, as we know, assumed a vicious form in the biological racism of the Nazis. Even when it did not assume the menacingly virulent form of the Nazi imagination, biological racism or varieties of social Darwinism underpinned administrative policies in European colonies. Cultural and historical differences were often used by European colonizers to make subordinated peoples look like inferior and deprived versions of humanity. There were, of course, contrary and anti-imperial voices in Europe – Sankar Muthu's book on the Enlightenment comes to mind – but they usually did not set the tone of policy as European empires consolidated themselves (Muthu 2003).

Du Bois, however, also pointed to a more positive side of the color-line. He said that "the characteristic of our age" was "the contact of European civilization with the world's underdeveloped peoples." It was true that much of this contact, as he put it, was "not pleasant to look back upon." "War, murder, slavery, extermination, and debauchery, – this has again and again been the result of carrying civilization and the blessed gospel to the isles of the sea and the heathen without the law."[2] But the very fact of close contact between Europeans and others in large numbers and in everyday life also opened new human opportunities that, Du Bois hoped, would taken up by leaders in the 20th century. Du Bois words were prescient. They powerfully expressed a certain humanism of the oppressed while perhaps reflecting at the same time certain nineteenth-century ideas about evolution and civilizational hierarchies. There were even some faint echoes of Nietzsche in the association he made between nobility and strength. This is what he said:

It is, then, the strife of all honorable men of the 20th century to see that in the future competition of races the survival of the fittest shall mean the triumph of the good, the beautiful, and the true; that we may be able to preserve for future civilization all that is really fine and noble and strong, and not continue to put premium on greed and impudence and cruelty (Du Bois 1989 [1903]: 134).

To overcome the color-line and preserve for humanity all that was good, beautiful, and true is how Du Bois posed the task for his time. One can look on Mahatma Gandhi, Martin Luther King Jr., and Nelson Mandela as men who embodied, howsoever partially, the 20th century's realization of Du Bois' dream.

Our times are different. They are different in two principal ways. First of all, the color line does not quite run in the way in did in colonial, Nazi, or apartheid regimes. "Racism" as an ideological belief in a hierarchy of biological races has lost its coherence and has very few followers today, but the word is still

---

2 | "Of the Sons of Master and Men," in: Du Bois 1989 [1903]: 133.

used to denote the multitude of ways in which human beings are inferiorized, marginalized, demeaned, threatened, excluded and de-humanized on the basis of the way they look or on the basis of a devalorization of their group identity. As the philosopher Etienne Balibar has put it: on one hand "racism" no longer really exists and on the other, subtle forms of racial profiling and discrimination proliferate. It is not surprising, as Professor Balibar explained in a recent lecture he gave at the University of Chicago, that the riots of November 2005 by the youth of north-African descent in the suburbs of Paris had something to do with forms of policing and administration that were copied directly from France's colonial practices (Balibar 2006).

The second big difference that marks the 21st century apart from the 20th one is in the way discussions of globalization now have to take into account another global phenomenon: climate change or global warming. One could risk the proposition that if the question of the 20th century was the color line, the question of this century will be the environment. Now, the literature on globalization and that of global warming view the human being in rather different ways. The former views the human being as endowed with cultural and historical differences; so major questions in globalization analyses turn around the issue of what to do and how to understand differences between humans (hence the emphases on toleration, cosmopolitanism, cross-cultural conversation, etc.). The literature on global warming, on the other hand, views humans as already always constituted as one, as members perhaps of a species that through its simultaneous co-existence on the planet and its shared, though uneven, search for the good life, has degraded its own biosphere and the general environment (see Chakrabarty 2009: 197-222).

In spite of this important difference, however, it is my submission that policies of global strategies for mitigating the effects of climate change will have to take into account sentiments borne out of anti-colonial struggles in many parts of the world – witness how both India and China, in their bargaining with Western nations over measures to be adopted to fight global warming, keep harping on the historical self-interestedness of the Western nations. So the literature on globalization will remain relevant even as we begin to accept our collective responsibility in creating environmental problems that affect us on a planetary scale. It is because they see the world still divided between the West and the Rest, that China and India put the stress on seeing this collective and shared responsibility as "differentiated." Let me repeat, then, a point Balibar has made on several occasions (Balibar 2005; Balibar 2003: 37-44). We live in a world that is postcolonial in two senses. We have all been profoundly affected by the waves of decolonization that shook latter half of the 20th century. And, increasingly, movements of people in large numbers across the world – mainly from the South to the North, propelled by all kinds of crises ranging from the political to the environmental – ensures that most developed countries today have significant numbers of people from parts of the world previously colonized by European powers. The question of what to do with cultural and historical differences between human groups – to which what is called racism is merely a default response – only becomes more insistent as we enter a post-colonial world in which more people move around from one place to another as migrants and refugees, legal or illegal, skilled or unskilled; a world in which multinational and global or regional agencies, whether private or governmental, supplement the nation-state; an age in which even the phenomenon of so-called terrorism cannot but be a multicultural and multinational enterprise. Given what the United Nations project to be the world's population growth in the next four decades – a one and a half times increase to nine billions is their median projection – and the ageing populations of the richer countries, one can safely predict that this will see further large-scale population movements in the world from the South to the North. Climate change will contribute to the process. So the problems of global warming will have to be dealt with in a world that has also been shaped by the processes and cultural politics of globalization.

The globalized world is what we inhabit: connected, fluvial, and "flat" and crowded, as the Indian software entrepreneur Nandan Nilekeni put it and as the expression has been adopted by the *New York Times* columnist, Thomas Friedman (see Friedman 2006: 4-8). On the one hand, this is an exciting world full of human possibilities as we increasingly come into contact with people who are not like ourselves. It should promote an ethos of cosmopolitanism throughout the world, whether officially so-called or not. This could be a world that actually promoted more human toleration and understanding by generating identifications that challenged and crossed national boundaries. On the other hand, the presence of cultural differences could also produce more prejudice and fear. One powerful version of this fear that has acquired some notoriety is, of course, Huntington's thesis about the clash of civilizations. Another has been the fear of refugees and immigrants (legal and illegal) in many countries of the Western democracies. Besides, as Foucault pointed out in his lectures at College de France in 1976 – published in English under the title "*Society Must be Defended*" – the ways modern societies manage populations on a large scale (methods that Foucault called Regulation in order to distinguish them from his idea of Discipline) undermine liberal principles of government (Foucault 2003). Governments have never officially subscribed to the Huntington thesis, with even President Bush acknowledging that civilizations, including the Islamic one, are always internally plural and contradictory. But it is clear that as Western governments necessarily become more security-minded in the fight against ill-defined and seemingly interminable forces of terror, they adopt "emergency" measures that both undercut civil liberties and are deployed at the same time to control immigration as well. Given the nature of modern "terrorism," this is an emergency with no end in sight!

When Hannah Arendt wrote *The Human Condition* in the late 1950s, she did so, as she put it, from "the vantage point of our newest experiences and our most recent fears." (Arendt 1998 [1958]: 5). Globalization, I submit, has been simultaneously a site of our "newest experiences and our most recent fears" about fellow human beings. (I leave aside the kind of experiences and alarmed reactions global warming has given rise to.) It is therefore all the more urgent that we devote our collective attention to questions of humanism and to the problem of how to think about and relate to – or even converse across – cultural and historical differences. Globalization often appears as a "blind force" in people's lives making them a "victim" of it. Yet, if we are to participate, however vicariously, in some sense of having agency over its processes, we need to be able to spell out visions of humanity that propel such a movement. Questions abound. Will globalization lead to one global culture that the media will both mold and sell? Will globalization mean that all our claims to cultural differences will survive only if we can make such differences into marketable commodities so that "local" becomes merely an inflection of global capitalism? Or will globalization lead to the emergence of a universal humanism that is enriched by numerous particulars? The time has come for the world to produce a new charter of humanism, now that the nation-state is no longer the exclusive repository of cultural difference. The problem, if anything, is accentuated by the emergent crisis of climate change, for we cannot strategically become "one" – which is what we in part need to do to act in unison on questions of global warming – if our claims to difference are ridden roughshod over.

Is the past a resource in addressing our present concerns? How do we find those moments in human history when human beings have desired togetherness without their differences being made into excuses for domination? I want to begin by suggesting that one exemplary archive of such thought would be the writings of anti-colonial and anti-imperial thinkers of the 20th century. These were people deeply engaged with the traditions that made Europe modern and who yet knew first-hand the exclusionary tendencies of the humanism that European colonizers preached to the colonized. These thinkers felt compelled to consider afresh the problem of being human and to reflect on the need for a new kind of humanist charter as part of their effort to build a world in which the domination of humans by humans would be finished for once and for all. This was utopian thought to be sure – for I am enough of a Nietzchean to grant the will to power that animates human existence in everyday life – but a utopian thought that was badly needed. For there could not be any modern anti-colonial movement without utopian dreams of a world without domination; it was such utopian dreams that one hurled at the face of one's enemy, the colonial masters. The utopian nature of anti-colonial thought is also exposed in the fact that no ex-colonial nation, on independence, has ever kept the promise it made with itself while fighting the indignity of colonial rule. Postcolonial states and nations have often repeated the sins of colonial rule with respect to their own populations (see my "introduction" to Chakrabarty/Majumdar/Sartori 2007). Yet anti-colonial, utopian humanism remains valuable as an archive precisely because this humanism turns around certain axes – the universal versus the particular, the ideal versus the pragmatic, the past as a resource (tradition, as in the hands of a Tagore or Gandhi) versus the need to overcome the past – that often act as organizing themes for contemporary debates as well.

2.

My case in point is the anti-colonial humanism of Frantz Fanon. Utopian thought is unrealizable by definition. In that sense it always fails. Fanon's thoughts are interesting because his is a rich and instructive case of failure. Fanon, who was born in Martinique in 1925 and who died in a Washington hospital in the United States in 1961, was a product and prisoner of European thought. Indeed, it is impossible to think of his works without reference to the Parisian milieu of Marxism, existentialism, and psychiatry of the 1940s and the 1950s. But he was also someone who burned with a spirit of rebellion against the way European colonial rule and its attendant racism showed up what was problematic in the colonizing humanism of Europeans. As he declaimed, angrily and with some rhetorical liberties, asking for a new beginning to human history: "Leave this Europe where they are never done talking of man, yet murder men everywhere they find them" (Fanon 1968: 311). But where would one go, leaving "this" Europe? Not back to a blackness that had been proclaimed by Fanon's mentors such as Leopold Sédar Senghor (1906-2001), the Senegalese poet and intellectual and later President of the country, and Aime Césaire (1913-2008), the poet who was once Fanon's teacher in Martinique and was later to be the mayor of Fort de France and a deputy to the French parliament, both of them among the foremost creators of the Negritude movement in Paris in the 1930s and the 40s. That option did not work for Fanon and we will soon see why. For him, there was nowhere to go but to create a new beginning with European thought outside of Europe, to rescue from Europeans their heritage of the abstract humanism of the Enlightenment – the human who is the subject of the idea of human rights as spelled out at the end of the eighteenth century – and make that everybody's heritage everywhere. Fanon was never a nationalist and never failed to acknowledge what one owed to Europe: "All the elements of a solution to the great problems of humanity have, at different times, existed in European thought." The problem was that the "action of European men has not carried out the mission which fell to them." (Fanon 1968: 314). America was no alternative model either, for its institution of slavery mocked at every step its loyalty to the values of the Enlightenment:

Two centuries ago, a former European colony decided to catch up with Europe. It succeeded so well that the United States of America became a monster, in which the taints, the sickness, and the inhumanity of Europe have grown to appalling dimensions (Fanon 1968: 313).

Hence the option before the Third World – for Fanon wrote at a time when this concept still held ground – could be not that of catching up with Europe or becoming like America (i.e. modernization programs). The choice, according to Fanon, was profoundly new and yet in a deep sense connected to Europe:

Let us create the whole man, whom Europe has been incapable of bringing to triumphant birth. [...] No, there is no question of return to Nature. It is simply a concrete question of not dragging men toward mutilation [...]. No, we do not want to catch up with anyone. What we want to do is to go forward all the time, night and day, in the company of Man, in the company of all men. [...] It is a question of the Third World starting a new history of Man, a history which will have regard to the sometimes prodigious theses which Europe has put forward, but which will also not forget Europe's crimes, of which the most horrible was committed in the heart of man [...] (Fanon 1968: 313-315).

The target of Fanon's new universalism was not merely the failed application of universalist thought by European colonists who always replaced the abstract figure of the human or man by that of the white man, saying to the Native, "be like me!" and thus mistaking sameness for equality and setting up the never-ending game of the Native always having to catch up (the French called it "assimilation") with the European (see the excellent discussion in Wilder 2005: part 2). Fanon was disagreeing with his mentors as well – Césaire and Senghor. Both Senghor and Césaire – deeply immersed in Parisian debates to do with Hegel and dialectics, Heidegger and existentialism, Breton and Surrealism – rejected the French republican and universalist version of colonial humanism. The French, as is well known, granted colonized people French nationality without full citizenship that they advocated only for a tiny native elite, depending on their perceived stage of evolution. Alternatively, as Gary Wilder has shown in his book on French cultural policies in their colonial territories, "educated elites were supposed to be those exceptional natives who had become autonomous individuals." "Yet they were identified as incipient individuals who were never yet ready to assume full citizenship rights because of the irreducible residue of African culture they supposedly could not transcend." Wilder thus characterizes the imperatives of what he calls colonial (and official) humanism as "individualism without individuality, collectivity without collectivism, citizenship without culture, nationality without citizenship, training without civil society" (Wilder 2005: 133-135; 143).

This was a humanism that belittled the colonized. Senghor and Césaire were right to reject it. Instead, they used their poetic gifts and their affiliations with a variety of aesthetic movements – black literature coming out of the African-American diaspora, existentialism, French and German colonial ethnography, Surrrealism, and Marxism – to develop a poetic diction that emphasized their refusal to be assimilated into French universalist ideas by exploring, creatively, the different dimensions of their blackness and African roots. It was as if they declared a war of the particular against the universal. The result was the famous Negritude movement that both invigorated and disturbed many Black intellectuals including Fanon and, later, Wole Soyinka who once famously asked, in criticism and banter, "Does the Tiger need to display its Tigritude?"

There has been much written on the works of Negritude writers and on Senghor and Césaire specifically and I do not intend to revisit that literature here. What is of interest to me is the fact that this war of the particular against the universal was not anti-universal in itself. Césaire and Senghor were definitely trying to resist the French imperial attempt to assimilate them into a Frenchness that for the colonized could only be an instrument of exclusion and oppression. They would therefore – and by way of claiming their roots – seek to introduce into their works images and sounds of an Africa they expressed nostalgia for: the Africa of sensuality, of nights where the tom tom beat out its rhythms to the "music of Koras and the Balaphon," and of villages that did not aim to expand, occupy, and civilize the land of others. As Senghor wrote in one of his poems:

At the bend in the road the river, blue by the cool September meadows.
A paradise protecting from fever a child who eyes are bright like two
Swords
Paradise my African childhood, protecting innocence from Europe.
(Senghor cited in Mehta 2004: 326).

Or consider these lines from Césaire's celebrated *Notes on the Return to One's Land of Birth* – immortal monuments to anti-colonial criticism of the Europe that saw in its worldly power to subjugate others the proof its "superior" civilization:

Eia for those who have never invented anything
for those who never explored anything
for those who never conquered anything
but yield, captivated to the essence of all things
ignorant of surfaces but captivated by the motion of all things
indifferent to conquering, but playing the game of the world.
(Césaire 1939, in Wilder 2005: 287-288)

This turning back to Africa or blackness – a "will to particularism," as he once called it – was something Fanon could never accept (Fanon 1968: 239). For one thing, he thought that the Negritude movement papered over all that divided Africans from Africans or the African from the African-American or the African-American from the black people of the Antilles" (Fanon 1968: the chapter on "National Culture"). But more to the point, he believed that the black peoples of colonial Africa and even those of America and the Caribbean islands had had their pasts so changed by the colonial impact that there was no way of returning to a pre-colonial past escaping Europeans' representations of it: "Colonialism is not satisfied merely holding a people in its grip [...]. By a kind of perverted logic, it turns to the past of the oppressed people, and distorts, disfigures, and destroys it." (Fanon 1968: 210). There was nothing to be found in claiming the color-line for oneself:

The Negro problem does not resolve itself into the problem of Negroes living among white men but rather of Negroes exploited, enslaved, despised by a colonialist, capitalist society that is only accidentally white. (Fanon 1970 [1952]: 144)

Or as he put it differently in the same text: "The discovery of the existence of a Negro civilization in the fifteenth century confers no patent of humanity on me. Like it or not, the past can in no way guide me in the present moment." (Fanon 1970 [1952]: 160)

Fanon's description of Negritude poetry as a "will to particularism" was at the very least a misreading of what Césaire and Senghor and their comrades intended to achieve. It is true, as Fanon charged, that Senghor or Césaire owed their romanticism of Africa to the sympathies of colonial ethnography. The German Africanist and ethnologist Leo Frobenius, whose books were quickly translated into French, had a great influence on Senghor, for instance. Senghor actually wrote to foreword to a Frobenius anthology in 1973 and thus remembered his impact:

I still have before me [...] the copy of the *Histoire de la Civilisation Africaine* on the third page of which Césaire wrote: "décembre 1936." [...] I was intellectually on familiar terms with the greatest Africanists and above all the ethnologists and the linguists. But suddenly, like a thunderclap – Froebenius! All the history and pre-history of Africa were illuminated, to their very depths. And we still carry the mark of the master in our minds and spirits, like a form of tattooing carried out in the initiation ceremonies in the sacred grove. We knew by heart Chapter II of the first book of the History, entitled "What Does Africa Mean to Us?," a chapter adorned with lapidary phrases such as this: "The idea of the 'barbarous Negro' is a European invention, which in turn dominated Europe until the beginning of this century." (Cited in Mehta 2004: 301)

So Fanon was right: the past Senghor and Césaire related to was already a creation of European Africanists. But where Fanon misread the intention of Senghor and Césaire was in not recognizing that they also were looking for a universal humanism but through a different path. As Senghor once put it: "to be nègre is to recover what is human beneath the rust of what is artificial and of 'human conventions'" (Senghor cited in Wilder 2005: 188-189). A lecture Senghor gave at the Dakar Chamber of Commerce on September 8, 1937 sought to demonstrate "that universal humanism, when pushed to its logical limit, necessarily leads to a spatiotemporally specific cultural humanism" (Senghor cited in Wilder 2005: 235). And he was clear that he was not looking for any "authentic African culture:" "Our milieu is no longer West Africa, it is also French, it is international; we should say, it is Afro-French." Implying that "that the universal human being always and only exists in culturally mediated forms," he rejected, as Wilder puts it, both "the universalizing racism of the civilizing mission and the particularizing racism of the white supremacists" (Senghor cited in Wilder 2005: 241). In fact, the first volume of his collected works was called *Liberté: Négritude et humanisme*. He claimed that the book was a "cornerstone in the edification of the *Civilization of the Universal*, which will be the common work of all races, of all different civilizations [...]. It has been enriched by the contribution of European civilization, which it has likewise enriched. [...] Negritude is therefore not a *racism* [...] In truth, *Negritude is a Humanism*." (Senghor cited in Wilder 2005: 250)

The same could be said of Césaire whose *Notes* included the prayer: "preserve me from all hatred/ do not make me into that man of hatred for whom I only feel hatred/ for entrenched as I am in this unique race [...] that what I want is universal hunger/ for universal thirst" (Wilder 2005: 288). In an interview with René Depestre, Césaire added: "My will to be rooted is ferocious. Hegel once wrote that the universal is not the negation of the particular, because one moves toward the universal through a deepening of the particular." And in a famous letter in 1956 to Maurice Thorez, on the occasion of the resignation of his membership of the French Communist Party, Césaire remarked:

Provincialism? Not at all. I do not enclose myself in a narrow particularism. But nor do I want to lose myself in a lifeless universalism. There are two ways to lose oneself: through walled segregation within the particular and through dilution within the universal. My conception of the universal is of a universal enriched by every particular. (Wilder 2005: 290)

Césaire was intensely aware of the utopian nature of his project and that is why he found in poetry an effective resolution of the universal and the particular. In opposition to Sartre and others who thought the French language could not be an effective vehicle for the expression of Africanness or blackness, Césaire said in an interview published in 1978:

I am not a prisoner of the French language. I try and have always wanted to *bend* French. That's why I have had a strong affection for Mallarmé, because he has shown me [...] that language at bottom is arbitrary. It is not a natural phenomenon. [...] my effort has been to bend the French language, to transform it in order to express, let us say, "this self, this black, creole, Martinican, West Indian self." That is why I am much more interested in poetry than in prose, precisely to the extent that the poet creates his language. [...] I re-create a language that is not French. If the French rediscover their language in mine, well, that's their affair. (See Davis 1984: 14)

What hurt Fanon profoundly, however, was Sartre's gloss on Negritude in his introduction entitled "Black Orpheus" to Senghor's 1948 collection of Negritude poetry. Sartre described Negritude as "a temporary 'racist anti-racism' that would be transcended by the dialectic of history" (Macey 2000: 187). Fanon said to his friends, "The generation of young black poets has received a blow they will not recover from" (Fanon 1970 [1952]: 94). That blow, one feels, shaped a lot of the argument in *Black Skin White Masks*. Fanon now felt that "every hand was a losing hand." "I wanted to be typically Negro – it was no longer possible. I wanted to be white – it was a joke." (Fanon 1970 [1952]: 93-94). Sartre had made a "minor dialectic" of Negritude in the larger Hegelian schema of world transformation. The Negro's "anti-racist racism" was only a temporary phenomenon soon to be superseded by the coming of a universal-humanist consciousness: "Beyond the black-skinned men of his race it is the battle of the world proletariat that is his song." (Sartre quoted in Fanon 1970 [1952]: 94). Fanon decided that the only way open to him was to struggle for a completely new universal, not as a black man – for he only happened to be black, – and not even as a historical man descended from slaves ("I am not the slave of the Slavery that dehumanized my ancestors"). "The Negro is not." He wrote, putting a deliberate full-stop after "not" and starting a new sentence: "Any more than the white man." "There is no Negro mission; there is no white burden" (Fanon 1970 [1952]: 163-165). What there was, was the Enlightenment mission of valuing the abstract human being of human rights, someone who is entitled to our civility long before we have in any way placed him or her in any historical or social context.[3] But this was precisely the mission that the white man, self-absorbed in his arrogant sense of supremacy, was not able to carry out. How would the oppressed man of color keep that pledge to the Enlightenment? This is where Fanon mobilized the rhetorical power of the figure of redemptive violence and called for an act of complete volition by which, at one stroke, to leap out of history:

No attempt must be made to encase man, for it is his destiny to be set free.
The body of history does not determine a single one of my actions.
I am my own foundation.
And it is by going beyond the historical, instrumental hypothesis that I will
    initiate the cycle of my freedom.
[...]
I, the man of colour, want only this:
...That the enslavement of man by man cease for ever. [...] That it be possible for
    me to discover and to love man, wherever he may be.
[...]
My final prayer:
O my body, make of me always a man who questions!
(Fanon 1970 [1952]: 164-165)

3.

That debate within and about Negritude is my one of my 20th-century archives as I think of humanism in a postcolonial age of globalization. When I read about Fanon and Césaire and Senghor's restless spirit in their struggle against the colonizing humanism of the ruling race they encountered, and

---

3 | See Julia Kristeva's discussion of the French declaration of civil and human rights in Roudiez 1991.

I reconsider my own Indian background – and my background in Indian history – I realize that colonial rule was not the same everywhere, nor were the compulsions of the race-dynamic the same. A Gandhi or a Tagore or a Nehru – the three most universalist and yet profoundly Indian anti-colonial thinkers I can recall immediately – never theorized race with the intensity of Negritude writers or writers in the African-American diaspora. It was not that Indians did not come across incidents of unpleasant and extreme British arrogance. But in their experience of colonial rule, racism remained episodic rather than something constitutive of colonial relations of power. Readers of Gandhi's autobiography will notice how often in South Africa he used to think of law as a weapon against racism. Perhaps the low-castes – in particular the so-called untouchable groups – experienced something like racism but that at the hand of other Indians. The British did not oppress us quite in the way the French did in Francophone Africa or the Caribbean islands, so we bring to today's questions somewhat different legacies when we argue from the experience of colonial rule in India.

It may be said against my invocation of the familiar names of Fanon, Césaire, or Senghor that they in turn remind us of the radicalism of the sixties, forms of utopian thinking that may appear useless in the face of a world in which capitalist globalization and domination seem inexorable. Today's tasks, it may be said, ought to be humbler and pragmatic, and not echo the seductive but powerless dreams of these anti-colonial thinkers. But what use, one might counter, is a pragmatism the logic of which amounts to simple capitulation to that forces one once set out to fight? Should one not instead try and develop pragmatisms that rework and recall – in however fragmented and practical a manner – the idealisms of the past that once sought to change the world, lock, stock, and barrel? Let me give a concrete example of this phenomenon from postcolonial writing. Salman Rushdie's subversion of the English language from within may seem pragmatic and practical without being driven by a revolutionary or totalizing intent. But can one deny that it stands on the shoulders of the efforts of anti-colonial writers such as Césaire whose desire to "*bend* French" arose out of a desire for total anti-colonial autonomy?

Let me draw out some lessons from the story I have recounted in this essay. We have three positions on humanism here. Firstly, Sartre's in his "Black Orpheus" where he wanted to say that the Negritude emphasis on blackness and race – on the particular, say – was a temporary recourse to anti-racist racism, soon to be sublated into a superior term of history's dialectic, universal proletarian consciousness. Fanon's biographer, David Macey, has pointed out what was problematic about this position: "Sartre falls into a trap of his own making, and he describes that very trap in his *Reflexions* when speaks of the 'democrat's' inability to recognize the Jew in the assertion of his Jewishness and in his insistence on the need to see him [the Jew] as a universal" (Macey 2000: 187).[4] Then there was Frantz Fanon's position that called for an entirely new historical stab at Enlightenment humanism,

---

4 | Macey explains that by "democrat" Sartre meant "wooly liberal."

except that it was a task that now belonged to anti-colonial people of color. But the creation of this universal called for something like a violent action of the will, akin to jumping out of one's own skin. It has never been realized in the world and cannot be, for its extreme and deliberate inattention to history. It is a program for violence that implodes from within.[5]

We are left with Césaire's or Senghor's positions that do look for a path to universal humanism but a universal that will never able to fold completely into itself – and thereby subsume in a Hegelian way - any particular that enriches it. The Jew will be allowed his assertion of Jewishness as will be the Muslim his Muslimness, so long as the assertion of the particular does not aim to destroy the universal. What this calls for is a deeper appreciation of historicity. I want to end my talk by explaining what I mean by that expression. To do that, I need to introduce here, briefly, a distinction I make between "rootedness" and "dwelling."

Recall Césaire: "My will to be rooted is ferocious." I will read "dwelling" where Césaire uses the figure of "roots." I want to argue that human beings will always ferociously want to dwell but are seldom rooted. By rooted I mean something like a fixed and enduring relationship of persons to places. This actually seldom happens, for human beings move, if not in one or two generations then in three or four or more. Being rooted to one place is a very special privilege most of us cannot afford to enjoy. Yet, when human beings move, they almost never move to places where no humans have been before them. And they have to learn from their predecessors in these places how to live – that is, dwell – in those habitations. To dwell is to recognize that wherever we find ourselves, there have been other humans there before us and they have left traces – in material and immaterial cultural practices – of suggestions of how to be human in that place. Dwelling is how humans recognize historicality, the fact that we never live in places that have not been inhabited before. It clearly allows for cosmopolitanism but it does not allow for universals that want either to deny (as in Fanon's case) historicality itself or want to seek to fold into themselves (as in Sartre's Marxist reading of Negritude) historical particulars that actually resist such subsumption.

What I am suggesting then is a middle path, a middle path between Kant and Herder, say, to bring my concluding references nearer Europe. This middle path gives us a way of thinking about the relationship between the universal and particular that may be helpful in the age of globalization/global warming. An American Kant scholar has suggested that such a middle path is conceptually viable – I refer to John H. Zammito's book, *Kant, Herder, and the Birth of Anthropology* (Zammito 2002). It is, of course, impossible to do justice to two very deep, complex, and foundational thinkers in the space of a few sentences. I use the names of Kant and Herder here mainly as flagposts for the two positions that define, in their mutual opposition, the field of tension within which I locate the question of humanism today. Zammito

---

5 | None of this, however, denies the poetic appeal of Sartre's or Fanon's universals or their capacity to seem apt in certain specific circumstances.

points to the closeness between Herder and Kant in the 1760s – when Herder was a favorite pupil of Kant's – and to their intellectual separation from the 1780s on, and asks if there are not ways of bringing them together, or at least of holding on to both, in order for us to address the philosophical aspects of social enquiries of our times. In the process, he elucidates what separates the older Kant of "critical philosophy" from the later Herder. Their opposition is strongly reminiscent of the contrast between the universal and the particular with which I have been working. The "mature" Kant of *Anthropology from a Pragmatic Point of View* (1798) held to the position that "universal knowledge will always precede local knowledge as long as it is to be arranged and guided by philosophy, without which all acquired knowledge can provide nothing but fragmentary groping, and no science at all" (cited in Zammito 2002: 301). Here the universal triumphs over the local, the empirical, and the particular. It reminds us of the Sartre of "Black Orpheus" or of Fanon's search for a human with no particularity stamped on him. For Herder on the other hand, as Zammito puts it, "logical abstraction, as it gained in precision, lost in content: the more universal concepts lost ever much more of the concrete richness of their subordinate instantiations" (Zammito 2002: 319). In a letter to Scheffner (October 31, 1767), Herder actually said, "Nothing makes me sicker than the arch-error of the Germans, to build systems, so please permit me my *philosophizing art* of speaking; I am contemplating some few such contributions, but I have no taste for [system] building." (Zammito 2002: 315).

You can see the opposition that I have alluded to. In resolving it, however, a younger Kant comes to our rescue. In his *Announcement* in 1765 of his physical geography course, Kant spelt out a position not too distant from Herder's. He said that the course would "consider *man*, throughout the world[,] from the point of view of the variety of his natural properties" (within which Kant included "physical, moral and political geography"). "Unless these matters are considered," he wrote, "general judgments about man would scarcely be possible," and added: "[Concerning man] I shall always begin by considering historically and philosophically what *happens* before specifying what *ought* to happen." (Zammito 2002: 293-294).

In thinking about the relationship between the particular and the universal in questions of humanism today, I have stayed with the younger Kant: the universal needs to be *open* to the particular and be liable to serious revision under its pressure. Perhaps questions of the universal and the particular as they intensify in an age of globalization/global warming are in the end reminiscent of old problems of human reasoning. To speak with Kant again, they are perhaps questions that human reasoning can neither ignore nor answer with any degree of permanent satisfaction (Zammito 2002: 280). The universal, then, functions like a hypothesis, to be constantly tested against reality. If that sounds like I want to have my contradiction and eat it too, then I will have to remind you that, as I said in the beginning, we all live in postcolonial times, and in such periods of human history we can only speak with a "double consciousness" or with a "forked tongue," as Du Bois and Rushdie have respectively taught us.

Humanism in the Era of Globalization:

Some Thoughts

Romila Thapar

Given the world of today there is a need for Humanism, but not just as a repetition of its 18th century form. It requires to be reformulated in response to the crises of the world in the 21st century.

Humanism as a concept begins in Europe in about the 18th century. But its constituents, as either unique ideas or as a combination of ideas, go back to earlier times and to many other parts of the world. No part of the world has been an island unto itself. Therefore the roots of humanism when taken back into history involve much more than the ideas of the European past, since these ideas themselves have been drawn from a variety of cultures some of which were not central to Europe as it emerged in the 18th century. The interface between cultures so essential to the making of history is only just beginning to be recognized. We have so far been conditioned to see the past as isolated and discrete civilizations.

The constituent ideas cover a range of thought: the autonomy of the human subject, the ability to engage in self-reflection, the freedom to exercise choice in action, the ability to assume responsibility, the idea of the person and the dignity of the person. These would be relevant to virtually any age and have been posed by a number of major thinkers across the globe. An emphasis on the dignity of the person also assumed a concern for human rights as well as the moral autonomy of the person.

I would like to add two further thoughts to the constituents of Humanism which I think are opposite to our times. Firstly, is divinity relevant to Humanism? Does Humanism involve attitudes to deity, divinity or a divine presence? This introduces the question of believing in the superiority of one's own religion as also the conversion of others to one's religion arguing that it is the only way to approach deity. This also introduces the not altogether subsidiary question of the point in history when divinity takes a human shape. Is such an icon a self-reflection and does it supersede divinity? Secondly, these broad constituents of a Humanistic way of perceiving people and communities can be found in diverse societies, but putting them together as an integrated system may well differ. We may therefore consider the possibility of using the term, Humanisms – in the plural.

Humanism should be discussed with a focus on its scholarly sources in different cultures, which enabled them to present. In Islam it arose in a period of philosophical speculation; in China the context was Confucius and clan-patriarchy; and in India the dialogues between educated Indians formulating their cultural inheritance, enabled them to present an identity to alien colonial rulers and to the wider world. This underlines the difference in context and society.

The 18th century was in many ways a point of historical disjuncture in Europe. The formulating of Humanism was a reaction to a crisis in ways of thinking and behaving that had been relatively unquestioned earlier. We need to ask whether this was also true of the situation in the Arab, Chinese and Indian world which led to what has been claimed as the expression of Humanistic ideas. There was a background of dissent and reformulation in these societies. In the case of India the debates on Hinduism and Islam and on Hinduism and the West were a recognizable aspect of a concern with modernization as a major historical change in the late 19th and early twentieth centuries. Furthermore, we have looked at the formulations of the relatively free members of these societies, the scholars, the nobility, the bourgeoisie. What was the understanding of Humanism in other sections of society?

I would like to suggest that there are three areas that we might investigate: history, civilization and the secular. By the 19th century the concept is tied to history. It coincided with the birth of the discipline of history as a modern category of study. There was a reaching back to the past, a search for claiming earlier roots with Greco-Roman and Renaissance ideas. Such claims of antiquity are often colored by the needs of the present and the teleology undergoes change. The Renaissance, which encouraged the ideas that took shape as Humanism, was a turning point in Europe but it was confined to Europe. If we follow the heritage of Humanistic ideas and go back into the past then comparative studies become significant. Are there moments in time when societies create similar ideas because they have to face similar conditions? For example, was Karl Jaspers right in projecting an axial age of the 6th-5th century BC with Confucius, the Buddha and Plato as near contemporaries? Can these be called the roots of Humanistic thinking?

Humanism is also tied to the idea of civilization as a historical reality with civilizations being in a sense its units of expression. Civilization as a humanistic concept encapsulates the articulation of the higher nature of the human in the more sophisticated forms of philosophy, art, literature and complex religious beliefs and organization. This is said to be the opposite of the uncivilized and the primitive, who are unaware of Humanism. This raises the important question of who decides the criteria of what is civilized and what primitive? Does the primitive not also have notions of human values that are respected in his society?

The relationship of Humanism to religious expression is important because in some cultures, religion has been projected as opposed to the secular. Does Humanism distance itself from religion or from religious orthodoxy? Ethics and human values can be cultivated without religion. This was fundamental to the teaching of the Buddha and has been considered by other thinkers of the past as well. This aspect of Humanism brings in the question of the secular as essential to human society. Can Humanism be extended beyond religion?

In the historical context there is a contradictory aspect. Humanistic trends are seen as central to discussions on the nature of western society from the 18th century onwards. These were concerns at the scholarly and elite levels. At another level, with the spread of colonialism there was little concern for human dignity generally and this unconcern was intensified in the 19th century. We would need to analyze both the normative and the narrative texts with a sense of critical enquiry. For example, there are religious texts that codify human obligations, rights and behavior in society which conflict with the ideals of Humanism. There would be a need for secular analyses of religious texts.

Humanism draws on identities both of the past and the present and identities are created by individuals in societies and emerge out of believed historical experience. Often the experience and the claim to memory is also constructed. Identities grow out of the relations between the dominant and the subordinate, between those at the centre and those at the periphery and are determined by cultural inequities, differences and similarities. If we historicize the construction of civilization we get a different view of Humanism as well.

There is a need to be more questioning of the assumptions of one's historical perceptions of one's own society. Has Humanism indeed been a central issue of the humanities in western society and within the Christian articulation of society? The relations of Christianity and Islam were not based on humanism on either side and human dignity was of no concern. They were influenced by commercial competition and political control over trade routes. European colonialism treated the local human of the colony as sub-human and justified it through theories of race, a concept suited to colonial needs. Much the same would apply to those that argue for Humanism as qualifying other religions such as Hinduism and the teachings of Confucius. Religion as an identifiable social institution has a history which involves codes of behavior, organization, codes of belief and their articulation. It also involves looking at relations between human groups as they were on the ground and not just from normative texts. The elements of Humanism may well be evasive in religions, hinting at a degree of contestation.

By the 19th century there was some familiarity – however fanciful – about Asia in Europe as is evident from the image of Asia in German Romanticism. There were great expectations of new knowledge from what has been called the Oriental Renaissance. Europe under industrialization led to many debates on the form that human society should take. This change also emphasized the confrontation between Church and State and gave rise to a particular form of secularism which sought to differentiate between the functions of the Church and those of the State.

Prior to the 19th century had been the time when the concept of civilization took shape as a historical entity. The world was mapped into a number of civilizations and the mapping continues. Today we are counting either the twenty-six of Toynbee or the eight of Huntington and who knows what new numbers are yet to be quoted. The Asian continent was divided largely in accordance with research on the Orient, and Orientalism as we know is now a much debated subject. There was the West Asian Islamic civilization, the South Asian Hindu and the East Asian Confucian. Defined in the singular, civilization is characterized as a specific territory, a single religion and the language of the literature of the religion and of the elite. In the interests of a neat and orderly world the loose ends were tucked into the larger entity. This is historically unacceptable now. History has revealed that even the larger entities – territory, language, religion – were reformulated and mutated repeatedly. They have fuzzy edges and cannot be clearly and definitively demarcated.

The conventional view ignores acculturation and consequent change as a major feature among cultures that were juxtaposed. The areas of civilizations experienced considerable external cultural interaction with varying cultures contributing to their evolution. This was through migrations of peoples, the exchange of goods and ideas and through invasions. Central Asia and South-east Asia, were areas traversed by Buddhist missions and by Sufi teachers both of which gave a different definition to each area. The concept of civilization blurs the identities of the multiple cultures within a territory and their interface. The variants were homogenized under the rubric of a single language and religion and the viability of the variant was denied. A single culture was selected and projected as defining a particular civilization. What we call non-western civilizations today do not see themselves as civilizations in the European sense and with the European demarcations. Apart from Europe no other culture or society defined itself as a civilization. We are therefore strengthening this European perspective and search for the equivalents in other civilizations of what is defined as European civilization. Is civilization therefore a useful unit for looking at Humanism? Would it not be a pre-conception that would color our investigations?

The notion of civilization has its own history and undergoes change. The 18th century emphasized the qualities of the civil and the civilized associated with the scholastic and the elite. In the 19th century the concept had changed its meaning thorough the adaptation of the term in colonial thought. The civilized world was Europe at the high point of colonialism and the uncivilized and primitive was the world that had been conquered. Each civilization was demarcated and separated. Combined with the notions of race science and social Darwinism there was talk of some civilizations such as north-western Europe demonstrating the survival of the fittest. This contradicted the historical perceptions of the areas within the purview of these civilizations and their history as recorded in pre-colonial sources.

By the late 19th century, civilization had become a judicial notion. It entered the language of international law. Legal discrimination was permitted between "civilized" and "uncivilized" persons or groups. Therefore some rights were denied to the colonized. This was justified by resort to the legal sanction given to the civilized. One glaring example of this is where in many areas the British administration claimed ownership of land on the basis of being representatives of the civilized and therefore knowing what to do with the land. This notion in turn helped elite groups in the colonies to further underline their superiority over low status groups. Thus, the upper castes in India regarded tribal societies and untouchables (the present-day *Dalits*) as primitive and uncivilized. This pattern of exploitation was reinforced even at the local level resulting in a kind of localized colonialism. The Law of the Christian nations became the law of the civilized nations. Interestingly Europe in the 19th century moved from the centrality of Christian values to some concession to secular values. But the latter were limited to Europe. The Other, was seen by the European as primitive, despotic, lawless in relation to rights to property and generally as a survival of a remote past. 19th century India is characterized by conditions that relate to the past of Europe.

The notion of civilization is now being given a new lease of life in two ways that are both false as they are using civilization as a front for politics. Conflicts of a politico-economic nature are disguised as a clash of civilizations; and religious nationalisms are claiming that they are defending indigenous civilizations when in fact their agenda is political nationalism.

The argument for Humanism will advance if we look for situations where it might have been recognized but where we have failed to look. The interstices of multi-cultural societies are likely to have observed elements of humanism. How do societies organize difference – by encouraging multiple cultures, by demarcating communities, by caste, by various plural groups? Yet in case there is a historical change and reformulation we have to ask why it is better known in some social conditions and not in others. Therefore, should we start by assuming the viability of the concept of civilizations as units of human society. This might prejudge and limit the discussion. It might be better to examine the validity of the concept. The historical context that produced the concept of civilization and kept it afloat in its various incarnations has itself changed.

There is also the question of the inter-face both historically and currently between the ideals of Humanism and the way in which religions have evolved. This relates to the question of Humanism and secularism. Religious fundamentalism in its current form has to do with the use of religion as motivating political mobilization. This has become characteristic of all religions. Religious fundamentalism is implicitly and explicitly anti-democratic. It rejects the secular, nevertheless it uses religion for a political agenda of nationalism that has bearings on the secular. Sometimes the mobilization is through political propaganda, through state policies and through the media, as in the United States, where the appeal is to Christian fundamentalism. In the case of the United States violence is perpetrated against the enemy in Iraq and Afghanistan as retaliation against terrorist acts within America. But it is also beginning to take its toll on civil liberties at home. In other cases the articulation is through terrorist violence within the state. South Asia has witnessed much of this: Islamic terrorist groups blowing up targets in Maharashtra and in Pakistan, Hindu groups organizing genocide in Gujarat, Khalistani Sikhs indulging in murder and mayhem in Punjab, the Buddhists and Hindu Tamils locked in violent conflict in Sri Lanka and the Islamic threat to Hindu populations in Bangla Desh. Violent terrorism seems to have become characteristic of new nationalisms.

The support for Humanism in religious teachings is made a mockery of when terrorism claims to be defending religion. Such teachings have to be juxtaposed with activities of religious institutions that control society through codes of behavior, social laws and rituals. What I am suggesting is that it is not enough to merely quote the *Vedas* and *Puranas* in discussions on Hinduism and Humanism or the *Quran* with reference to Islam or the Bible when speaking of Christianity and Judaism. We also have to look at the normative texts – the *dharma-shastras* and the *sharia* to see what social codes were being proposed and at yet other texts to discover how the religious codes were being practiced. This raises the question of the role of the secular in society as it involves human rights and values which do not derive sanction from divine sources but from the requirements of social living and the agencies of human society. The non-observance of these values does not carry the threat of damnation as it does in religion. This relates to two central issues of Humanism. Does the individual have a free choice in the observance of values and does the choice relate to the centrality of individual liberation? Choice however is not without constraints because the individual lives in a society. Only the renouncer who has opted out of social obligations is relatively free and even his/her freedom is bound by some mutual dependence on society. The secular places the onus on the individual, on social consciousness and on the responsibility of the state.

In religions claiming divine revelation does the dignity of the individual imply a distancing from deity or from divine presence as a source of authority or even a rejection of this? The Buddha, for example, in his discussion on the evolution of society and on social ethics eliminates the presence of deity. The moral autonomy of the individual may be divested of religious authority but it is confined by notions of heaven and hell or of rebirth, notions that have been present even in the almost atheistic teaching of the Buddha.

The normative in all religions has to be juxtaposed with the historical articulation of that religion, where the latter creates social institutions carrying the identity of the religion. The latter often contradicts the former. For example, societies claiming to follow a religion propagating non-violence as do Buddhist societies, often fail to do so, yet continue to claim to be Buddhist, as in Sri Lanka. The claim that religious activity always abides by Humanist values is proved false by history. The need to observe customary codes can go counter to Humanist norms. Few religions actually observe the equality of all human beings and perhaps Hinduism is the worst offender in maintaining that some groups of people are permanently impure and therefore untouchable.

The assertion of believed religious norms can lead to religious fundamentalism as a form of defense and of control. Humanism will need to confront situations where this occurs. This is not a clash of civilization or of religions, but a clash of agencies of social and political control: the more powerful political economy wishing to subordinate the less powerful for reasons that have to do with resources that sustain power. The secular becomes a component of Humanism and is important to Globalization.

Religion tries to assume the laws of civil function so as to keep a control on society. These include family codes and kinship rules, education, property rights and inheritance. A secularizing society has to withdraw these from the control of religion.

The major contestants of Humanism as a course of action will be religious institutions of a fundamentalist kind and what they propagate, often falsely claiming that they have always abided by Humanist values even if history proves the reverse. Humanism will have to fight religious fundamentalism not as a clash of civilizations – which is a diversion from the main issues – but as institutionalized religion opposing Humanism. This contestation will be in the context of Globalization, and this introduces other dimensions that bring in other complications.

Globalization builds on economic inter-dependence which is not a new idea. However, the nature of the economy brings it about and the quality of the interface between nations is new. There is a quantitative and qualitative difference and the context seems to assume the dominance of a single super power. Globalization is unconcerned with erstwhile boundaries of civilizations except when it is thought necessary to project some economies as either the Enemy – Islam, or the Super Power – the United States, or potentially, the Other – China or India. At this point the notion of civilization takes on another meaning, namely the front for not recognizing that enemies and super powers are not identified by civilizations but by political and economic realities. The clash is not between civilizations but between attempts by one system to control the other, and within the systems of control. Globalization assumes a differentiation of polities and economies; it assumes the dominance of sophisticated technology, i.e., the technology of Europe and the USA ; it asserts this dominance not only in re-organizing labor and markets but in encouraging the spread of the instant "one-byte" culture created by the media. In many ways it echoes 19th century colonialism but on a different scale.

Economic inter-dependence under Globalization is asymmetrical. Some societies provide labor, some markets and some technology. This results in an extreme disparity between rich and poor both between states and within the same state. This change erodes social stability because it creates new communities and it also erodes the responsibility of the state towards its citizens, a responsibility to which Humanism drew attention. Cultural objects become commodities. Networks that cut across nation-states take the form of the distribution of drugs and the organization of terrorist attacks. What were once the alliances of the Third World, as for instance between India and the Islamic countries of west Asia have no meaning any longer. It is forgotten that not so long ago India was at the forefront of giving legitimacy to these new nations. Today India is among the nations that are sought to be terrorized by local and transnational groups tied to West Asia.

Within the society of the nation-state there is resentment against the break-up of what is assumed was an earlier social stability, resulting in new insecurities among competitive consumers. These are played out in the highly taut economies that Globalization introduces into the state. This ferments fundamentalism where the struggle is over asserting identities either ethnic, religious, linguistic or caste. The claim is that the identities are traditional or indigenous and are a revival of what existed before. But more often than not they are a return to the identities created by colonialism. The identities are invented but the inventions contest the program of Humanism. Can Humanism be reformulated to give direction to a globalized world?

The values of Humanism can become effective if the world is re-organized into new units different from post-Renaissance civilizations. Vertical divisions would no longer be effective nor the notion of the uniqueness of each civilization as an isolated, self-sufficient entity. In the period of nationalisms of the twentieth century the state moved to centre stage. Now the multi-national corporations are breaking this down through the pursuit of transnational economic patterns. Can Humanism also be re-formulated to give direction to a globalized world, or will it be a repeat of 19th century colonialism and its aftermath. Do we have a choice or do we have to subscribe universally to the "one-byte" culture – the culture of the visual media of instant and brief answers to questions devoid of nuances of thought? Can we think of the world not in vertical units but in lateral units where the networks of communication are very different: units that are trans-national and that relate to the problems across the globe and link up the peoples that have similar problems or solutions to them. Using global technologies can we infuse cultural forms emanating from Humanism into such units?

Humanism is an attitude of mind. It is an articulation of the rights that can be legitimately claimed by societies. Defining a religion or a culture as Humanist does not have the limited meaning of listing the presence of its poetry, art, music, philosophy and so on. It lies in internalizing the essentials of Humanism in one's own culture and recognizing their presence of they are there. It means an open discussion on issues central to Humanism. If we speak of the Holocaust we should not forget Hiroshima and Nagasaki. This was all part of the use of science to destroy humanity. Guilt has become a major concern in one case. It is set aside in the other. We have to see such actions as the parallel misuse of knowledge and an expression of racism. There is perhaps too great an emphasis on Humanism as the creation of Europe. There can be different foci in various cultures and societies that can be brought into the definition. It is tempting to rest content with quoting Classical texts on ethics that are supportive of Humanism, but perhaps we now have to go to real-life situations and explain what a Humanistic solution might be. This might mean major re-readings of world history. Humanism arises from contestations in which an assertion of humanistic values becomes necessary. We would have to agree on what it is that we are contesting in our times through the ideas of Humanism. Embedded in Humanism is the idea of a utopia and this may help to an understanding of the ideas.

I would like to conclude with some suggestions for research. What was the historical context to the emergence of Humanism both as it evolved in Europe and as it came to be conditioned by colonial and anti-colonial perspectives that went into its further formulation? European interventions during this period were world wide and affected most aspects of life in many parts of the globe. Did the concept of civilization encourage or obstruct the notion of Humanism and is it still doing so? What meaning does civilization have today in a world that is being molded by globalization? Civilization and globalization seem to be paradoxes. If normative ideas especially in religious discourse are juxtaposed with historical situations related to that discourse, does it make a difference to the inter-face between religion and Humanism? If the search for the presence of Humanism is sought in marginal cultures, in the cultures of the Other, and in the ideals held by subordinate groups, we may find many facets of Humanism without their being called so. Such groups are by their very nature interested in the ideals and values of Humanism and it is to these groups that we should also turn our attention. Studies of the ideologies of such groups and their articulation may take Humanism further as a perception of, and a prescription for, the globalizing world of today.

Part II: The Variety of Cultures

The Spirit of Renwen (人文 "Humanism") in the Traditional Culture of China

Yunquan Chen

The culture of China originated from the ancient times, and keeps up its traditions for several thousand years un-intermittently. It's not only one significant factor for the existence and development of the Chinese nation, but also has had a wide influence on other cultures in the world having greatly contributed to the human civilization. And the quintessence of the traditional culture of China is the rich spirit of renwen (人文 "humanism").

The term renwen (人文) appeared in the chapter "Bentuan" (易 贲彖) of the Book of Changes[1] for the first time, saying "the civilization being with renwen (人文) [...]. And the renwen (人文) guarantees huacheng (化成) of people's deeds." This renwen (人文) meant people's "course" or "deeds"; and the "huacheng" (化成) meant to achieve people's deeds. Our traditional ideology renwen huacheng (人文化成) constituted the idea of regarding the people as the center, paying attention to their dignity and value and giving full play to their initiative and potentialities, and treated the space and all things on the earth with this idea. It should be said that this unique traditional ideology of renwen (人文) had not only produced a great effect on the ancient China but exerted a tremendous influence over the modern China.

China is one of the first civilized countries. In China's history of civilization, the culture of the Xia, Shang and Zhou Dynasties (ca. the end of the 22nd century-771 BC) is known as one of "li (礼) and yue (乐)". The li (礼) was originally the ritual of the religious and sacrificial ceremony, and its nature came to a fundamental modification after zhi li zuo yue (制礼作乐, to formulate the ritual and to compose music) by Zhougong (周公). The li (礼) of the Zhou Dynasty constituted a suit of laws and institutions for their feudal patriarchal and hierarchical society and a kind of people's behavior norm instead of the religious rite. As a means to express people's emotion, the yue (乐) had a remoter past, and could not be moderated and limited with an accompaniment of the li (礼) in the expression of emotion

---

1 | "Bentuan" In: *I Ching: Book of Change* (易 贲彖).

by it and with patriarchal and hierarchal ideas. Therefore, Zhou people's ideology came to a significant transformation "to wait on ghosts and gods, but to keep them at a distance" marked significantly the transformation of this ideology, and then, it was actually to respectfully remove the ghosts and gods from the human affairs. The Zhou people thought that the social life was principally controlled by the "li and yue," (礼乐) and that people could establish and maintain the social order on the "li and yue." (礼乐) The Zhou people made the culture of China free itself from the primitive religion and step fool on an unreligious path since they had placed the "li and yue" (礼乐) on an important and high plane as a regulator of the social life.

The Spring and Autumn and Warring States Period (春秋战国, 770-220 BC), those of radical social changes in the history of China, were considered as the time of "the set of etiquette collapsed and the music was lost." (礼坏乐崩) It was precisely during this period of radical social changes that the Confucian doctrine was evolved for the new historical context on the basis of the traditional culture of the "li and yue." (礼乐) Confucius (551-479 BC), thinker in the late Spring and Autumn Period, was the founder of the Confucian doctrine. His doctrine was well developed and known in the Warring States Period.

Confucius advanced a new doctrine of ren (仁, benevolence) after some reflection on the traditional li (礼). He interpreted the li (礼) in line with the ren (仁) and internalized the external social norms to an immanent moral consciousness. Confucius said: "How can be observe the li (礼) and the yue (乐) if people is not benevolent."[2] He argued that it was necessary not only to normalize and restrain human behavior with the external li, but subjectively to develop people's moral character of the ren (仁) making them immanently and consciously observe the norms of the li (礼). Developing the immanence of the moral subject in Confucian thinking, Mencius argued that all kinds of moral consciousness were internalized by oneself. He said: "My ren, yi (仁义, justice), li and zhi (礼智, intelligence) are not acquired from the outside, but innate."[3] The ren (仁) and the "li and yue" (礼乐) were both the culture of embodying and upholding the patriarchal relations; and their difference was one that the li (礼) was the form and formation of system and the yue, (乐) the expression of emotion and aesthetic conceptions for the li (礼); and the ren (仁), the substantial mentality or ideological tenets for the li (礼) and yue (乐). In short, the Confucianists have developed the Western Zhou culture, and their most prominent contribution was just to advance the doctrine of ren. (仁).

And it is precise to begin with the discussion of the ren (仁) doctrine if one wants to know the renwen (人文, "humanistic") ideology of the Confucianists. Here, we quote two passages from the *Confucian Analects*. One of them said: "It is a benevolent person who wants to succeed himself and in the meantime

---

2 | Chapter "Bayi" in the *Confucian Analects*. （论语 八佾）

3 | Chapter "Gaozi" [part one] in the *Mencius*. (孟子 告子上)

to enable others to do the same, and who wants to occupy a distinguished position by himself and in the meantime to enable others to do the same."[4] The other said: "Do not do unto others what you would not have them do unto you."[5] According to the explanation of Feng Youlan, China's contemporary famous philosopher, it seemed to look on others and oneself as one "person." (Feng 1964: 148-149). In China, some said that these arguments constituted an "infallible law "of the Confucian ethics.

As a renwen (人文, "humanistic") culture, the Confucian doctrine attached great importance to the explanation of human existence by the cosmos itself, establishing human nature, statues and value, and setting up people's subjective consciousness, so it was imbued with the renwen (人文, "humanistic") spirit particular to the traditional culture of China. The main viewpoints of the Confucianists were as follows: firstly, the human being was highly valued for the nature of the universe; and the reason why the human being was highly valued was the fact that he had the yi (to do justice to himself), that is to say, he could distinguish whether an idea and behavior were appropriate or inappropriate so as to observe certain norms of social justice. Secondly, the human being was the soul of the universe; this point of view constituted an exposition of people's rational spirit. Thirdly, the human being was the heart of the universe; this point of view constituted a call to give full play to people's ideological capacity. Fourthly, Heaven and human being existed in perfect harmony, maintaining that the more subject went to comfort with divine justice in self-cultivation so as to rise to the mental level of being in harmony with Heaven. The so-called "Heaven and human being" in the traditional philosophy generally meant "nature and man-made."

Confucian ethics was a kind of moral conduct doctrine. As regards the individual, the moral conduct constituted giving full play to the capacity possessed by him or her. And as regards the collective, it constituted being perfect harmony among them. The object of this doctrine was not only to give full play to the potentialities of the individual, but to keep up favorable interpersonal relationships. Each person was one member of a family or a group, but he had his own moral quality and his own values. – In the traditional culture of China, there was a kind of vigorous and constantly self-advancing spirit and of immortal outlook on life for establishing moral, performing a meritorious service and expounding ideas in writing. It constituted confirmation and propagation of people's subjective value and moral quality, and presented a certain positive effect of the Confucian humanistic ideology in history.

China's society was a patriarchal one from the Western Zhou Dynasty (西周) to the fall of the Qing Dynasty (清) (ca. the 11th century BC-1911 AD). The patriarchal clan system constituted the fundamental feature of the traditional culture of China. Its central point was to make the relation among

---

4 | Chapter "Yongye" in *Confucian Analects*. (论语 雍也)

5 | Chapter "Weilinggong" in *Confucian Analects*. (论语 卫灵公)

peoples into one of domination and submission; and this kind of relation was formed, established, maintained and consolidated fundamentally by such relation as blood, pedigree, senior and junior, etc. The human relations based on the patriarchal clan system were a thing of a blend of man-made social estate system with natural blood relationship and kinship. It constituted an inner contradiction of the Confucian humanistic ideology that equal requirements were made for people's accomplishment in self-cultivation, and the social estate system was maintained for social and political status. Thus, it constituted the key to understanding China's traditional culture and its renwen (人文, "humanistic") conception to make a serious study and analysis of the human relations based on the patriarchal clan system.

The Confucianists placed great emphasis on the necessity to start with emotion in human relations so as to make people be obedient and attain the goal of upholding the patriarchal and hierarchical system. And the Legist School argued that since the human being had consideration for his own interests with selfish desire, it was necessary to start with compulsion in order to upholding the human relations based on the patriarchal clan system. So it emphasized interests and full rigor of the law. And the Confucianists assimilated some useful ideas of the Legist School, as a result, the orthodox dominant ideas of China's feudal society were formed. In China's history, there were the Mohist School which held a kind of "equality" conception against the inequality of the patriarchal and hierarchical system, and the Taoist School which took an attitude of criticism towards the human relations based on the patriarchal clan system claiming to cast off the yoke of the patriarchal clan system in order to be free and unrestricted. However, both of them couldn't constitute the mainstream of China's traditional culture instead of the Confucian School.

During the period of 2000 odd years, the ancient society of China was, in whole, imbued with the Confucian culture which penetrated into all of the fields of social life – politics, ethics and economics, so as to play a great role in normalization of systems and political enlightenment – to enlighten people on the Confucian doctrine for common practice. It should be said that the Confucian culture played a most important role in China's history in the molding of national spirit and temperament of the Chinese nation. Over nearly 100 years, the Confucian culture changed in social life under the amazing circumstances in the history of China's culture and ideology because of running countercurrent to the social development. It was certain that the conclusion of the age of domination of the Confucian culture didn't mean the end of its role in the modern society of China.

May 4th 1919, in Beijing broke out the May 4th Movement which shook the world. The May 4th Movement was a new culture movement as well as a mass patriotic one. It was the concentrated expression of advanced Chinese's seeking and probing the way of making our country powerful and our people rich since the Opium Wars. The May 4th New Culture Movement which took democracy and science as the banner carried forward the ideological movements in thee Reform Movement of 1898 and the revolution of 1911 with far more thoroughness of anti-feudalism. The old culture opposed by the initiators of the May 4th New Culture Movement was the "culture inherent in China," feudalist culture of "making a distinction between the elite and the lowly and between the noble and the humble." The new culture initiated by them was one about liberty, equality and human rights popularized after the French Revolution in the 18th century. However, the May 4th New Culture Movement didn't "totally repudiate traditions," so that neither the traditional culture had broken off its existence nor its break-off might appear. Generally speaking, when it assimilated foreign cultures, it made a certain selection according to what it needed adopting strong points of the foreign cultures to make up its own deficiencies, encouraging people to think things out for himself, opposing dependence on the ancients and claiming emancipation of people's individuality and ability from the trammels of feudal traditions for free progression.

By the Shang (商) and Zhou (周) Dynasties, China evolved already the conception of minben. (民本) The minben (民本) meant taking the people as the foundation of the state. The Book of History[6] (尚书) was the earliest extant collection of documents of ancient times. It was said in chapter Song of Wuzil (五子之歌) in the Book of History (尚书) that "The people is the foundation of the state. When the foundation is solid, the state is at peace." It summed up the experiences in politics since the Shang and Zhou Dynasties recognizing that the people was the fundamental factor of "surviving or perishing" of a political power, of "order or disorder" of a state. Confucius and Mencius carried forward the conception of minben (民本) and fused it into their own ideological system.

The term minben (民本) first appeared in the Book of History. It was said in chapter Duofang (多方) in the Book of History (尚书) that "Only Chengtang (成汤) is capable of commanding all states to exterminate the Xia (夏) Dynasty and of being the lord of all the peoples." That is to say, the term minzhu (民主) meant that "lord of the people" or to "make people's decision," being totally different from the modern times to understand the minzhu (民主) as the exercise of power by the people.

When Chinese first met with the modern conception of democracy or looked over the democratic system of the West, they looked upon it as the same as China's traditional conception of minzhu (民主) and policy of benevolence, arguing that it "originates in the ancient times." Just as it was said in Guomin Bao (国民报) in those years that Chinese got used to talk about the "administration of the Three Dynasties – the Xia, Shang and Zhou Dynasties (夏商周)" in the ancient times, wrongly arguing that there already existed democracy and national in that epoch.[7] It was obvious that people hadn't in those days distinguish the modern democracy of the West from China's ancient conception minben (民本) and policy of benevolence yet. By the time of "May 4th," people did systematic studies on the Western

---

6 | *Book of History*: Old 1906.

7 | *Guomin Bao*, II, May 10, 1901, quoted from Geng 2003: 76.

politics and China's one making a serious check on the Confucian political ideology. They brought to light the monarchist essence of Confucian policy of benevolence, pointing out that the Confucian rule of virtue was incompatible with the modern politics and criticizing the person-of-virtue politics and psychological dependence of nationals on a holy sovereign or a sage premier. They finally distinguished China's traditional conception of minben (民本) and rule of virtue and policy of benevolence from the modern democracy of the West (Geng 2003: 354-357).

In the time of May 4th, modern conception of science and humanism were pouring into China. By 1923, the debate on science and outlook on life (also known as "science and metaphysics") took place in China's intellectual circles. This debate was evoked by Zhang Junmai, professor of philosophy, who had made a speech on the "Outlook on Life" to students in the Tsinghua University. He argued, "However developed the science is, it's incapable of solving the problem of outlook on life" (Feng 1989: 648). Considering that "the problem of outlook on life must be solved by metaphysics." To counter his arguments, Ding Wenjiang, scientist, published the article "Metaphysics and Science "in the Journal Nuli Zhoubao (努力周报). He said, "When we pay attention to requirements of this time, we cannot but recognize that the actual greatest responsibility and requirement of the human being are to apply the scientific method to the problem of human life" (Feng 1989: 648). The central issue of the debate which was called a "great unprecedented ideological written polemics" by Hu Shi was whether the science could solve the problem of outlook on life (Feng 1989: 648).

In this debate, the Metaphysical School which held firmly to the humanistic preference kept on moving back. They withdrew to the argument of "the innate consciousness of duty is extra-scientific" (Fan Shoukang) from the one of "the outlook on life is extra-scientific" (Liang Qichao). And although they held firmly to the argument of "the outlook on life is not extra-scientific," Ding Wenjiang and others who insisted on the scientific preference didn't convincingly expound and prove "why science can govern outlook on life"[8] because of being unable to resolve, to the degree of world outlook, the problem of scientific methodology for treading on the problem of social history and outlook on life.

Contemporarily, Marxists took an active part in the argumentation analyzing and commenting the viewpoints of both parts. They opposed the viewpoint of the "Metaphysical School" which argued that the outlook on life was determined by free will and not governed by science as well as criticizing the viewpoint of the "Scientific School" which said that both of the object and content of science originated from subjective sense. For example, Chen Duxiu pointed out that he ought first to affirm that it was science to be used to explain natural and social objective phenomena when one wanted to plain the reason why science could govern outlook on life.

---

8 | The articles of Fan Shoukang, Liang Qichao and Ding Wenjiang were published in Collection of articles *Science and Outlook on Life*, Shanghai 1923

He argued,"Various kinds of outlook on life are governed by their objective causality respectively. And the scientific explanation made by the social science rests in the fact that all kinds of outlook on life come from the objective cause and none of them, from individual subjective, intuitive and free will" (Chen 1984: 7).

Li Dazhao, main representative of China's advanced intellectuals who first embraced Marxism, began in the time of May 4th to establish social ideal on the basis of historical materialism. He said, "On the one hand, it's the emancipation of individuality, and on the other hand, Great Harmony and Unitization. The movement of the emancipation of individuality accompanies the one of Great Harmony and Unitization. The two movements seem to be opposite to each other but as a matter of fact are complementary to each other." He added, "We advocate remolding human spirit with humanism and economic institutions with socialism at the same time." He came to the conclusion that the emancipation of individuality was integrated with the Great Harmony and Unitization and the humanism, with the socialism (Li 1984, vol. 2: 597-598, 437-438).

In short, this "debate between science and metaphysics" touched on a whole series of "related" problems such as relation between natural law and social law, relation between social law and human activity, relation between social progress and individual freedom, etc. and in the final analysis, on the important problem of how to realize the unity of scientific reason and humanistic spirit and to enrich and develop scientific world outlook.

Democracy and science were the two principal objectives pursued by the May 4th New Culture Movement. As a result of vigorous propaganda and recommendation of the New Culture Movement, democratic ideology and scientific spirit became a strong tendency of those days guiding China's modern ideology towards a new direction. Although the criticism on old traditions of China's feudalism made by May 4th New Culture Movement couldn't very well avoid certain historical limitations, it essentially constituted an indispensable important link of the course of development of China's national culture and its traditions to modernity without causing a spirit in the tradition. Hence, we should carry forward the fine traditions of May 4th New Culture Movement amply uncovering and remolding our national traditions of culture, as well as fully assimilating foreign culture, and fusing elements of both parts into a new-style modern culture of China.

The conceptions such as "to take the human being as the center," "to keep pace with the progress of the times," "social harmony" and "peaceful development" presently emphasized by China rest on a solid foundation of China's civilization, as well as embodying the progressive spirit of development of the times. Today, to advocate "to take the human being as the center" is to hold firmly to the development of the people, by the people, for the people and to paying a great deal of attention to people's value, their rights and interests, their freedom and to carry for people's living quality, their potentialities of progress and their happiness indexes, in sun, to the realization of people's all-round progress. It's China's chief task to guarantee people's right of existence and their right of development. We are vigorously promoting economic and social human rights in accordance with the law, and realizing social equality and justice and making 1.3 billion Chinese lead a happy life.

(Translated from Chinese by Minwei Hao)

Humanism in Indian Thought

Surendra Munshi

For a preliminary understanding of humanism in Indian thought, it is useful to listen to the voices of a monk, a poet, and a philosopher. These distinguished persons from India were reaching out to the world, especially the Western world, to present the cultural heritage of their country. All three of them, in their different ways, thought India had something to offer to humanity.

Let us begin with the monk, Narendranath Datta, known as Swami Vivekananda, was traveling in south India, away from Calcutta where he was born, when he heard of a parliament of religions that was to be held in Chicago in 1893. He decided to go there. He arrived in Chicago after a long journey on the 30th July 1893, only to find out that the Parliament was to be held later in September. The weeks that he spent in the United States, his first in a foreign land, till the Parliament was inaugurated on the 11th September 1893 are full of interest, but let us go straight to the Parliament that took place in Columbus Hall, mindful of the "discovery" of America, as a part of the World Fair which put on display the products of American industry. He addressed the Parliament six times, officially representing Hinduism.

In response to the welcome accorded to the delegates, he made his first address on the opening day, setting the tone for the later ones. "I am proud to belong to a religion which taught the world both tolerance and universal acceptance. We believe not only in universal toleration," he said, "but we accept all religions as true. I am proud to belong to a nation which has sheltered the persecuted and the refugees of all religions and all nations of the earth" (Paranjape 2005: 41). He spoke against sectarianism, bigotry, and fanaticism, hoping that all persecutions with the word or with the pen would end. Later, he used the story of the frog that lived in a well thinking all the time that nothing could be bigger than the well in which it was born to illustrate the point that we disagreed because we were unable to think beyond our respective wells. What was needed was breaking the barriers of these little worlds.

The third address was meant to present the key ideas of Hinduism. He highlights here the capacity of Hinduism to assimilate diverse ideas, from high Vedantic thought to the low ideas of idolatry. He sees the common basis of these ideas in the belief that human life is a constant struggle to achieve perfection, to become divine, and to find bliss in union with God. This involves losing narrow individuality for "infinite universal individuality." This universality is reached by the realization that all souls are but manifestations of one Soul. It is through this realization that human beings become divine. All the external objects, such as an idol or a religious book, are merely aids in the childhood of this journey, for the journey must go on till God has been realized. "To the Hindu, then," says Vivekananda, "the whole world of religions is only traveling, a coming up, of different men and women, through various conditions and circumstances, to the same goal. Every religion is evolving a God out of the material man, and the same God is the inspirer of all of them. Why, then, are there so many contradictions? These are only apparent, says the Hindu. The contradictions come from the same truth adapting itself to the varying circumstances of different natures" (Paranjape 2005: 54). He is aware that the Hindus may have fallen short of their own ideals. But he is clear that, if there is ever to be universal religion, it will be as infinite as its God. It will have place for all human beings, irrespective of the paths they take, embracing saints as well as sinners, the savage no less than the most exalted of human beings. It will have no place for persecution. The only aim that will move it will be that of helping humanity realize its true divine nature. In his address to the final session, he shows the same catholicity by emphasizing that no religion has the exclusive possession of human values. No religion can survive in an exclusive manner, for what is needed is assimilation, not destruction.

Three points need to be briefly noted now from these addresses. Vivekananda clearly says that Buddhism is the logical conclusion of Hinduism. The Buddha came not to destroy but to develop the religion of the Hindus. He brought out the truth from the Vedas and combined it with his sympathy for the people, especially the poor. Secondly, he tells his Christian listeners that the crying need of India is not religion but bread for the starving people, criticizing them for sending missionaries not material help. Thirdly, he emphasizes that the Hindu does not look upon human beings as sinners ("it is a sin to call a man so") but as "divinities on earth", free and immortal spirits.

Vivekananda was received well at the Parliament. In the words of the *New York Herald*, he was "the greatest figure in the Parliament of Religions" (Paranjape 2005: 19). He stayed on in the United States for a lecture tour, traveling and speaking at different places. His sojourn abroad for more than three years took him to Europe as well, to Germany and other countries. He met the famous indologists Max Mueller and Paul Deussen during these European travels. To the possible charge that he was idealizing his country, it may be pointed out that the Parliament was not the first gathering that he addressed in the United States. He had spoken earlier during his first weeks there. It was during this time that he spoke about the "vengeance of history" in his portrait of the degradation of India. He was against British imperialism but as is known also against his own countrymen. He was critical of those who by their cruelty had degraded the people, and, in his words, "God has had no mercy upon my people because they had no mercy" (quoted in Badrinath 2006: 166).

It is time to turn to the poet now. Vivekananda, a young monk, went to Oxford to meet Max Mueller in May of 1896. Rabindranath Tagore went to Oxford in the same month to deliver his Hibbert lectures there more than thirty years later. He was then in the autumn of his life. He had by then received the Nobel Prize and lectured all over the United States, Europe, Japan, and elsewhere. Tagore had given up by that time his knighthood conferred upon him by the British imperial government, shocked as he was by the massacre of unarmed people under British command at Jallianhwalla Bagh in Amritsar. He had seen the devastation of the First World War. Personally, he had experienced considerable adulation and attention in different parts of the world, "the rude touch of the curious world" (quoted in Dutta/Robinson 1997: 180) as he mentioned in one of his letters, and had also lived through disappointments and bereavements.

Tagore's lectures have been published under the title, *The Religion of Man*. In Tagore's words, "the idea of the humanity of our God, or the divinity of Man the Eternal, is the main subject of this book" (Tagore 1994: 11). The message of the book is again best expressed in his own words:

The development of intelligence and physical power is equally necessary in animals and men for their purpose of living; but what is unique in man is the development of his consciousness, which gradually deepens and widens the realization of his immortal being, the perfect, the eternal. It inspires those creations of his that reveal the divinity in him – which is his humanity – in the varied manifestations of truth, goodness and beauty, in the freedom of activity which is not for his use but for his ultimate expression. The individual man must exist for Man the great, and must express him in disinterested works, in science and philosophy, in literature and arts, in service and worship. This is his religion, which is working in the heart of all his religions in various names and forms. He knows and uses this world where it is endless and thus attains greatness, but he realizes his own truth where it is perfect and thus finds his fulfillment. (Tagore 1994: 11)

Tagore explains his own religious experience in terms of his closeness with nature. He experiences nature as a source of satisfaction with its varied forms, colors, and sounds. This has impact upon human nature. He also refers to the unsophisticated singers of Bengal, called Bauls, literally madcaps, which follow the simple path of love, expressing their feelings through their songs in which they express the divinity of man. For Tagore, they provide the essence of all religions. Religions are "never about a God of cosmic force, but rather about the God of human personality" (Tagore 1994: 12). In the exalted thought of the Upanishads to which he refers, the supreme person or the supreme soul permeates all living beings and his spirit is over all.

Tagore sees the story of the evolution of life in terms of efficiency as well as adornment. He sees perfection in the butterfly's wings, the peacock's plumes, and the luxuriance of plant life. But none compares with man, for he has the capacity to acquire additional physical competence through tools that he can use and yet put aside when they are not needed. The schoolboy who receives a present of a penknife has advantage over the tiger, for, unlike the tiger, the schoolboy does not require long evolutionary time to acquire the sharpness of the tiger's claws or teeth. Nor does he need to carry the penknife all the time with him. His hands are free to carry other tools for different purposes. "From his original serfdom as a creature Man takes his right seat as a creator. Whereas, before," writes Tagore, "his incessant appeal has been to get, now at last the call comes to him to give. His God, whose help he was in the habit of asking, now stands Himself at his door and asks for his offerings. As an animal, he is still dependent upon nature; as a Man, he is sovereign who builds his world and rules it" (Tagore 1994: 27). As man progresses and develops some freedom from compelling physical needs, his religion moves to a stage where it reflects the concern with the mystery of his own self. This self when seen in a positive manner is best seen in union with an endless world of humanity and beyond. With the sense of unity, the sense of deeper relatedness experienced as an inner perfection, comes joy, the joy of being one with the Great Soul that dwells in the hearts of all people. The way to this joy is through not just the suppression of negative thoughts but through the positive idea of love.

Now let us turn to the philosopher. It was at Oxford that Sarvapalli Radhakrishnan, who was to become later the President of independent India, delivered his inaugural lecture on his appointment to the Chair of Eastern Religions and Ethics. This was in 1936, and Tagore had talked about the religion of man there in 1930. Radhakrishnan gave the title "The World's Unborn Soul" to his lecture. It was later published in a revised form, along with other articles, in a book that carried the title *Eastern Religions and Western Thought*.

Taking a broad view of European history, he sees clearly that the Greeks tried to subject life to the rational test, applying it to ask important questions. While it was believed that man's mind and body had to be developed to ensure a balanced personality, there was not much evidence of a great interest in religion or of much moral fervor. This did not prevent them from using religious beliefs for practical ends. The fate of the soul, for instance, did not have much importance for them. When an Athenian in Plato's *Republic* is asked "Have you not heard that our soul is immortal?" he answers: "No really I have not" (quoted in Radhakrishnan 1991: 5). The spiritual vacuum was filled by the devotion to one's city. The city claimed the loyalty of its citizens. This loyalty did not go beyond the walls of one's city; cones-quently, the Greeks failed to develop a larger loyalty that could include the entire Greek world. It was the adherence to this false religion of patriotism that was mainly responsible for the decline of Greek civilization. Rome too did not develop the kind of religious perspective that could satisfy the immortal longings of man or supply spiritual unity to the Roman Empire. While mediaeval Christianity provided a religious sense to Europe, it also imposed religious bigotry. As Europe regained with the Renaissance the questioning attitude of the Greeks as well as the practicality of the Romans, an attempt was made to break the power of the Papacy. Yet the faith in reason that was seen in European history then and later did not remove all irrationalities. Indeed, they increased over time in many ways. The problem lies in not seeing morality as an inner transformation. It is not enough to regulate conduct by external means only. Commenting on the present situation, Radhakrishnan writes:

The authoritarian creeds, which take us back to pre-Renaissance days, appeal to those who find the life of pure reason so utterly disconcerting. Revivals overtake us, and we yield to them in the faith that something is better than nothing. The age is distracted between new knowledge and old belief, between the cheap godless naturalism of the intellectuals and the crude revivals of the fundamentalists. As piety in any real sense has been effectively destroyed for large numbers, the national State absorbs all their energies and emotions, social, ethical, and religious (Radhakrishnan 1991: 16f).

If the past shows that goals in different periods were to live life rationally, or according to religious principles, or later to reclaim the lost world of old perfection, the present shows that it is not clear what we want. There is an awareness of emptiness without the knowledge of how to escape it. The old world is gone, but the new world is yet to be born. We need to organize our lives by rational faith. It is here that the East can offer some help. The Europeans need not just consider the Biblical or the Greco-Roman past. There are other voices that can be heard. It is to the voice of the seers of India that Radhakrishnan turns now.

For the Hindus religion is not so much a revelation as an attempt to unveil life's depth. For Hinduism and also Buddhism religion is a transforming experience. The evidence of an external power has significance in relation to the evolution of man. It is possible to deny the existence of God and yet admit spiritual experience. Brahman, the Sanskrit word that is difficult to translate but may be understood as the Absolute, is the striving of the soul as well as the object sought. Even if God is a mere idea and has no reality outside of it, the idea of God and the will to realize it is by itself divine. Spiritual consciousness consists of the awareness that God is life. The idea is, in the Upanishadic language, not to look outward but to turn the eye inward and see the self. We are saved not by creeds but by spiritual wisdom.

For Radhakrishnan this is true humanism. He writes:

True humanism tells us that there is something more in man than is apparent in his ordinary consciousness, something which frames ideals and thoughts, a finer spiritual presence, which makes him dissatisfied with mere earthly pursuits. The one doctrine that has the longest intellectual ancestry is the belief that the ordinary condition of man is not his ultimate being, that he has in him a deeper self, call it breath or ghost, soul or spirit. In each being dwells a light which no power can extinguish, an immortal spirit, benign and tolerant, the silent witness in his heart. The great thinkers of the world unite in asking us to know the self (Radhakrishnan 1991: 25).

In the refrain of the *Chandogya Upanishad*: "the whole world has that being for itself. That is reality. That is the Self. That art thou, O Svetaketu" (quoted in Radhakrishnan 1991: 30).

We have now heard three Indian voices. These were modern Indian voices of persons who having acquired English education and mastered the English language came to the West to present a vision from ancient India. There are other voices that could have been heard here. We have not heard from them about sceptical voices. In *Katha Upanishad*, Nachiketas asked Yama, the god of death, about what becomes of a man after death, reporting that some say he exists, others that he does not exist. It is interesting to read what Yama tells him: "On this point even the gods have doubted formerly; it is not easy to understand. That subject is subtle" (*The Upanishads*, in Müller 1995: 5f). We have not heard from them about Brihaspati and his school which questioned all forms of authority except the authority of perception. It is said that Brihaspati at one time struck the goddess Gayatri on the head. But the immortal Gayatri did not die and every fragment of the brain remained alive. It is possible to read this episode allegorically. Brihaspati tried to destroy Hinduism, but as it was eternal it could not be destroyed. We have heard about the Buddha's compassion but not of the challenge that he posed to the Brahmanical orthodoxy, including the idea of the eternal creator of all beings (Brahma). We have not heard of Islam, nor of the mediaeval devotional movement that was at least in one of its forms opposed to the oppression of the caste system. An important person to note here is Kabir who combined in himself various positive tendencies. It goes to the credit of Tagore that he recognized his worth and actually translated him into English. Kabir's God tells him that He is neither to be found in a temple nor in a mosque. "O servant, where dost thou seek Me? /Lo! I am beside thee" (Tagore 2002: 1).

I have not provided here my criticism of the three voices. All of them at least may be asked a critical question: How is it that the tradition which gave the lofty mantra *vasudhaiva kutumbakam* ("the cosmos is one family") created within its own fold the most oppressive form of inequality that humanity has ever known? I have also not gone to Gandhi without whom no discussion of humanism can be complete.

After noting what we have not heard, let me turn to what we have heard. I think the views presented here raise the important question regarding the definition of humanism. We need to go outside the tradition that defines humanism in the context of the concept of the original sin and the experience of a centralized church. It became necessary in the Western context to distance any recognition of the centrality of human beings from religion, for Christianity saw human beings as sinners and their membership of the centralized church as offering them the possibility of cleansing themselves.

The doctrine of apostolic succession that was formulated early gave the church through its pope and bishops power over those who belonged to it. Jesus is believed to have built his church on the rock of Peter, and papal succession is traced back to him. Jesus said to Peter: "And whatsoever thou shalt bind upon earth, it shall be bound also in heaven: and whatsoever thou should loose on earth, it shall be loosed also in heaven" (Matthew 16:19). Indeed, humanism had in the Western context an uneasy relationship with Christianity. The fascination with the classical (pagan) time was a reaction to the "dark" age of devotion and dogmatism. This fascination posed a serious threat to the authority of the church. The concept of the original sin and the experience of a centralized church created compulsions which were not present in other traditions. In Hindu thought, for instance, as Vivekananda pointed out it is a sin to call human beings sinners. The entire spiritual endeavor of a human being then is to discover one's true nature. What is emphasized is the intrinsic "divinity" of all human beings. We need to consider different traditions and their compulsions. We need to consider all the resources that they together make available to us. To begin with, we need to ask questions. Does concern with things human necessarily exclude things spiritual? Is humanism to be understood necessarily in intellectual terms? Are not the simple Baul singers of Bengal humanists?[1] If the demand on humanism at present is to unite humanity, we need to ask: On what principles can this unity be achieved? How are the limits of human potential to be visualized? As far as India is concerned, we need to ask: Is there something that we can critically draw and transform for our purpose from the tradition that has been represented here in the voices of a monk, a poet, and a philosopher?

For a universal definition of humanism that is to be developed in an intercultural manner, all these questions and more need to be asked. The use of the term mankind or even humanity does not ensure by itself a universal definition. We are familiar with the manner in which the term "human" as in the German expression *Mensch* can lead to a distinction between subhuman (*Untermensch*) and superhuman (*Übermensch*). Similarly, the distinction between civilized and uncivilized has been used to deny an equal status among human beings within and across societies. Even the principle of *in persona Christi* in the Roman Catholic Church did not lead to inclusion.

---

1 | The Bauls are mystics to be found in Bengal. As is the way of the wind (*vayu*) which never stands still, so is the way of the wandering Baul who moves from village to village. The Bauls convey through their folk songs which they sing accompanied by a simple string instrument their message of love, joy, and universal brotherhood. They draw creatively from different religious traditions, especially Hindu Vaishnavism and Muslim Sufism. Their goal is to discover *maner manush,* the true human being that resides in every human heart. This is indeed their conception of divine. They are seen as rebels who speak against orthodoxy. Their being seen as rebels does not disturb them, for the Baul, the "mad" mystic sings: Watchful as you are of your possessions and customs, you are oblivious, my fellow human beings, that you have lost contact with your own true self that resides in your heart.

The chief argument advanced against ordaining women to the priesthood as is known has been that, since Jesus was a male who chose only males as his apostles, Christ could not be represented through the body of a woman. This highlights the need to be careful about what is excluded when human beings are under discussion. Towards a universal definition of humanism that needs to be developed, a tentative definition may be attempted here for further thought. *Humanism at its core is the belief in the possibility of all human beings realizing their innate nobility, irrespective of gender, race, class, religion, caste, or any other distinction among them.* With the recognition of the possibility of this realization in every human being, justice can be done to the radical affirmation of human capacity during the European Renaissance, notably in Pico's *Oration on the Dignity of Man,* and the older tradition in Indian thought of seeing life as a struggle for perfection, realizing God in oneself. The term "nobility" refers here not to the exclusive status of high birth but to the shared privilege of all those who are born as human beings. In the ancient text of *The Hsiao King,* a favorite with the emperors of China, the Master says: "Of all (creatures with their different) natures produced by Heaven and Earth, man is the noblest" (Müller 1996: 476).

Africa and Humanism

Elísio Macamo

Introduction

The basic claim of this chapter is that humanism in Africa cannot be discussed in isolation from issues pertaining to tradition and modernity. To be sure, this conceptual pair has been central to many attempts at understanding Africa. The general assumption has largely been the interchangeable nature of African life ways with tradition. In other words, what is African is traditional because Africa is traditional anyway. This paper takes a different perspective by cautioning against the failure to distinguish African life ways from tradition. The paper argues that this failure is responsible for the assumption that there is something intrinsically humanistic about African life ways, the search for which does not present any special problem. In fact, precisely because Africa and tradition are very distinct entities, any attempt at understanding humanism in Africa must start by appreciating the difficulties which the concept of humanism poses.

At the centre of the discussion in this chapter is the Enlightenment understanding of humanism. Drawing from Kant, Fichte and Leibniz through Wilhelm von Humboldt, Goethe and Schiller to Jean-Paul Sartre in more recent times, this paper defines humanism as the search for the fulfillment of the individual under conditions which place the onus on human agency molded within the framework of a history made possible by social action. Such an understanding of humanism reveals immediately that the assumption that African life forms may be naturally associated with humanism is a highly problematic one. More fundamentally however, it can be argued without being overly deterministic that humanism requires the fulfillment of certain social conditions in order to obtain. Furthermore, such conditions are modern in nature and can hardly obtain in a traditional setting. African societies may be humane in the way that many societies are, but they are not humanistic in the strict sense of the word. The African continent has, however, been undergoing processes of social change which have placed humanism on the African agenda. Those processes, which are historical in nature, will be at the centre of this paper.

It may appear strange to approach the issue of humanism in Africa through a detour that takes us through the tradition/modernity dichotomy. Yet no conceptual pair has been so central to the retrieval of Africa as an object of social scientific inquiry than this one. Ignoring it would be at the cost of a fuller understanding of the matter at hand. There is a lot to the assumption that Africa and the traditional are somehow interchangeable. In fact, there is a lot more than the problematic implication that all cultures are humanistic in nature and the task of any inquiry into humanism in different cultural settings consists in finding essential home-grown forms.

While the tradition/modernity dichotomy may be seen as problematic in more ways than one, it still remains important for the conceptual clarification which it can reveal in attempts at understanding the sociology of culture in different settings. Probably the most objectionable aspect of the dichotomy, one which has not ceased to fuel intense debates about the role of ethnocentrism in the social sciences, is the teleological assumption made by modernization theories concerning the fate of societies held to be traditional. This assumption held that such societies would not only undergo processes of social change which would make them increasingly more like Western society but more importantly, it was based on the belief that a change in such terms was unavoidable and desirable. In this respect, the history of European contact with Africa can be understood as the history of the attempt to bring this historicist claim into fruition. Early critical comments on anthropology for example, blamed the discipline for aiding colonial rulers in their enterprise (Leclerc 1972). Even developmental aid in our own day has been subjected to harsh criticism for the same reasons.

The charge against anthropology was that it helped create an image of non-European societies which made them inevitable objects of European civilizing intervention. These societies were depicted as timeless cultural black holes incapable of effecting change themselves. A very symptomatic offshoot of such charges was the discussion that pitted Marshal Sahlins, a well known American anthropologist against Gananath Obeyesekere, a Princeton-based psychoanalyst and anthropologist originally from Sri Lanka. The latter took issue with the description of the role of mythological thinking and practice provided by the former to account for the death of the legendary Captain Cook (Obeyesekere 1992) in the Pacific. Sahlins (Sahlins 1987) had argued that Hawaiians had slain Captain Cook on the wrong, but well-grounded assumption, that he was the cyclically returning God *Lono*, who, following tradition, should be ritually killed. Obeyesekere, in contrast, argued that Captain Cook had fallen victim to profane considerations which, in the final analysis, had dictated his death. In other words, Obeyesekere was arguing that to account for social action among seemingly backward non-European cultures and societies, one required the same interpretive skills and frames of reference that were necessary everywhere. The assumption that social action could be accounted for differently appeared to offend Obeyesekere's sense of universalism in approaching anthropology.

While Obeyesekere's claims may appear plausible on a theoretical, and perhaps even a normative level; they may be problematic to the extent that they are silent on structural differences among societies and the role which these differences may play in encouraging patterns of behavior, attitudes and beliefs. Terms like "simple societies" or "complex societies" may be objectionable on the grounds that they draw from an ethnocentric position which places Europe as the standard and thereby fails to acknowledge the diverse ways in which a society may be simple or complex, for that matter. Yet they aim at a much more subtle point of extreme importance in appreciating the nature of social action in different settings. Durkheim's discussion of forms of integration (Durkheim 1978) and their effects on the division of social labor were not only mere classificatory contrivances against the Rest (as opposed to the "West"), but rather attempts at making available to analysts ways of appreciating the richness of social relations. The same goes to Ferdinand Tönnies useful distinction between *Gemeinschaft* (community) and *Gesellschaft* (society) (Tönnies 1963). Towards the end of his celebrated *Science as a Vocation*, Weber presents an image of the "savage" which provides valuable insights not only into the nature of modern society, but also into the rich texture of individual responsibility for one's fate that went lost in the transition to modernity. He writes:

Does it mean that we, today, for instance, everyone sitting in this hall, have a greater knowledge of the conditions of life under which we exist than has an American Indian or a Hottentot? Hardly. Unless he is a physicist, one who rides on the streetcar has no idea how the car happened to get into motion. And he does not need to know. He is satisfied that he may "count" on the behavior of the streetcar, and he orients his conduct according to this expectation; but he knows nothing about what it takes to produce such a car so that it can move. The savage knows incomparably more about his tools. When we spend money today I bet that even if there are colleagues of political economy here in the hall, almost every one of them will hold a different answer in readiness to the question: How does it happen that one can buy something for money – sometimes more and sometimes less? The savage knows what he does in order to get his daily food and which institutions serve him in this pursuit. The increasing intellectualization and rationalization do not, therefore, indicate an increased and general knowledge of the conditions under which one lives (Weber 1946: 142).

No social scientist today would speak as candidly as Weber did. Many today might even take offence at the language used by Weber. However, there is a lot of structural wisdom in Weber's remarks which boils down to the need to pay attention to the context within which forms of conduct, attitudes and beliefs emerge. By the same token, claims about humanism in Africa must be tempered by careful analysis of the societal context within which certain properties of social action are thought to be manifestations of humanism. Indeed, as I will further contend, there has been a tendency within African Studies to see social phenomena occurring in Africa as features of the essence of African culture, when such phenomena might be more adequately understood and analyzed as structural properties of a very specific type of society. The binary opposition between tradition and modernity has become problematic over the years. One reason for this has been the manner in which the opposition was used to make veiled commentaries about the natural order of things – cultures and individuals – on the assumption that certain societies and individuals, i.e. the West and Westerners, occupied a privileged place on the evolutionary ladder.

However, as the persistence of problems in state building in Africa adamantly reminds us, we may have been too quick in disposing of the opposition for descriptive and analytical purposes. It does not appear logical to argue for an essentialist view of African culture, which is the case when some extol hospitality and communalism as intrinsically African, and in the same breath refuse to place the blame on Africa and Africans for their inability to achieve political, economic and social stability. Again, as I will show, some view this inability as a form of resistance by Africans against external forces. What is illogical about such essentialist views of course is the rather a-historical assumption that societies and cultures are self-contained entities subject to no external influences and, even worse, likely to degenerate once they come into contact with the outside world.

Tradition and modernity matter. A useful discussion of humanism in Africa must engage with these concepts. To put it differently, only a clear identification of what in African life is a clear manifestation of the presence of traditional or modern elements will pave the way for an analytically coherent discussion of humanism in Africa. Ironically, Africa's history, especially the role of colonialism and to a lesser degree, developmental aid, has been crucial in placing humanism at the centre of African attempts to define a place for itself in the concert of world societies and cultures. Indeed, my claim is that humanism in Africa, just as Africa itself (cf. Macamo 1999), is a very modern construct. In other words, African humanism is the product of the manner in which Africans responded to the gauntlet of history by seeking to make sense of their worlds. In the process, they made their worlds anew. The much exalted "*Ubunthu*" philosophy in South Africa, for example, is in very important respects not so much the revelation of an essential cultural truth as a critical intellectual repositioning of Africans vis-à-vis their ambivalent experience of modernity (Macamo 2005).

Africa and Humanism

The idea of humanism in Africa faces a paradox. On the one hand, there is a tendency to stress the humanity of African ways of life, based as they have been assumed to be, on generosity, hospitality, communalism and a profound respect for human life. Key political philosophies in the course of the struggles for emancipation from colonial rule and oppression repeatedly emphasized these aspects. While Julius Nyerere (Nyerere 1968), Tanzania's first post-colonial leader, sought in communalism the roots of a moral a political order for his country, Kenneth Kaunda (Kaunda 1976), Zambia's first post-colonial leader, believed to have found in mutual aid and respect principles of African humanism which, like Nyerere's *Ujamaa*, would underpin his society's moral and political order. Several versions of "African socialism", from Leopold Sénghor's (Sénghor 1964), Modibo Keita's of Mali to Ahmed Sekou Touré's of Guinea Conackry[1] insisted on the idea that African ways of life had innate humanist qualities which could be harnessed to buttress the political order.

On the other hand however, the dominant perception of Africa in the world, particularly the perception informed by the images conveyed by the global media, is that of a continent with a very tenuous relationship to any notion of humanism whatsoever. The preference for news reporting on Africa which refuses to seriously engage with the logic of social action on the continent, opting instead for simplistic accounts based on such ideas as (a;) African political elites are self-serving, (b;) Africans are not interested in developing themselves, (c;) Africans are out to live off world compassion, (d;) Africans have, among other things, a different mentality – these only help to heighten the sense of a fundamental contradiction between Africa and humanism. The exploitation of this sense of contradiction can make best-sellers as a recent book published by a journalist in France purporting to discuss what it calls *"négrologie"* clearly documents (Smith 2003). Even serious publications have a hard time finding the right tone when coming to terms with what is going on across the continent as Achille Mbembe, one of the best African scholars, appears to be admitting his failure to find the right frame of mind to analyze or merely grasp what is going on (Mbembe 1992: 1-30).

Africa is indeed a continent characterized by cultures and societies which observe hospitality and solidarity to a striking degree, considering the increasingly atomized lives which modernity demands from individuals and societies. Hospitality and solidarity are particularly marked in rural areas. One may be tempted to explain the prevalence of these habits in rural areas with reference to the assumption that these areas are conservative by nature, and therefore, preserve original cultural forms. While the presence of cultural forms is a reliable indicator of their presence in the society in question, this might be just about all that can be said of hospitality and solidarity in African rural areas. More in line with the argument of this chapter is the assumption that African rural areas are the way they appear to be for reasons linked to their stronger propensity to what we might generally call traditional ways of life. In fact, hospitality and solidarity seem to have a conspicuous presence in many traditional societies. There are very good functionalist explanations for this, chief among which I could single out those provided by the German sociologist and social anthropologist, Georg Elwert (Elwert 1991). Elwert argued that reciprocity was central to the survival strategies of small-scale communities, especially in the absence of over-arching social

---

1 | For a presentation of "African socialism" see Friedland/Rosberg 1967; for a discussion Babu 1981.

safety structures. In other words, much in the same sense in which Marcel Mauss had argued in his widely read *The Gift* (Mauss 1992), Elwert singled out these cultural forms as manifestations of a very specific type of society.

African societies do not elicit our admiration only on account of the preservation of positive traditional social forms. Also in the face of enormous adversity, especially in recent years, which expresses itself in the form of civil strife, vulnerability to natural disasters and precarious livelihoods, Africans appear to document humans' perseverance and attachment to life. In fact there is a sense in which Africa may be understood as the living example of what human nature is capable of under duress. Nothing that has happened in Africa in the context of adversity – from brutal violence to dogged pursuit of individual ends – is atypical of how others have reacted to similar situations in other parts of the world. The wars of the eighties and nineties in the Balkans as well as the so-called "war on terror" conducted by the US and its allies against religiously motivated violence have produced the kinds of human conduct which uninformed common sense would associate with the images of Africa privileged by mass communication means. That in spite of all the adverse conditions Africans come back again and again, bears testimony to their resilience, but also to their profound identity with the human condition.

This resilience has prompted scholars to look for ways of accounting for African social phenomena in terms of their relationship to what has been happening to Africans. An adequate appreciation of humanism in Africa will indeed have to come to terms with the context within which Africans have been looking for their bearings in the world. Accounts have tended to emphasize the extent to which African ways of life can be conceptualized as negative reactions to concrete historical circumstances. Indeed, while some see these ways of life as critical commentaries on modernity (White 2000), others see them as resistance against capitalism (Comaroff/Comaroff 1993), and still others speak of retrogression as in the case of James Ferguson (Ferguson 1999), who describes his own observations of the collapse of the world promised by copper in Zambia as an ethnography of decline. In so doing these accounts turn African initiative into a mere expedient reaction to circumstances that empty history of any substantive local content. The history of Africa becomes, strangely enough, a narrative of misunderstandings holding Africans hostage to the role of victims to themselves.

However, what these accounts miss is the very important point that amidst the general manifestations of resistance, criticism and decline, history is being made in Africa. In fact the history being made is not a history by default, as suggested by these accounts. Rather, it is real history, i.e. actually existing history, the actions and thoughts of Africans in their attempts at securing their existence and giving meaning to their lives. In a certain sense my argument should be understood as a critique of a historicist view of African life ways. This view pits African ways of life against an established historical horizon and that reduces history writing to a long drawn-out commentary on how Africa deviated from its pre-ordained path. My argument is informed by an understanding of history based on the general idea of historicism, i.e. a theory of knowledge that engages with social action as it is as a document of itself.

Historicist ideas as opposed to historicism are not the privilege of external observers of the continent. Men and women who made history in Africa have fallen prey to them. The great *négritude* movement for example, the black African literary reaction against colonialism and for racial pride, dulled the cutting edge of its own critique by insisting on a timeless African history independent of what actually existed. Calls for a return to the roots made this clear. Curiously enough, the problem with *négritude* might not have been so much the insistence on racial and cultural essentialism as the inability to see the movement itself as the ineluctable historical process that is so central to social action. In other words, *négritude* was no accessory to Africans for them to return to their history, but rather yet another turn in African history, opening possibilities, widening agency and offering new and novel beginnings. In his celebrated introduction to the collection of *négritude* writings Jean-Paul Sartre, the French existentialist philosopher, might have been the only one to have clearly grasped the historical significance of the movement. His image of the "Black Orpheus" (Sartre 1972) was not only an ethnocentric bow to the epistemological omniscience of Greek thinking and culture, but also, and more importantly, an acknowledgement of the historical significance of Africa's plight. Sartre described the movement as history gaining consciousness of itself. What he meant was that the suffering and oppression of Africans could only make sense to the extent that Africans were able to draw implications of worldwide significance. In other words, the French philosopher was arguing that Africans had become agents of history who had been entrusted with the task of redeeming not only the continent, but also the whole world. Africans, very much like the proletarians from whose Marxist conceptualization Sartre had drawn, suffered in order to impel history forward and deliver the world to its true promise.

While of course Sartre's Marxist reading of *négritude*'s historical significance was historicist to a degree, he was drawing consequences from an understanding of African history which did not reduce social action to an artifact of a primordial culture desperately holding on to a world to which it did not seem to belong. He was actually adding a theory of knowledge to what Africans had been doing for several years, more particularly when returning slaves from America began thinking of Africa as a community of values and fate (see Macamo 1999). Sartre's understanding of the significance of *négritude* is consistent with the main thrust of the argument of this paper. Indeed, the argument can now be stated in a bolder manner: there is no such thing as an essential African humanism. That a culture values solidarity, hospitality and respect for others does not make it humanist in any theoretically acceptable way. Humanism in fact is a reflexive concept which implies that individuals engage critically with their own history and seek to draw lessons for the way they lead their lives. In this sense for instance, "*Ubunthu*" in and of itself is not a manifestation of any kind of primordial African humanism. However, the thinking activity that went into bringing aspects of the black peoples of South Africa together to form a coherent critique of their historical experience is. In other words, African humanism comes to fruition in the manner in which Africans engage with their own historical experience and seek to draw lessons thereof. For a better understanding of this argument it is necessary to take a cursory look at crucial moments in the development and evolution of Africans' engagement with their experience.

Africans' Dialogue with History

The most appropriate moment to start from is the point in time when a considerable number of former slaves from America start returning to Africa. These men and women contributed with their thinking to posit Africa as a *sui generis* category, to paraphrase the Nigerian scholar, Abiola Irele (Irele 1975). In so doing they set in motion a historical process which lends itself to being understood as the making of humanism in Africa, a humanism born of the experience of slavery, colonialism, racism and the struggle for human dignity. Two points will be at the centre of this account. The first point consists in the argument according to which the search for Africa (see Diawara 1998) plays a central role in forming humanist ideas in Africa. This can be hopefully demonstrated by drawing from the understanding that returning slaves in Liberia and Sierra Leone in West Africa towards the end of the nineteenth century brought to bear on their own condition. Secondly, the formation of humanist ideas was profoundly dependent on the elaboration of the idea of Africa, which came to stand for a community of values and destiny. On this score it is possible to link up with central pragmatic concepts[2] such as *African personality* or, for that matter *négritude*, which perceptive observers like the Ghanaian theologian Kwame Bediako (Bediako 1995). have traced back to the condition of the possibility of an African nation as experienced by returning slaves.

The background to this account is a debate on African philosophy. This debate opposed two sides within the African intellectual community. On the one side of the barricades there were scholars such as the Rwandan historian and linguist, Alexis Kagame and, to a certain extent, the Ugandan theologian John Mbiti, who argued for an African *Weltanschauung* which summed up a specifically African philosophy. Their position had a pedigree which reached back to the writings of missionaries, such as the Belgian Placide Tempels – who wrote "La philosophie bantoue" (Tempels 1945) – the German anthropologists Jahnheinz Jahn and Leo Frobenius, who in different but convergent ways thought that they had identified the true African self. Placide Tempels, for example, argued that this philosophy was based on the

---

2 | The notion "conceptual pragmatists" refers to one specific understanding of philosophy within Africa which holds that philosophy is a universal intellectual pursuit concerned with conceptual clarification.

idea of a *life force*. The *négritude* movement took up these ideas and used them to argue, as Senghor forcefully did, that Africans were fundamentally different from Europeans: "Reason is Greek, emotion is black", said Senghor to the cheers of Europeans who denied reason to Africans.

On the other side of the line stood philosophers such as the Ghanaian Kwasi Wiredu, the Nigerian P. Bodunrin and the Beninois Paulin Hountondji who insisted that philosophy was much more than a collection of folklore and mores. Some of them came to be known as "conceptual pragmatists" for insisting that what defined philosophy was respect for the universal rules of reasoning upon which that intellectual activity was based. By way of illustrating this point reference could be made to two arguments. Kwasi Wiredu, for example, took exception to an anthropologist, Robin Horton, who had argued that African traditional religion could be seen as a kind of science on a par with Western science (Horton 1960: 50–71, 155–187). In a polemical article with the title "How not to Compare African Traditional Thought with Western Science" (Wiredu 1984), Wiredu argued that African traditional thought was traditional thought much in the same way that traditional thought could be found in every society, including Western society. Wiredu felt that comparing this type of thought with science was rendering a disservice to the advancement of scientific thought in Africa. He singled out Senghor and criticized him for his remarks on reason being Greek wondering whether by that the great Senegalese poet and statesman might not have wanted to prove his point. Paulin Hountondji, on his part, rejected the idea of an African philosophy on the basis of what he felt to be an attempt to posit a kind of *unanimism* which in his view was lacking in Africa (Hountondji 1983).

The deeper one delves into the debate, the more one comes to understand that it was not just about establishing whether there was an African philosophy. One can actually see it as a debate about Africa itself. In other words, philosophers were reflecting upon what it meant to be African. It was an act of introspection and a necessary one at that. Indeed, the debate could be seen as the third stage of a long process of constituting Africa as a community of values and a community of destiny. In the study from which I draw this account (cf. Macamo 1999). I identified three main stages, namely a religious stage, a political stage and a cultural/philosophical stage. I believed, and still believe, that through these stages Africa was constituted as a modern construct. Humanism is intimately linked to this historical process.

The political stage consisted in the struggle for self-determination. It stretched from the end of the 19th century all the way to the 30-year period covering the sixties and the eighties – with the first independences which culminated with the end of white supremacy rule in South Africa. In this political stage Africa was defined as a political community under foreign rule. The slogans of the time were "Pan-Africanism" – there were Pan African congresses in Paris, San Francisco and Manchester. The most famous phrase of the time was Nkrumah's "seek ye first your political kingdom, all else will follow." This was the time of political ideologies such as African socialism, Ujamaa, Conscientism and Humanism (in Kaunda's understanding). The political stage articulated what had been simmering historically. It gave practical substance to Africans' efforts to engage with history by seeking to bring about the conditions which would enable them to recover their human dignity. In the process however, many, especially the intellectuals, realized that they were not recovering an essential Africa. Rather they were constructing a new Africa fashioned on their existential experience.

Therefore Africa is in a sense a recent phenomenon. It came into being in the course of the 19th century. This may sound objectionable, since received wisdom would hold that the continent has existed for as long as anyone can remember. Africa as a continent inhabited by black folks, was known already in antiquity. However, the sense in which Africa should be understood as a recent phenomenon refers to the way in which the continent was the outcome of historical struggles of an ideological, political and philosophical nature. More substantively though, the sense in which Africa can be understood as a recent phenomenon is linked to the manner in which it was the outcome of people becoming aware of their existential condition and responding actively to it. They referred to what was already there, engaged with it and in the process, they molded something new: Africa.

The recent nature of Africa can be seen clearly in the travails of returning slaves who settled on the West African coast – Liberia and Sierra Leone. These were people who had been sold into slavery by their own brethren or by Europeans and subjected to the most inhuman treatment that men have inflicted upon one another, both on the way to as well as after arriving in America. These people came into contact with Christianity, learnt and accepted its message of redemption and equality before God. They wondered why such a benevolent and forgiving God could have allowed such a fate to fall upon them; exactly the theodicy question which Weber identified as being at the root of ethical frameworks.

The answer to this existential question was the first stone in the construction of Africa. While feeling that slavery was inhuman, they did not see it as a curse. They saw a larger purpose behind it. They saw slavery as the work of providence. Kwame Nkrumah summed this up nicely in a speech held in Liberia in 1952:

I pointed out that it was providence that had preserved the Negroes during their years of trial in exile in the United States of America and the West Indies; that it was the same providence which took care of Moses and the Israelites in Egypt centuries before. "A greater exodus is coming in Africa today", I declared, "and that exodus will be established when there is a united, free and independent West Africa [...]" (Nkrumah 1973: 153)

God had allowed these men and women to be sold into slavery so that they could learn Christianity and a new ways of life. These men and women were destined to liberate their brethren from the darkness they had lived in up until then. Most of the writings of the time are full of biblical imagery. Slavery is seen as the exodus and the return to Africa is the return to the Promised Land. Slaves were the "chosen people", in fact Edward Blyden, one of the most vigorous writers of the group, even went as far as to argue that Africa as a whole had been chosen by God to liberate the world. This is the argument that would be taken up later, albeit clad in Marxist terminology, by Jean-Paul Sartre, who argued that history had chosen the black man to lead the way into all men's emancipation. Even the naked people they encountered in the African hinterland symbolized, in the eyes of former slaves, the state of innocence Africans were still in.

To the extent that the search for Africa was concerned with redeeming the continent, its people and the rest of the world, it contained within itself the seeds of humanism in Africa. But what was this Africa that they were supposed to redeem and how were they going to do it? This Africa did not exist, yet it did. It did not exist in the sense of a politically, economically and socially coherent territorial community. Africa was a collection of fragmented polities, each pursuing its own interests and worshipping its own deities. Alexander Crummell, an Episcopalian minister who had settled in Liberia and a powerful spokesperson of the returned slaves for example, went as far as to say:

Africa is the victim of her heterogeneous idolatries. Africa is wasting away beneath the accretions of moral and civil miseries. Darkness covers the land and gross darkness the people. Great social evils universally prevail. Confidence and security are destroyed. Licentiousness abounds everywhere. Moloch rules and reigns throughout the whole continent, and by the ordeal of Sassywood, Fetiches, human sacrifices and devil-worship is devouring men, women, and little children. The people of Africa, [...] have not the Gospel. They are living without God. The Cross has never met their gaze [...] (quoted in Appiah 1992: 35)

Yet, Africa existed as a promise, as a community ready to be called into being. It fell upon those God had chosen to lead their brethren – former slaves – to identify the commonalities that would show them the way. Crummel's contemporary, E. W. Blyden, (quoted in Mudimbe 1988: 110) wrote:

It is the feeling of race – the aspiration after the development on its own line of the type of humanity to which we belong. Italians and Germans long yearned after such development. The Slavonic tribes are feeling after it. Now nothing tends more to discourage these feelings and check these aspirations than the idea that the people with whom we are connected, and after whose improvement we sigh, have never had a past, or only an ignoble past – antecedents which were 'blank and hopeless', to be ignored and forgotten.

Race was a central element of this nascent African nation in the minds of returned slaves. In fact they have been strongly criticized by Kwame Appiah, an African philosopher of Ghanaian origin on, for example, their "racism" and "racialism" (Appiah 1992). Indeed, their most powerful justification for an African nation was this common notion of race. They were so concerned about the purity of this notion that they were frightfully bigoted about anything in between, which is why they would call former slaves of mixed race "mongrels". Race was important, but so was a shared history of suffering and a yearning for "improvement", as they often put it.

As the chosen people they were to be the go-between for Europeans and their black and pagan brethren. Hence Blyden's passionate invitation to freed slaves in America to come and claim their land. In the run-up to the Berlin conference, which took place from 1884 to 1885, for example, they still kept the hope that Africa's future might be entrusted to them. It was in fact the Berlin conference coupled with the realization that Europe meant to avail itself of Africa's riches that paved the way for the radicalization of their discourse, culminating in the political stage that I mentioned earlier.

In concluding this section it can be said that Africa was understood as a community of values and also as a community of destiny. Former slaves were to nurture it as part and parcel of the mission which God, in his infinite wisdom, had entrusted upon them.

Humanism in Africa was profoundly linked to the attempt at finding a place for Africa within an adverse historical process. Returning slaves lent substance to this understanding by defining Africa in a very specific way, namely as a community of values and destiny. What led them to this was their existential condition. This was the result of historical forces that fell upon the continent from the end of the 15th century onwards.

Elsewhere I argue that Africa is a modern phenomenon (Macamo 1999). This is because it emerged as a community of values and destiny out of a conscious dialogue between people and their own situation. Indeed, if reflexivity is an intrinsic part of modernity then Africa is a particularly poignant example of that. A Swedish political scientist, Björn Wittrock (Wittrock 2000: 31-60), has defined modernity as a set of promissory notes waiting to be cashed in. Africa as a modern construct resulted from the attempt by a very specific group of people, the returned slaves, to make modernity live up to its promise of liberty, progress and justice. It gained texture from the way in which these people engaged with their surroundings.

Conclusion

In this chapter I have been concerned to claim that a proper appreciation of humanism in Africa requires a conceptual framework which is still in need of development. My suggestion is that humanism in Africa is deeply related with the conditions under which Africa took shape as a community of fate and values. In other words, drawing from my earlier work on the philosophical debate concerning the issue as to whether there is an African philosophy, I submit that just as Africa is a modern construct, the fate of humanism in Africa is coupled with the historical conditions of the possibility of Africa as a modern construct. Indeed, humanism is what remains – perhaps what should remain – once all the fallen bodies throughout the course of history have been counted.

To be sure, this is not a conclusion. Rather it is an indication of the kinds of conceptual, theoretical and analytical paths which discussions of humanism in Africa should take. It is a statement of work to be done. This work should engage in a more vigorous manner with African life ways and tradition with a view to understanding their precise relationship. Not everything that is African is traditional, but a clear understanding of tradition might caution us against light hearted conclusions about the relationship between humanism and African life ways. Equally important is the worthwhile attempt at understanding discussions of the nature of African society as can be found in several writings of very influential anthropologists, missionaries and travelers. The writings of Leo Frobenius, Jahnheinz Jahn, Placide Tempels, David Livingstone and others are crucial to such an enterprise. They lie at the root of subsequent and more recent attempts at recovering the essence of African life ways. These writings were not inconsequential, and for this reason they deserve to be read and discussed at length as part of the efforts to appreciate humanism in Africa. This appreciation should include a consideration of Africans themselves, some of whom have been briefly discussed in this paper, as part of the attempt to understand how they responded to the challenges of history.

Only such an endeavor can hold the promise of a clear understanding of humanism in Africa.

Exclusion and Inclusion in the Quest for a "New" Humanism: A Perspective from Africa

Bernard C. Lategan

Introduction

The quest for a "new kind of humanism" stems from a dissatisfaction with existing concepts, from a sense that traditional notions of what it means to be human no longer serve their purpose. There are good reasons or this disaffection with "humanism" in its traditional guise. The social, political and cultural transformation we have experienced in various parts of the world during the past two decades have indeed put into question our current understanding of the human condition and of our ideals for a humane society. Talk of the "global village" demonstrates both the rapid expansion of what is considered to be the boundaries of the human world and the radical decrease of distance between the elements constituting this world. Recent examples of inhumane behaviour and flagrant disregard for human dignity have cast doubt on whether the optimistic ideals espoused by "humanism" will ever be achieved in concrete terms. From all sides our "current understanding" of humanism (if such a consensus does exist at all) is challenged – an understanding that is based on the realities of human nature and of human history which have found their precipitation in cultural practice, attitudes and norms and have been systematised in philosophical concepts. The contributions to the present project give ample evidence of this need for reconsideration – and that the process to do so is already under way in East and West, in North and South.

Any discussion of the human condition by necessity has to take into account an extremely complex and dynamic interaction of forces, conditions, contexts, values and intentions. Any reflection on and proposal for the contours of a "new humanism" in an era of globalization will therefore per definition also be a complex and multi-dimensional undertaking. The purpose of this contribution is to highlight only a few of the many aspects that merit consideration in this regard. We take our clue from the focus of this project, namely "humanism in the era of globalization." More specifically, we shall look briefly at some consequences of globalization for the process of individual and collective identity formation and then explore possible new impulses for re-imagining humanism from the experience and perspective of Africa.

Globalization and Identity

One of the enduring consequences of globalization is the way in which it has affected the processes through which personal and group identities are being formed. Identity is a central theme in any discussion on humanism, simply because the way individuals and groups understand and project themselves contains key information regarding the human condition in a specific context and provides some of the important raw material for constructing alternative concepts of humanism.

First and foremost is the unprecedented way in which globalization has stimulated the growth of new and alternative identities – to such an extent that "identity" has become the counterpoint of "globalization". The seemingly unstoppable homogenizing effect of multinational companies and brands, spreading a pervasive sameness in music, fashion, food, strategy, organizational culture (to name just a few of these manifestations) has unleashed a counter force – that of claiming an own, an alternative identity. In many ways this is a manifestation of protest, of resistance, of the refusal to accept an identity that is foisted on unwilling recipients. These alternative manifestations are as varied as the multiple effects of globalization itself. In fact, the stronger the force of globalization, the stronger the need for differentiation, and the more resolute the determination to claim alternates identities. In this sense, globalization and identity represent opposite poles in an enfolding process.

What makes this process different from previous major cultural changes, is the way in which the constituent elements of our "world" are transformed in a fundamental way. Castells describes the process as follows:

Our world, and our lives, are being shaped by the conflicting trends of globalization and identity. The information technology revolution, and the restructuring of capitalism, have induced a new form of society, the network society. It is characterized by the globalization of strategically decisive economic activities. By the networking form of organization. By the flexibility and instability of work, and the individualization of labor. By a culture of real virtuality constructed by a pervasive, interconnected, and diversified media system. And by the *transformation of the material foundations of life, space and time*, [my italics, BCL] through the constitution of a space of flows and of timeless time, as expressions of dominant activities and controlling elites. This new form of social organization, in its pervasive globality, is diffusing throughout the world, as industrial capitalism and its twin enemy, industrial statism, did in the twentieth century, shaking institutions, transforming cultures, creating wealth and inducing poverty, spurring greed, innovation, and hope, while simultaneously imposing hardship and instilling despair. It is indeed, brave or not, a new world (Castells 2004: 1-2).

Whether one agrees with the depiction of Castells or not, any reconsideration of humanism has no choice but to engage with the underlying tenets of this new world. These affect the process of identity formation in fundamental ways – with far-reaching consequences. The widespread surge of new expressions of individual and collective identity in recent years represents in essence a challenge to globalization – stemming on the one hand from a desire to have control over one's own life and on the other hand from an insistence on singularity and on the diversity of cultural experience and expression. It is exactly the power and pervasiveness of global trends – be they search engines, operating systems, fashion, art or whatever fad – that can lead to the experience of imposition and consequently, to resistance and rejection. As Castells (Castells 2004: 2) shows, these responses are multiple, highly diversified, following the contours of each culture, and utilize the historical sources of formation of each identity. They may be global themselves, like feminism or environmentalism, but more often, the reactive movements yield resistance on behalf of God, nation, ethnicity, family or locality. But they are fast to learn from the enemy and, paradoxically, use the very strategies and means developed by global trends to further their own cause – like worldwide interactive telecommunication networks, powerful technological media and the like.

Social Transformation and Identity

Globalization thus has its own effects on how identities are formed and how they function in the information age. But there are also other forces reshaping identities. While globalization forms the wider background, the world also experienced major social transformations since 1989, mostly consisting of the demise of authoritarian regimes and the establishment of new democracies. These transformations have far-reaching implications for issues of identity, but are of course not manifestations of globalization as such. Nonetheless, aspects of globalization have influenced these social transformations decisively – in some cases by facilitating, in some cases by deterring them.

These transitions were accompanied by a wide variety of projects to redefine individual and collective identities. To mention just two examples: The reunification of Germany and the establishment of an inclusive democracy in South Africa. Despite similarities, there were also marked differences. In the case of Germany, there was a legal framework in place before the reunification in the form of the *Grundgesetz*, defining in essence what it means to be a German citizen and which inhabitants of the new

Länder were expected to adopt. In the case of South Africa, there was no pre-existing constitution and no pre-defined South African identity. The first had to be negotiated through a protracted process of an interim and a final constitution; the latter is still work in progress. But despite these differences, both are attempts at establishing a new inclusive identity. Both are still struggling – despite the formal consensus that has been reached and despite its legal expression – to give content to this new inclusive identity in day-to-day situations. Similar processes can be observed in other projects of this kind. The expansion of Europe is not merely a debate about who qualify as new members and what constitutes the new boundaries of Europe, but also about the values underpinning the project and about the contours of a new European identity.

The Complexity of Identities in the Information Age

What are the salient changes in identity formation that we have to keep in mind when we search for a new conceptualization of humanism?

The first is the marked increase in the complexity of identities. In a "world without boundaries" the restrictions imposed by a single geographical location or by a single state largely fall away. The immediacy of communication that transcends physical and other impediments makes it possible to experience and identify with events and persons far beyond the traditional circles. Multiple loyalties are formed, stimulated by an increased awareness of choice and diversity.

What is at sake here, is more than an awareness of the different roles that an single individual can play as worker, mother, neighbor, union member, citizen and the like.[1] It is rather the individual integration of a wide variety of (often conflicting) loyalties, values and ideals. This integration forms part of a sense-making process and which gives meaning to the specific individual. Maalouf (Maloouf 2001: 3) shows how different components combine to form an identity that is unique to every individual. Instead of trying to reduce these to some essential allegiance that defines a person, the move should be in the opposite direction – the net should be cast wider to find as many ingredients as possible and not to deny any of them. In his case, he comes from an Arab family which lived in Lebanon for centuries and which was Christian from the third century onwards – long before the rise of Islam and even before the West converted to Christianity. His mother tongue, Arabic, is also the holy language of Islam, providing him with a unique link to more than a billion believers – just like his Christianity links him to two billion other Christians. "There are many things in which I differ from every Christian, every Arab and every Muslim, but between me and each of them there is also an undeniable kinship, in one case religious and intellectual and in the other linguistic and cultural" (Maalouf 2001: 15).

---

1 | Contra Castells 2004: 6.

But the complexity goes further – he belongs to the Melchite or Greek Catholic community which recognises the authority of the Pope while retaining some Byzantine rites. He was sent to the French school run by Jesuits because his mother, a devout Catholic, wanted to remove him from the Protestant influence of his father's family, where children were traditionally sent to British or American schools. He thus learned French and went on to study in Paris, rather than in New York or London. As an author he started writing in French and lived in France since he left Lebanon in 1976. The question he frequently has to face – whether he feels "more French" or "more Lebanese" – does not make sense to him. To the contrary – he celebrates and claims all the diverse strands that make up his unique identity.

While Maalouf provides an example of a complex identity from real life, the concept of can also be used as a strategy to bring together a diversity of racial and culture components to form a new identity. A good example is the famous "I am an African" speech that Thabo Mbeki delivered in 1996 (Mbeki 1998: 31-36). In poetic style, he deliberately combines elements of his own biography with elements of all the other South African traditions – Khoi, San, Malay, Afrikaner, Indian, European, and other strands in a way which is obviously not historically correct, but which serves the rhetorical point he wants to make: The need to unite these diverse elements into a new, inclusive, non-racial African identity.

Complex identities are not the exclusive product of the network society – they were also to be found in other periods. But what the large-scale crossing of pre-network boundaries and restrictions did achieve was to raise the awareness of these complexities and encouraged their positive acceptance. Even more importantly – in line with one of the most significant tenets of complexity theory – it focused attention on the *relation* between the elements of a complex system as the key to understanding the system (rather than on the elements themselves). In the case of complex identities this applies to an even greater extent. Furthermore, identities can no longer be claimed one-sidedly – they must also be acknowledged, which implies as process of negotiation and dialogue.

The Predominance of Resistance Identity

However, the move towards more complex and inclusive identities is not the dominant trend in a globalized world. This poses a challenge for any attempt to construct a new humanism and which most probably will have to rely on inclusive concepts and strategies. Castells (2004: 8) claims that in the network society, three types of identity formation can be observed: legitimizing, resistance and project identity.

Legitimizing identities are the least prone to facilitate processes of change, in so far as they are produced by the dominant institutions in order to keep the existing order in tact. The outcome of these identities is civil society in the sense that the latter consists of a set of organizations and actors that are bound to reproduce the identities that will rationalize the sources of structural domination.

Project identity aims to construct a new identity around a common cause, based on an alternative understanding of social realities and therefore has the potential to transform existing social structures. Feminism and environmentalism are two prominent examples of such project identities. The basic strategy of this approach to redefine existing positions or structures is of special importance for the conceptualization of a new humanism, as will be argued in due course.

By far the most prominent in the globalized world is the formation of a wide variety of resistance identities, all fuelled by the inexorable march of globalization itself. These are all reactions to what is experienced as oppression or exclusion and fuelled by a deep skepticism of existing institutions and the possibility to change these through conventional channels. The basis for the mobilization can be quite diverse – religion (especially religious fundamentalism), nationalism in various guises, ethnic or territorial identities – but the logic is the same. To prove this point, Castells (Castells 2004: 12 – 167) analyses cases of Islamic and Christian fundamentalism, of nations and nationalism in the aftermath of the break-up of the Soviet Union, of social movements against the new global order, so diverse as the Zapatistas in Mexico, the Patriot movement in the United States, Japan's Aum movement and Al-Qaeda with its agenda of global terror.

From the perspective of a new humanism, these resistance identities and the underlying trench mentality pose the greatest challenge.

When the world becomes too large to be controlled, social actors aim to shrink it back to their size and reach. When networks dissolve time and space, people anchor themselves in places, and recall their historic memory. When the patriarchal sustainment of personality breaks down, people affirm the transcendent value of family and community, as God's will (Castells 2004: 69).

The defensive reactions become sources of meaning and identity by constructing new cultural codes out of historical materials. What compounds the situation is that these reactions – arising out of the sense of alienation and out of resentment against unfair exclusion – can lead to an inversion of values and even a pride in self-denigration in what has been called "the exclusion of the excluders by the excluded. That is, the building of defensive identity in terms of the dominant institutions/ideologies, reversing the value judgement while reinforcing the boundary" (Castells 2004: 9).

The tragic result of alienation and exclusion is the loss of humanity (Castells 2004: 144).

Overcoming this resistance and negativity will be a formidable task for any new concept of a more constructive, inclusive humanism.

Moving from Exclusion to Inclusion

This brief overview confirms the dynamic, interactive and changing nature of identity construction in the context of globalization and goes some way to explain why the process is gaining such momentum. The implication for any quest for a new humanism is that more is required than merely proposing alternative concepts. In order to be convincing, such a project should concern itself as deeply with the *dynamics* of identity construction, that is with forces, processes and strategies that lead to the emergence of specific identities.

The examples discussed so far – especially any form of resistance identity – relies heavily on the strategy of *exclusion*. It relies on the distinction between "them" and "us" and on the delineating of the boundaries between insiders and outsiders. This should come as no surprise. Identity implies distinction. It requires a consciousness of the self – the contours of which only become visible in contrast to the other. Contours delineate and boundaries distinguish, but at the same time they divide. Identity construction and the understanding of the human condition cannot do without this basic strategy but also cannot escape its divisive effects. The question is whether we can move beyond the strategy of exclusion and also incorporate inclusive moves in the process.

In order to do this, it can be helpful to acquire a more adequate understanding of the process of cognition as such. In this regard, the latest work of Paul Ricoeur (Ricoeur 2006) provides valuable insights, especially his suggestion of an interconnected process moving from cognition to differentiation/identification and finally to recognition. This complex process can shed some light on how the strategies of exclusion and inclusion function with regard to the concept of what is a human being and what a 'new' humanism could look like.

Cognition

Any reference to "humanism" already presupposes an act of cognition. It is an abstract concept, resulting from a consciousness of the human condition. This consciousness is based on prior knowledge and experience and informed by the on-going stream of events. The fact that "humanism" is an abstract concept and the result of secondary reflection should not mask its roots in cognition – which implies that new knowledge, insight and experience will also influence our meta-language and thus our understanding of what humanism is.

Differentiation/Identification

Cognition inevitably leads to differentiation and differentiation forms the basis of identification. The ability to distinguish, to see the difference, enables the young child to identify shapes, colors, objects. Here we are at the heart of the exclusion/inclusion dilemma that affects even such a generic concept as "humanism". The whole debate is about what is "human" or "humane", about what should be included or excluded when defining "humanism". This underlines the tension between 'humanism' as generic term that tends to include, and "identity" which is based on distinction and the tendency to exclude.

The dilemma is further complicated by the fact that in the current "identity politics", the time-honored markers of country and culture are no longer as functional as they used to be. Demarcation in terms of space or location is virtually no longer possible. As we have seen above, identities defined by the relation to a specific region, country or state, are overrun by simultaneous liaisons that take no account of such spatial limitations. New identities emerge which have *none* of the conventional markers – for example *al-Qaeda's* rigid cohesion without any of the traditional ties.

Recognition

The critical step is to move beyond differentiation to recognition. It implies not only recognizing another person, but to recognize yourself in the other, and finally, to value the (other) person as person for what he or she is. Here the German word *Anerkennung* gives more adequate expression to the vital element of "valuing" that is at the core of this stage. "Recognition" is the code word for a whole process that is directed towards accepting, valuing and respecting the dignity of the other. For the overcoming of resistance identities and moving towards a more inclusive concept of humanity, this is a crucial step in the process.

A Perspective from Africa

Given the dynamic, negotiated, and constructed nature of the process of identity formation and given the predominance of resistance identity in the present global context, what are the chances of transcending this and to re-imagine a more inclusive, constructive concept of humanism? Is it possible to counter the natural tendency to exclusivism that becomes so pervasive as soon as own interests come under threat? Contributors to this project were asked to suggest alternatives from their own cultural contexts, resulting in interesting suggestions from the East, West, North and South. From the perspective of Africa, are there values, social concepts or traditions that could assist in the ambitious project of developing a new humanism?

Understanding that the concept of "Africa" is a construct in itself and accepting the diversity of values, traditions and cultures that make up this construct, there is no denying that the basic attitude and general orientation in Africa is one of communalism, rather that individualism. The group is the point of departure and the individual is in essence constituted by others, bringing with it a web of social and ethical obligations. This does not mean that forms of resistance identity do not occur in Africa, but the basic orientation remains communal. This orientation found its historical and social expression in many forms through the centuries and in different African communities: "African socialism", "ujamaa", "harambee", "unhu" and "ubuntu" being a few of the prominent examples. The individual is defined in terms of several relationships with others – "a person is a person through (other) persons".

When attempting to explore the potential of African communalism for a new conceptualization of what its means to be human in the present globalized world, it is important to avoid a possible misunderstanding. I am not interested in a "defense of *ubuntu*" or any related terms. *Ubuntu* itself has become embroiled in controversy (see so example Cornell 2004: 661-70; Van Binsbergen 2002: 53-89). The generic nature of the word leaves it open for diverging and often conflicting interpretations, but it is especially the way the concept has been applied in contemporary society that has drawn sharp criticism: To paper over deep divisions that still exist in many African societies by appealing to a shared humanity; to exploit the concept unscrupulously for profane commercial and political purposes; to create a new exclusive community of *ubuntu* believers who do not tolerate criticism from outside the fold. Some even fear that it runs the risk of totally losing its humanizing potential (Van Binsbergen 2002: 78-83).

Any theoretical concept or moral principle is of course open to abuse. But as little as ongoing examples of human rights abuses invalidate a constitutional bill of human rights or the moral obligation to respect human dignity, so little does the abuse of concepts like *ubuntu* invalidate the values underpinning them. The real problem is the level at which the issue is being addressed. Van Binsbergen correctly points out the danger when *ubuntu* becomes yet another grand narrative, generating another exclusive community of believers and losing all potential for true inclusivity (Van Binsbergen 2002: 70-72). The cause of such an aberration is a confusion of levels. This happens when the concretization (on a secondary level) of an underlying primary value is confused with the value itself. The secondary expression by necessity will be only one of many potential actualizations of the value. It is neither definitive nor exhaustive and therefore does not lend itself to serve as the basis of a new exclusive group.

To explain what is at stake here, it is necessary to revert back briefly to Max-Neef's theory of needs and satisfiers (Max-Neef 1991). Without going into any further detail[2], it is sufficient for our purpose here to refer to his distinction between a primary level of basic, universal human needs (like subsistence, creation, participation, identity, protection, affection, respect) and a secondary level of satisfiers of these needs. For example, the primary need for respect can be satisfied (on a secondary level) in many ways and by a variety of forms. These "satisfiers" may appear as direct contradictions: In some cultures, the subordinate is expected to greet his superior first, in

---

2 | For more information on Max-Neef's theory, see Lategan 1999: 157-164.

other cultures, the person lower on the social scale should not speak until his presence is recognized by his superior; in one culture, respect is shown by looking the other straight in the eye, in others by averting the eyes. What appears to be in conflict on the secondary level of actualization is in fact driven by the same basic value – that of respect. Despite the assumption of a "clash of civilizations" caused by a conflict of values, a closer analysis reveals that we are in fact dealing with a clash on the level of satisfiers. Almost no individual or community are against the values of respect, fairness, integrity and the like. *How* these values are satisfied often leads to conflict, sometimes because of cultural diversity, but more often and more fundamentally, by differences in interests and objectives.

Brought back to the issue of *ubuntu*: In terms of Max-Neef's theory, *unbuntu* is not a basic need or value, but a collective term for the way in which basic needs are satisfied. This is already evident from the fact that most definitions of *unbuntu* are descriptive (a person is a person through persons) or behavioral in nature: "Being open and available to others, [...] belonging to a greater whole, [...] diminished when others are humiliated, [...] tortured or oppressed (Tutu 1999: 31).

That also means that the process of finding suitable satisfiers remains open and that each new generation will give it their own expression and each different situation will require an own concretization. Nobody owns the definitive set of satisfiers – by its very nature *ubuntu* comes into being through the interaction of people with one another – not only within the own group but also and especially with outsiders.[3]

The challenge therefore is to penetrate the (secondary) level of satisfiers in order to rediscover the basic values underpinning the practice of *ubuntu* – and other expressions of African humanism. These values are bound to be more generic and universal, but that is an advantage rather than a loss. In fact, it is only on this level that links can be established with the basic values underlying other cultural systems and supporting other concepts of humanism as presented by other contributions to this project.

The quest for basic values from the perspective of Africa that is proposed here is not a historical undertaking, but a future-oriented process. The investigation of their origin and development has its rightful place, but here we are looking for footholds to move beyond resistance identities to a more inclusive humanism in a globalized world.

Values with Future Potential

If we re-examine African concepts of humanity and more specifically *ubuntu* from this perspective, several promising avenues for further investigation present themselves. As Cornell shows (Cornell 2004), one crucial aspect of

---

3 | The bloatedness of the concept, which Kroeze sees as a weakness, might therefore actually be an advantage. See Kroeze 2002: 260.

"African" philosophy which is articulated by anthropologists, theologians, and philosophers who disagree on every other aspect of "African" philosophy is its focus on metadynamics and the relationship, or active play of forces, as the nature of being. *Ubuntu* in a profound sense, and whatever else it may be, implies an interactive ethic, or an ontic orientation in which who and how we can be as human beings is always being shaped in our interaction with each other. This ethic is not then a simple form of communalism or communitarianism, if one means by those terms the privileging of the community over the individual. For what is at stake here is the process of becoming a person or, more strongly put, how one is given the chance to become a person at all. The community is not something "outside", some static entity that stands against individuals. The community is only as it is continuously brought into being by those who "make it up," a phrase we use deliberately. The community, then, is always being formed through an ethic of being with others, and this ethic is in turn evaluated by how it empowers people. In a dynamic process the individual and community are always in the process of coming into being. Individuals become individuated through their engagement with others and their ability to live in line with their capability is at the heart of how ethical interactions are judged. However, since we are gathered together in the first place by our engagements with others, a strong notion of responsibility inheres in *ubuntu*. Since our togetherness is actually part of our creative force that comes into being as we form ourselves with each other, our freedom is almost indistinguishable from our responsibility to the way in which we create a life in common with each other. If we ever try to bring *ubuntu* into speech, we might attempt to define it as this integral connection between freedom as empowerment that is always enhanced and indeed only made possible through engagement with other people. Each one of us is responsible for making up our togetherness, which in turn yields a process in which each person can come into their own.

This interactive, ontic orientation reveals how freedom can be understood as indivisible. As Nelson Mandela himself wrote, "Freedom is indivisible. The chains on any one of my people are the chains on all of them. The chains on all of my people are the chains on me (Mandela 1994: 617)."

Without justice and without all of us transforming ourselves so as to be together in freedom, our individuality will be thwarted since we will all be bound (if differently so) in a field of unfreedom. Again to quote Mandela,

A man who takes away another man's freedom is a prisoner of hatred. He is locked behind the bars of prejudice and narrowmindedness. I am not truly free if I am taking away someone else's freedom, just as surely as I am not free when my freedom is taken from me. The oppressed and the oppressor alike are robbed of their humanity (Mandela 1994: 617).

Mandela refers to the word humanity as an ideal in that *ubuntu*, as it is associated with justice and freedom, is something to live up to. On the other hand, the dynamic, interactive ethic that *ubuntu* expresses has as much to do with reshaping our humanness through the modality of being together as it does with defining what are, for example, the essential attributes of our humanity that make us moral beings. This understanding that our humanness is shaped in our interactions with one another and within a force field created and sustained by those interactions explains one of the most interesting aspects of *ubuntu* which is the notion that one's humanness can be diminished by the violent actions of others, including the violent actions of the state.

As Cornell shows, we can at least make sense of why *ubuntu* was so crucial in the decision rejecting the constitutionality of the death penalty in South Africa. In a society in which the death penalty is allowed, state murder is clearly institutionalized and this form of vengeance becomes part of the field in which we have to operate. Vengeance feeds on itself whether it is perpetuated by the state or the individual. Freedom as understood by *ubuntu* thinking, then, is not freedom from, it is freedom to be together in a way that enhances everyone's capability of power to transform themselves in their society. Since *ubuntu* is an ontic orientation within an interactive ethic, it is indeed a sliding signifier whose meaning in terms of a definition of good and bad is always being reevaluated in the context of actual interactions, as these enhance the individual's and community's powers.

In Conclusion

We may have to accept the idea that a new humanism no longer can – and no longer should – be conceived as a new grand narrative. Perhaps we have to make peace with the reality that basic values will always have to be contexualized in a historical and cultural setting and therefore always will take on new and different forms. Letting go of the idea of a *uniform* global humanism might just open the possibility to expand the scope of humaneness far beyond expectation – if that implies creating the space to give new content to being human and to value these expressions as variations of a central theme.

In cases where these theoretical concepts have been applied in real life situations of conflict and cultural diversity (see Lategan 1999), the encouraging result was that a finite number of negotiated and accepted basic values could generate a quite diverse series of satisfiers – again developed by the groups themselves – that expressed in a realistic and adequate way how these values could be practiced effectively in a specific context. Exactly because the set of negotiated basic values provided a common basis and a sense of continuity, the space was provided for a creative and diverse application of these values. In this way, the experience of a common, inclusive humanity was expanded, despite the most diverse participants and backgrounds.

From this perspective, the scope for a negotiated, inclusive, expanded humanism in a globalized world is growing rather than decreasing.

A Return to the Question of Humanism

in Islamic Contexts

Muhammad Arkoun

It is essential to realise that Muslim civilisation is a cultural entity that does not share our primary aspirations. It is not vitally interested in analytical self-understanding and it is even less interested in the structural study of other cultures [...]. If this observation were to be valid merely for contemporary Islam, one might be inclined to connect it with the profoundly disturbed state of Islam [...]. But as it is valid for the past as well, one may perhaps seek to connect it with the basic antihumanism of this civilisation, that is, the determined refusal to accept man to any extent whatever as the arbiter or the measure of things, and the tendency to be satisfied with truth as the description of mental structures, or, inn other words, with psychological truth (Grunebaum 1962: 40).

Today the question of humanism should be raised and debated in all contemporary cultures. This is in my view a key introduction to a counter culture to stop the expanding political, social, economic and ecological violence. My contention is that violence is a systemic force internalized in the operating mechanisms of globalization. The geopolitical mapping of the present world is another evidence of the systemic power of contemporary violence. This means that the question of humanism should concern at first the Western countries where the wills to power are more and more disregarding, if not disqualifying the quest for meaning that is the core of humanist attitude. Islam as a historical force of mobilization has of course to contribute to the emergence of a new humanism in all the societies gained by violence.

Arab or Islamic?

Anyone interested in the Arab and Islamic area comes across this terminological difficulty. *Arab* refers to an ethnic group that was concentrated in the Arabian Peninsula until the advent of Islam and the emergence of the

Koran's influence between 610 and 632. The process of conquest between 632 and 1400 resulted in the Arab *Diaspora* but still more in the rise of Arabic, the language of the Koran, which became the language of a civilization. Till the early eleventh century all converts to Islam, and as well all Muslims living in the *Mamlakat al-islâm*, the political area ruled by a Muslim authority (Caliph or Imâm), used Arabic whenever they needed to articulate knowledge and disseminate it in written form. Iranians, Turks, Berbers, Kurds, Copts, Andalusians, Indians, Jews, Christians, Zoroastrians, Manicheans wrote in Arabic in order to be accepted into the scholarly community. Thus we have a Jewish and a Christian theology written in Arabic (the famous example is Maimonides) as well as the Muslim theology. In the area of philosophy and the sciences unity was more complete and much less disputed, not only as regards use of Arabic but also concerning tools of thought, conceptual apparatus and demarcation of meaning. The notion of Arab humanism became accepted within this linguistic and conceptual outlook in the same way as the culture promoted by English is in today's world.

What about the label *Islamic?* First we should be clear that the form *Islamic* refers to Islam as a doctrine, a collection of beliefs, non-beliefs, teachings, normative ethico-legal codes that define the borders of a thought and regulate the behavior of believers. The label *Muslim* applies to Muslims themselves as social, political and cultural actors, and to the conduct and actions proceeding from these actors. We talk of *Islamic humanism* whenever there is continuity in devotees' behavior between what was called *al-'ilm* and *al-'amal*, that is, the required knowledge of the theologico-legal distinctions (*ahkâm*) derived from the Koran, and prophetic traditions (with the addition of traditions associated with the 12 or 7 Imâms among the Imâm and Isma'il Shî'ites), with a view to making individual and group conduct conform strictly to them. From the same religious viewpoint it is possible to speak of a Christian, Jewish, Buddhist, Hindu humanism. But in his book on *the humanism of classical Islam,* George Makdisi puts forward an attractive argument that is nevertheless hotly disputed by historians specializing in medieval scholasticism in the Christian context. He suggests a direct link between Christian Europe's first universities and colleges and Muslim institutions designed to teach and pass on religious thought and scholarly culture from the eleventh century onwards. This would mean that Islamic humanism had already begun to move towards the intellectualization of scientific disciplines (*al-'ulûm*) in general and normative religious science (*al-'ilm*) in particular. If we talk about "secularization" of knowledge we fall into anachronism. But with what I have called the philosophical *adab* (*paideia*) of the fourth/tenth century we can refer to a liberalization of cognitive activity similar to the European Renaissance, which was not free either from the hold of the theological, as Enlightenment reason would later be. The debate is open and should be taken further. Once again according to Makdisi, a literary genre common in classical Islam since the ninth century, *munâzara,* is found in Christian scholasticism in the form of *disputatio,* which has been kept alive up to the present day (cf. the current procedure for defending a doctoral thesis). Even if they are historically authenticated, these facts do not allow us to confuse the evolution and content of Islamic humanism with those of Christian humanism as it was defended in the 1930s by the neo-Thomist Jacques Maritain, author of *L'Humanisme intégral*, and his followers, such as Louis Gardet, whose Islamology was quite clearly influenced by comparative concerns.

It is possible to suggest critical assessments of the two concurrent theories that have continued to confront each other since the Middle Ages: a *humanism centered on God* or theocentric, with its three versions – Jewish, Christian and Islamic – and a philosophical humanism *centred on the reasonable human being* within the Platonist tradition of intelligibles and the logocentric conceptual frame of Aristotelianism. I shall not rehearse here the current movements that go beyond the humanisms that are trapped inside dogmatic fences inherited from medieval theologies and traditional metaphysics (see Todorov 1998).

The strength of the historic upheaval taking place in present-day political Islam obliges us to travel again along the critical genealogical paths already trodden by European thought when it faced the pressures, resistances, rejections and positions of power wielded by the Catholic Church, which was subsequently reinforced by Protestant fundamentalisms. My experience of Muslim populations since the 1960s has convinced me that everything that might be initiated, written or taught in order to release Islamic thought from behind its own dogmatic fences cannot succeed as long as the mytho-historical framework and basis for belief are not undermined, just as those of Christian belief have been since the eighteenth century. I have demonstrated that this subversion is not brutal demolition but a methodical entry into the relevant literature's discursive and cultural processes, which are still used today by those who manage belief. However this belief has not had the same content, or the same functions, or the same objectives since a highly ritualized political Islam penetrated into all levels of production in contemporary societies which, more than ever before, wish to be seen as Islamic. It is claimed that the rules of the Divine Law (*shari'a*) are being applied, whereas even a fleeting analysis shows that it is mostly a matter of external signs (beard, moustache, veil, posture, forbidden foods, group prayer, pilgrimage ...) of adherence to an "identity" and a kind of social solidarity. Reformist clerics (*islâh*) from the nineteenth century up until 1950 still led people to think that revival of the original teachings and forms of belief was necessary and possible; nowadays there are only legalistic consultations with muftis who have no connection with classical theological thought and are required to give isolated ad hoc opinions to "believers" at the mercy of a populist culture's tinkering.

And so the labels *Arab* or *Islamic*, which became accepted at a time when intellectual, scientific and cultural production expressed directly in Arabic new contributions to every field, are no longer applicable today with the same meaning. Thought and culture in Arabic are struggling to reproduce or clumsily explain models, ideas and works from the west. It is not a creative, liberating Islamic thought that is being mobilized, but a political, fundamentally ideological Islam intent on "Islamizing" modernity, which means picking out bits and pieces of modernity and importing *en masse* the material comforts of modernization so as to integrate them into the normative framework of prohibition and prescription that is defined in the minutest detail by ritual Islam. These processes are not even being analyzed from a psycho-sociological perspective to make people aware of the ways in which thought, language and religion are currently being distorted, both compared with the historical sources of past values and legitimacies that are supposedly being revived, and in relation to the tools of modern thought without which any research work will remain obsolete. In other words, there will not be any humanist attitude in contemporary Islamic contexts as long as the conditions set out in the introduction are not met.

The humanistic wealth of a religious thought varies with the levels of culture in which it is expressed. Thus the distinction I pointed out in the introduction between the phenomenon of the Koran and that of Islam allows us to grasp a condition *sine qua non* for moving from an orthodox religious context of thought to a humanist one that leaves all options open as regards realized or potential articulations of meaning. The discourse of the Koran leaves these options open because of its mythic structure, just as do the other founding discourses, whereas the theological and legal constructions that define some orthodox Islams (Islamic sects) restrict humanist expansions of thought. It goes without saying that today's fundamentalist versions are explicitly anti-humanist. In contrast the humanist attitude is one of the essential foundation stones of democratic thought and practice: it does not rule out anything human beings produce or anything that affects their future, but it subjects everything to critical scrutiny, including the dogma of religious belief and truths held to be sacrosanct or conferring sanctity.

Arab Humanism in the Fourth/Tenth Century

Readers will now acknowledge that it is historically legitimate to talk about an Arab humanism in the fourth/tenth century. In Baghdad, Isfahân, Shirâz, Damascus, Cairo, Kairouan, Mahdia, Fez, Córdoba all intellectuals, writers and scientists used Arabic to disseminate thinking and knowledge that went far beyond the limits of what were called the religious sciences, in contrast to the secular or rational sciences: *al-'ulûm al-naqliyya-al-dîniyya* versus *al-'ulûm al-'aqliyya*, which were labelled "intruders," *dakhîla*, by their opponents. The spread of literature and secular knowledge was promoted by a combination of several factors: political, economic, social and cultural.

Politically, an Iranian family from Daylam, the Banû Buwayh, took over power in Baghdad in 945. The caliphate, which was supposed to represent Islamic legitimacy was retained merely to avoid serious social upheaval; real power passed to the Bûyid emirs, who were supported by cosmopolitan elites of many faiths. These were nevertheless united by belief in the philosophicoliterary ideal of an eternal wisdom (*al-Hikma al-Khâlida*) found in many anthologies, encyclopedic works and practical manuals, from which the "man of culture," the *adîb*, drew all the knowledge he needed to pursue his profession (secretary to the central administration, magistrate, counselor to princes or wealthy patrons, writer, poet, legal expert, theologian and especially philosopher). Not only did the caliphate disappear as a centralizing political force, but the three Bûyid brothers – Mu'izz al-Dawla in Baghdad, Rukn al-Dawla in Rayy and Mu'ayyid al-Dawla in Shiraz – decentralized power and encouraged intellectual competition and doctrinal and cultural pluralism in the Iranian-Iraqi arena until the arrival of the Seljukids, who encouraged Sunni "orthodoxy" from 429/1038 onwards. The Fatimid dynasty, which was established in Mahdiyya (Tunisia) in 296/909, then in Cairo from 358/969, embodied a political theology that ran alongside Sunni theology but emphasized the humanist, pluralist strand of the culture as expressed in the famous philosophico-scientific encyclopedia by the Sincere Brothers (*Ikhwân al-Safâ'*). The political and cultural dynamism of the Ismaili movement provoked fruitful counter-arguments from the Sunni side in the east (Iraq-Iran), but not from the western Sunni area (Muslim Spain and Morocco), where the Córdoba caliphate (300-422/912-1031) supported the flowering of the famous Andalusian civilization, whose prestigious remains we still admire today.

Economically, the merchant class went through a period of extraordinary expansion in the fourth/tenth century and then began to decline from the 5th/11th century, becoming ever weaker with the corresponding rise of European hegemony and the arrival on the scene of Bruges, Troyes, Genoa and Venice, then Spain (the Reconquest or *Reconquista*), Portugal, England and France, up to the nineteenth-century period of colonization. The merchants controlled both sea routes (Mediterranean and Indian Ocean) and land routes (Sahara), as is attested by the rich geographical literature in which humanist travelers recorded precise, varied and extensive information on the people, cultures and civilizations very far removed from Arab Islam, which remained the political centre, the compulsory model, but did not prevent horizons extending out in time and space. In the urban centers merchants who had grown rich formed the social group that accepted a predominantly secular and rational culture. It was then that the demarcation lines were drawn between a theocentric humanism controlled by the *ulamâ* – those who managed the sacred – and a philosophical humanism focused on the human being as the source of creative freedom, intellectual initiative and the critical, responsible exercise of reason. Inevitably one thinks of the obviously more decisive role the capitalist bourgeoisie was to play in the triumph of Enlightenment Reason in Europe from the seventeenth and eighteenth centuries.

Socially, the class formed by administrative secretaries – *Kuttâb* – intellectuals and educated men, who were all trained in the disciplines of *adab* and supported by rich and powerful patrons, strengthened the impact of secular humanism in urban settings. It should be emphasized that all the strands of thought, all the social groups, all the civilizing initiatives we are discussing here are associated with urban civilization. Outside the urban centers we have to talk of a peasant, mountain society or a desert civilization whose social, economic and cultural characteristics were despised and negatively viewed by the educated elites, who talked of the ignorant and dangerous masses (*'awâmm*). There was social division in the towns themselves between the cultured educated classes who shared the ideals of humanism (*adab*) and the dangerous irredentist classes, necessary for the well-being of the elites but left to the cultures that today we call popular, with their beliefs and "superstitious" rituals, codes of customs and practices that were roundly criticized by both religious and secular elites. Thus, with the help of a sociology of culture and thought, we have to correct everything that is normally written and said under the admiring and homogenizing heading of Arab civilization or culture, classical Islam and Islamic thought, architecture and art.

Culturally, it was the progress of Greek philosophy and science that helped strengthen secularizing humanism in the 4th/10th century. Already in the 3rd/9th century a very prominent writer like Ibn Qutayba (died 276/ 889) was criticizing the extremely strong influence of Aristotle and Greek philosophy on Islamic thought.[1] After 848 the return to a Sunni anti-Mu'tazi policy with the caliph Mutawakkil did not stop philosophy spreading and reaching a wider audience by appearing in books of general culture (*adab*), whereas it had long been restricted to specialized works (Al-Kindî, died 256/870; Fârâbî, died 339/950). Among a profusion of literature that I have called philosophical *adab* (cf. Arkoun 2005) it is possible to discern several early signs of the rise of a human subject concerned with autonomy and free choice in the exercise of moral, civic and intellectual responsibilities. Christians such as Yahyâ Ibn 'Adî (died 364/974) and Ibn Zur'a (died 399/1008), and Jews such as Ishâq Isrâ'îlî (died 320/932), Ibn Gabirol (c. 450/1058) and Maimonides (601/1204) took part in this movement of a society that was small in numbers of people, it is true, but extended its influence as far as Europe via Sicily, Andalusia, the south of France and Italy.

In this regard the works of Tawhîdî (died 414/1023) and Miskawayh (died 420/1029) are good examples. They express with clarity, critical rigor and enthusiastic conviction the preoccupations, ideas, objectives and activities of the whole generation that followed Fârâbî and ended with Avicenna (died 428/1037). "Human beings are a problem for human beings" (*al-insân ushkila 'alayhi-l-insân*), Tawhîdî clearly stated and his writings, his intellectual revolt and his incisive criticism are centered on humanity but not forgetting its spiritual dimension. Tawhîdî wanted to de-ritualize religion in order to make it into a space for deepening spirituality,[2] link political action to a concrete ethic of social humanity, enrich Aristotle's rhetoric with the semantics and

---

1 | Cf. his preface-manifesto to his book *Adab al-Kâtib*.

2 | Cf. his *Ishârât al-ilâhiyya* and the lost work entitled *Al-Hajj al-'aqlî idhâ dâqa-l-fadâ' ilâ-l-hajj al-shar'iyy*.

grammar of Arabic, exploit historiography to clarify theological and legal debates, and bring together all disciplines, all available knowledge, properly verified, to explain all the mysteries of humanity, the world and history. All this would lead to a continual widening of the mind's horizons through the cult of creativity, the search for the beautiful, the true, the just, and the acceptance of all living cultural traditions in cosmopolitan towns such as Baghdad, Rayy, Isfahân and Shirâz. Miskawayh responded and acted as his "discussant;" he exemplifies the serenity, patient pedagogy and considered vision of the wise philosopher, drawing on the most ancient Iranian culture, open to a "universal" history of cultures and peoples as they were known in his time, and persuaded by the explanatory power of Aristotle's physics, metaphysics, ethics and logic.

These two humanist figures were clearly not alone. With his critical verve and demanding existential acuity Tawhîdî has left us brief but highly suggestive portraits of several contemporaries who met regularly in the philosophical and literary salons known as *Majâlis al'ilm*. It was there that *disputatio* or *munâzara* between experts from various disciplines and different schools of thought saw its finest applications and eventually became a literary genre. The grand vizirs who exercised both intellectual and political powers, for instance Abû-l-Fadl and his son Abû-l-Fath Ibn al-'Amid (died 360/970 and 366/976 respectively) and Al-Sahib Ibn 'Abbâd (died 385/995), graced these confrontations, these battles for humanity and the salons' prestige, with their presence and their political support.

In his majestic work Ibn Sîna (Avicenna) recapitulates and enriches all the knowledge and strands of thought developed before him; he too was open to all the great winds of the mind and, more than his predecessors, combined the rigor of reason and flights of creative imagination. He drew as much on the rich Iranian tradition that was still alive even though it was for a long time expressed in Arabic, on the work accumulated by Islamic thought, which had now reached its classical maturity, and of course on the philosophical tradition reworked by Syrian and Arab contributions. Medicine, as practiced by him, was inseparable from philosophy as knowledge, wisdom and style of presence in urban society. His teachings quickly became essential even for defenders of an orthodox religious reason, the humble servant of the *revealed given*, such as Ghazâlî, Mâwardî, Juwaynî, Fakhr al-dîn al-Râzî, etc. Logic, ethics, politics springing from philosophy were mixed with concepts and traditions defended by the guardians of the sciences labeled religious, by contrast with the intruder sciences (*dakhîla*). In metaphysics Ghazâlî and Ibn Rushd (died 595/1198) carried the debate to a level of theoretical fertility that not only has never been surpassed in Islamic thought but was forgotten from the 13th century until today.

Humanism and the Ideology of Struggle for Liberation

Since the nineteenth century the famous metaphor has been continually and lazily repeated about the closing and necessary re-opening of the "gate of *ijtihâd*," that is, the effort of research whose object is to develop a theology and code of law based on the revealed given, which has been piously received and written down in what I have called the Closed Official Corpuses (Koran, Hâdith, the collection of laws by the founding masters of schools, *madâhib*) and used as Founding Sources (*Usûl*). We have seen that the conditions for developing a humanist attitude in the third to $4^{th}/9^{th}$ to 10th centuries were simultaneously political, economic, social and cultural. However, it is a historical fact that those conditions gradually ceased to be operative from the $5^{th}/11^{th}$ century on. The Sunni policy of "orthodoxization" grew stronger with the advent of the Seljukid Turks from 421/1038; and it was consolidated for centuries to come by the arrival of the Ottomans from 857/1453 (capture of Constantinople) up until 1924. The imam Shî'ites confirmed the division into two Islams with the same active policy of "orthodoxization," which was implemented in Iran by the Safavids (907-1145/1501-1732). In the summer of 907/1501 the Safavid Ismâ'il was proclaimed Shah and his first decision was to change the call to prayer, *'adhân*, by adding, after Muhammad is God's Envoy, the Shî'ite formula "and Alî is God's walî." This was the beginning of official imam Islam. So the establishment of a state Islam was everywhere increased, resulting in the reduction of the schools of theologico-legal thought to a single official school.

The many ethno-linguistic and confessional groups that coexisted in vast empires were also tending to become autonomous under the leadership of heads of local brotherhoods. These grew up from the twelfth to thirteenth centuries and were recognized as confessional communities (*Millet*) by the Ottoman administration. The beliefs, ritual practices, celebrations and customs of each group were inseparable from the purely oral cultures and collective memories. Expansion of colonial rule in the nineteenth century more often than not reinforced the processes of isolation and growing autonomy, and therefore the strengthening of cultural and confessional divisions within the virtual Community (*Umma*), which was fragmented by internal and external forces. It was during this long period that *djihâd* became central everywhere as an ideology of battle against the "infidels," both internal (the "true," "orthodox" religion defined by the *ulamâ* who supported the imperial states, or locally by the leaders of rival brotherhoods jealously protecting their geographical and spiritual borders) and external (*dâr al-harb*). We should remember that the first crusade was launched in 1095, and was followed by several others; the Spanish *Reconquista* ended with the expulsion of Muslims and Jews from Spain in 1492, the date of the discovery of America, that is, the opening of the Atlantic route for the expansion of Europe. The Spaniards and Portuguese began their colonial conquests in the sixteenth century. Gradually and irreversibly the balance of power between the world of Islam and hegemonic Europe went into reverse.

Djihâd was the expression of resistance, an attitude that was no longer on the offensive, by the countries of Islam towards Europe, which turned into "the West" after 1945. If we take this long historical view, 9/11 is simply a form, following many others, of a struggle around several issues and with several dimensions that have not yet been objectively analyzed by historians. On the Muslim side the ideology of battle has mobilized all people's energies for centuries to such an extent that contributions to this thorough critical history have been insignificant.

As we can see, all these historical situations are inimical to the development of a humanism that is open to other cultures, as was the case in the brief period I have just described. Expressions of present-day Islam reflect the successive historical breaks that cast into oblivion and condemned to pious criticism all the achievements and humanist thinking that have so long remained unreadable and unthinkable both for scholastic Islam and even more for the "popular" Islam of the brotherhoods and oral tradition. Political and cultural tensions between the domains of educated written culture and those of popular culture – which has itself become populist since the 1960s and 70s – have an anthropological impact that has not yet been integrated into the study of the long period (from 1258, the end of the Baghdad caliphate, to the beginning of the nineteenth century) which has been called one of "decline," "paralysis," repetitive scholasticism and continuous regression in the intellectual, cultural and scientific fields. Lost memories, discontinuities, rejection of the conquests of the classical age are the subjects of long chapters in the history of thought and cultures in Islamic contexts, chapters that have not yet been adequately written. Indeed that history needs to be (re)written in the wider perspective of the rivalries that have set Islam and the Christian world against one another since the 11th to 12th centuries within the Mediterranean arena, and all the questions posed by historical anthropology, sociology and psychology need to be integrated into it, not just political and military history, which has long been highlighted. There are close and obvious historical correlations between the discontinuities that characterize the development of the whole Islamic area from the 13th to the 20th century and the irresistible rise of European hegemony till the present day. Indications that could be confirmed or enlarged upon are to be found in the suggestive work by Janet L. Abu-Lughood, *Before European Hegemony: The World System A.D. 1250-1350* (Abu-Lughood 1989). Added to the inadequacies of historical research into these questions, there had been the conditioning spread in the last thirty years or so by the influential production of political pundits, who often neglect to include data relating to the long-term picture in analyses that focus particularly on the most visible and prominent actors and events in the short term.

The political "elites" that have monopolized the leadership of the post-colonial states could not bring back a humanist tradition that was totally overlaid by a discourse of "liberation" patched together with fragments of modernity and proclamations, which were as dogmatic and obscurantist as they were deafening, on national "identities" whose obliteration is blamed on the colonizers alone. Granted, it could never be enough to revive the expressions and values of a humanism associated with the limits specific to the medieval mental space common to the three monotheistic traditions. Christianity, which has been directly involved in European history, has been forced to take on board, always after resistance and delay, certain undeniable achievements of modernity; it is not the same for Islam, Judaism and the Orthodox Christian world, which have been engaged in struggles to defend and protect themselves right up to the present day. All the great intellectual, cultural, scientific and institutional breaks forced upon the world by modernity remain outside contemporary Islamic thought. It is probably desirable that the critical intellectual *activities* of the most important thinkers and scholars mentioned above should be brought into the present; it is even more urgent to bring back the philosophical attitude that has disappeared since the death of Ibn Rushd (1198) and is still opposed by fundamentalist Islam. However, return to what Arabs call the legacy (*al-turâth*) of classical thought cannot be enough to free Islamic thought from the fundamentalist, one might even say hallucinatory, distortions of radical Islamism. The *content, methods, visions, postulates*, systems of knowledge, criteria of judgment and interpretation, beliefs peculiar to the medieval mental space can be reintroduced into our intellectual, scientific, legal, political and economic modernity only after adjustments and revisions that are rejected or deferred by the ideology of battle in its nationalist or religious forms. One of the characteristics of this past and present ideology is that it has mobilized all social groups, including clerics – intellectuals and managers of the sacred – who are thus abandoning their original function: critique of the values and definition of the legitimacy in whose name the humanist struggle demands to be waged. There is no doubt that eliminating colonial domination finds its legitimacy in the radical anti-humanism the colonizers tried to mask under promises to pass on modern civilization. Those combatants drew from this argument a feeling of moral superiority over their rulers, so much so that they too forgot the radical anti-humanism of their relationship to their own past, to the present conditions of their societies, to the legitimate expectations of their peoples, to the religion that was being instrumentalized in order to perpetuate its alienating functions and empty it of its most fruitful spiritual teachings.

Reading wars of liberation or national wars as a full-on confrontation between two anti-humanisms disguised by discourses of self-glorification and self-legitimazation requires historians first to be converted to a more subversive, independent writing of the "places of memory" consecrated by official historiographies, without which these mobilizing anti-humanisms would be stripped naked. In a book entitled *La Gangrène et l'oubli: La mémoire de la guerre d'Algérie* (Stora 1991) Benjamin Stora has provided an example, whose effect is a paradigmatic, of the permanent battle between the spontaneous humanism of people motivated by the desire to contribute to promoting the human, and the anti-humanism of ideologies serving the will to power. The author dismantles "the mechanisms for manufacturing forgetting" by showing how, on the French side, a war without a name (up until 21 September 1997 people referred officially to "events", "operations", but not war) was carefully covered up from 1962 onwards. On the Algerian side praise of the million martyrs was taken to extremes in order to win the people over to a revolution that for too long had been simply chatter, noise, arrogance and manipulation, without a human face, without a clear meaning. And this is proved by a fresh civil war, which for ten years now has been played out before an indifferent or contemptuous a world, too accustomed to the horrors of a terrorist violence held up as the "modern" way to take over power without bothering any more than in the past to build a legitimacy that can be respected.[3] Certain aspects of modernity have multiplying effects on the spread of anti-humanism and the corresponding derision that greets not only humanist discourse but also concrete manifestations of the humanist attitude. We have to recognize that what is called the anthropology of modernity has not identified the negative side-effects of the increasingly threatening uses made by uncontrollable actors of technology in particular.

Humanism and Globalization: from Classical Humanism to Contemporary Anti-Humanism

The evolution since the 1950s of societies associated with Islam does not encourage us to hope for an imminent conversion to the themes and objectives of the struggles for humanism. Millions of believers throughout the world recite and invoke the politico-religious story of Islam as it has been lived, the mythological history of a Salvation that is undifferentiated because the eschatological expectation of the Other Life is increasingly effaced by the demand for a justice that is itself as vague as in the past and recent eras of the Mahdis, Masters of the Hour. Among these mingled visions and periods there remain small spaces for introducing concrete actions that relieve the suffering, the anguish, the needs of the most deprived, but do not open the gates on to another history.

If we accept that the humanist attitude is more needed than ever in all cultures, we should ask ourselves about the conditions for a possible development of that attitude in "Muslim" societies, whose attention is strongly attracted by the somewhat anarchic revival of religion. The many observers of and experts on contemporary Islam have not been sufficiently aware that the new social actors who claim loyalty to it say it has contingent, ideological, even perverse functions relevant to the present time and very different from the long-term, transcultural, metahistorical goals common to the religious phenomenon. I have shown in various essays that present-day Islam is an identity *refuge* for many rootless peoples and individuals, a *home* for all kinds of rebels in places where civil liberties have been abolished,

---

3 | To assess the paradigmatic impact of the Algerian example for our discussion of humanism in the context of globalization, readers are also referred to the recent book by Mauss-Copeaux 1999.

forcing citizens to take cover and wait for the right moment to attack, a *springboard* for the ambitious attracted by social, political or clerical success (cf. Arkoun 1988: 171-186.) There are also believers who are sincerely and wholly devoted to deepening the human experience of the divine, following on from the great examples of religious spirituality. They remain on the sidelines of noisy activities, and prefer to practice spontaneous humanism based in an ethical and spiritual authority. Sociologically they are minorities marginalized by dominant groups, activist militants and secularizing forces that are as powerful as they are elsewhere. However, no social group can escape the inexorable processes that are reconstituting belief; at all visible levels of society subjective identities are being cobbled together by observing this canonical obligation rather than that one, drinking wine but not eating pork, or vice versa; by breaking free of the authority of the Medina surates, but not those in Mecca, by casting doubt on the authenticity of the Hadîth but not the sacred status of the uncreated Word of God duly set down in the Koranic vulgate, etc. In the same way people choose from modernity's wide menu. They do not ask questions about the socio-cultural construction of every belief, the ways it has been transformed through history; they piously repeat and teach the life story (*Sîra*) of the prophet, Alî, the Companions (*Sahâba*), in the form and content handed down in the first three or four centuries of Hegira without ever letting themselves find out about the critical re-readings suggested by researchers – all of them westerners – particularly in the last ten years or so (see the recent work by Motzki 2004).

In all the areas where human subjects construct and work on themselves, there is a predominance of patching together experienced as a way of fitting "rationally," or at least functionally, into society, modernity, the contemporary world. A more refined analysis is needed of the modes of integration of the self into family, village, city, global society, collective memory, geopolitical spaces, "Islam" and "the west" in order to measure precisely the distance separating each citizen, each person, each subject of rights and obligations from the imperatives of the humanist attitude as I am attempting to construct it for an example of humanist contexts. This situation explains why the return, or rather psycho-socio-political spread, of the religious in its various contemporary manifestations should be labeled anarchic. In the case of Islam this revival is taking place in a narrow intellectual and scientific field, which is fragile, contested, controlled, a tradition of thought that is weakened and impoverished by centuries of scholasticism, at a historical juncture governed by a multiplicity of challenges that are hard or impossible to resolve (authoritarian, even predatory states; states without the support of or even against the nation and civil society; lack of a civil society as an interlocutor respected by the legitimate state, the heavy burden of demography in a frustrated young population with no memory or foreseeable future, and a neglected and devalued older population; mounting unemployment, poverty, marginalization, exclusion; fragile economies that are ill-managed and entirely dependent on outside "aid", which itself is being diverted from its social goals by actors who operate in enclaves more connected to wider circuits of production and exchange than to domestic needs; disintegrating cultures polluted by ideological discourse and as dependent as the economy on hegemonic culture).

In such unpromising conditions, with so many negative factors converging at the same historical moment, how should we explain the fact that spontaneous humanism retains an effective enough presence to nourish hope among the most deprived? It is true that the re-composition of the functions of religion is everywhere assuming a dual significance: it is limiting despair and psychological and social distortion; it is conjuring up new forms of social solidarity by relieving solitude, poverty and exclusion. But these undeniable plus factors always have an exorbitant intellectual, cultural and political cost for individuals as well as for the whole of society. Only a serious sociology of hope – a problematic that has been completely ignored by political commentators on what they call Islam – will mean a more equitable assessment of the positive and negative effects of changes associated with these complex phenomena, which people are happy to merely brand with the labels fundamentalism, religious violence, etc. Here we can put our finger on one of the great epistemological weaknesses of the social sciences as applied to the study of religion in general, and Islam in particular, after the brief phases of the death of God and the death of Man with a capital M. The philosophical assumptions implicit in Enlightenment reason's battle against clericalism, are still determining perceptions and interpretations immediately violence re-emerges, which is swiftly and unanimously labeled religious. In the case of Islam, Christian and Islamic theologies have handed down since the Middle Ages the arguments required for pronouncing reciprocal exclusion. Enlightenment reason thought it could re-establish those arguments on irrefutable scientific knowledge. The simple fact of stating those reservations as to the validity of Enlightenment reason's epistemological stance vis-à-vis religion causes polemical reactions in many contemporary listeners and readers because we do not yet know how to differentiate the concept of religion from that of particular religions. Religion raises problems with an anthropological impact that are prior to problems raised by specific religions.

Democratic Humanism as an Integral Humanism

In the 1930s the Christian philosopher Jacques Maritain found himself in a situation comparable to the one today's Muslim thinkers must face; he had to react to the claims of the French Third Republic's dominant secular humanism and remind people that humanism inspired by Christianity could also take on advancing the whole of what is human, since it gave equal emphasis to the theological virtues (faith, hope, charity) and the intellectual aspects and spiritual vocation of human beings with God. At the same time another Christian philosopher and historian of medieval thought, Etienne Gilson, was defending the notion of a Christian philosophy that was rejected root and branch by his colleague at the Sorbonne Emile Bréhier. These discussions have once again become topical with the return of the religious, which the academic and university establishment of the 1920s and 30s dismissed as outmoded, pointless (God, a useless hypothesis), old, primitive, residual, a left-over. French, British and Dutch researchers on the period have documented at length that positivist stance when exploring the colonized societies of the time (see the ethno-sociological literature on North Africa).

Nowadays the human and political influence of religions is forcing researchers and political leaders to reconsider the relations between religion, politics and philosophy. However, although the human and social sciences have accumulated more reliable knowledge about a number of religions, philosophical thought and theologies are not more capable of transcending the old divisions than they were in the first half of the last century. What is the situation today as regards Islam for example? A brief sociology of the social context of knowledge and corresponding behavior allows us to distinguish three trends:

- The state take-over of religion (ministry of religious affairs, policy of ideological control) is still stronger than the politics of hope. What does a politics of hope mean in Islamic contexts?
- An opposition based on "religion" that recruits its militants among young people born in the 1960s-70s, who grew up in a socio-cultural environment dominated by the slogans of the ideology of battle against the alliances between ruling classes and "western imperialism." The social and political imaginary of this sociological group is built on a Manichean model that contrasts an Islamic ideal, forgotten, repressed, distorted by so-called national elites who preferred to import the socialist, then the liberal model after the failure of the Soviet world. This phenomenon affects both downgraded social groups (graduates, the unemployed, middle classes come down in the world, workers without trade union, political or administrative leadership) and those that have no roots (peasants, hill-people, nomads, villagers) far from the large urban centers where continual re-composition of status, roles, alliances, loyalties and solidarities is taking place, while the processes are gaining pace of disintegration of cultural or customary codes, so-called dialects, local memories ruled out by official national memory.
- The formation of social, economic and cultural enclaves that are associated more with the style and standard of living of the privileged in the most developed western societies than with other sectors representative of each society. Inside the country those who gain entry to these enclaves build for themselves a dense and reliable network of relationships in order to take advantage of political protection and the contacts they need to develop their business and achieve their ambitions; abroad they strengthen as far as possible their investment position with a view to possible retreat to societies run by legitimate states. In this way they can carry on lucrative businesses and hold down useful posts without being

truly part of the political and economic structures and choices imposed by these states; unexported profits serve to finance a luxury lifestyle; they choose the best schools and universities for their children, in the home country if they exist, but above all in the west, just as they go for treatment to the best clinics or hospitals to avoid the many inadequacies and dangers of the home health service. Culturally they flaunt their identity proudly before all foreigners; they participate in celebrations, group rituals, beliefs, signs of allegiance to an Islam that is in fact reduced to a collection of badges of identity; but they would not think of building up a private library in order to keep up with the great debates about society, culture, civilization that closely affect Muslim societies, which remain under-analyzed, under-studied, poorly connected to their past, present and future. Knowledge about Islam does not go further than in other social groups; on this point alone it is possible to talk of the enclave being in touch with the whole of society.

That leaves the clerics, who have extensive knowledge, either in the religious field (in which case they are called *ulama*) or in the secular area (where experts, engineers, researchers, teachers, writers, artists show off their talents). Those who are called intellectuals can emerge in all the specialist professions, but their distinctive characteristic is that they participate in debates about the most certain achievements of knowledge and the most sacred legacies of common belief. And as far as Islamic tradition is concerned this questioning attitude has always had very few representatives. At the present historical juncture, which is heavily influenced by political Islam and nationalist demands, a large number of intellectuals prefer to suspend their critical stance, or even abandon it explicitly, in order to put the emphasis on the urgency and demands of the ideology of battle. It is then that there arise, in the equally urgent and necessary quest for a humanism for all people, the complex problems thrown up by the interventions of NATO powers in the Gulf War and the Bosnia and Kosovo crises. The debates that went on beside those events concerned neither the quest for humanism nor the necessary conditions for achieving it on the threshold of the third millennium.

Before setting out those conditions, let me first reply to some common objections. In claiming a specific role for the critical intellectual in the construction, never so far completed, of a humanism that, for ever and everywhere, involves the human condition, I do not advocate a return to the old contemptuous, arrogant rejection of the ignorant, dangerous, toiling masses (*'awamm*) on the part of so-called educated, refined (*al-zarf wal-zurafâ*) elites (*al-khâwâss*), who are enclosed within an individualistic, aestheticizing, fragile group humanism. The humanism we now have in our sights is inseparable from the struggles, which have also never been completed, to establish and consolidate democracy. There is no democracy without a humanist mission and content, and there can be no viable universalizable humanism without a democracy that is everywhere acclaimed in the name of the dignity of the human person, an international law and legal organization guaranteeing respect for the rights and obligations of human beings in all the political spaces where it is implemented. The link that is thus explicit between the humanist quest and building democracy implies that all citizens are equal actors who contribute in the areas of their respective abilities to the tasks of producing and defending a humanist democracy. So we need to resolve the contradictions and conflicts that have always, in all regimes known up until now, set defenders of a religious humanism against those who advocate a secular humanism.

First of all it will be noted that this confrontation feeds into civil wars, terrorist acts, debates tied down by problematics that are obsolete in very many contemporary societies. Once more it is in the new political space of a European Union in process of construction that are being outlined out attitudes of thought, cognitive practices, legislative initiatives and legal processes directed towards moving on and transcending the traditional problematics in which the two rival humanisms are trapped. It is in this Europe that a secular, militant and politically triumphant humanism, as in France, has led to scientist certainties that have declared religious beliefs to be archaic, primitive and harmful; this has even gone as far as political persecution of traditional religions via the establishment of an official atheism. This distortion of philosophical and scientific thought justifies present-day movements evoking the return of the religious and even "God's revenge". That tragic experience (the Holocaust), with the political and intellectual failure of the colonial enterprise, makes it possible in Europe today to review and transcend them as is taking place. We are still far from the goals to be attained because the resistances of anti-humanist philosophy, implicit in any construction of what is called a nation-state,[4] have spread to all the post-colonial states in the world. This point in history is crucial for identifying new paths that would result in abandoning or correcting the anti-humanist aspects of the nation-state (expansion through violent conquest, exploitation of vulnerable peoples and social groups, imposition of an official ideology as was done by religious communities that justified their desire for power with holy wars).

---

4 | I do not mean that the nation-state is necessarily and always anti-humanist, but today we must weigh up the positive and negative effects of the nation-state as *one historical modality among others* for building the human. In a recent book entitled *La République mondiale des lettres* Pascale Casanova has demonstrated how national literary spaces are created with the support of states that defend local authenticities before reaching the present stage of a world republic of literature where "all writers are first situated unavoidably in the global space according to the place occupied by the national literary space they come from" and the peoples recently liberated from domination by the hegemonic nations can only make a place for themselves by gaining recognition from western academic bodies. Democratic humanism will make it possible for us to transcend control of the values of the mind based on hegemonic positions inherited from the age of nation-states that were ranked according to their ability to expand their dominion.

In putting forward these proposals I risk reactivating sterile arguments and compromising efforts to *deconstruct* systems of thought and make possible advances towards democratic humanism, that takes responsibility, this time without any residue, any exclusion, any massacre, for the human condition developing independently in a universe that is at last perceived and respected according to the principles of an ecological civilization. In order to put an end to all the ideologies legitimating desires for power that are masked by ethical, spiritual or civilization issues, it is necessary to re-examine the theological and philosophical problematization of *truth*. Indeed it is at this level that are perpetuated all the ancient and "modern" confusions over what used to be called "true religion," or nowadays the right to difference, identity, national independence, the right of peoples to self-determination, modified recently by the right to intervene where there is a danger of non-assistance.

It is not possible to reduce to a few paragraphs a fresh examination, from the perspective that interests us here, of the ever-vast question of truth, and the truths that can be jettisoned in our societies of spectacle, of continual dramas put on by various authorities, of endless consumption of material goods and goods that we can no longer call symbolic. However, I shall emphasize that for Islam, as for all today's living religions, it is necessary to reconquer, if possible, the specifically spiritual dimension of the experience of the divine. This reconquest must avoid the moralizing illusions of speculative oppositions between material and spiritual: the question of spirituality and its place in the formation of human subjects, who are forever struggling to become fully paid-up producers of – and not predators on – the humanity of humanity. This view of the subject's humanist vocation breaks with all the attitudes of thought and practices of reformism that are still being advocated in Islam under the name *islah*.

The humanist perspective requires rigorous identification, without value judgment, of distinctive features of the religious and the functions attributed to it in all religions that have appeared in history. All this leads to a redefinition of the cognitive status of the so-called founding or sacred texts, whereas their sanctifying power has increased with time and the repeated and varied demands of believers, who are always and inseparably social actors. Prophetic discourse retains its revelatory power through the centuries and spaces, cultures and civilizations, history's forces of upheaval and the works that intersperse its development, but the texts themselves, frozen by a static theology of revelation, act more as spaces of retrospective projection of the believing imaginary than as inexhaustible sources of intrinsic meanings. The distinction between *revelatory* and *revelation* is very illuminating for a humanist interpretation of the so-called founding texts: the *revelatory* function of prophetic discourse as a poetic discourse is connected to the suggestive riches, the inspiring forces inherent in the modes of articulation of meaning in this discourse; *revelation* may signify either the revelatory flow of a type of discourse, or the unique act by which a word that triggers an unexpected meaning suddenly breaks through into understanding because of the gratuitous initiative of a producer towards a receiver. It may be noted that these definitions avoid the restrictive vocabulary of the dogmatic theologies accepted in each community and provide a humanist framework of acceptance and interpretation for all initiatives by all possible *producers* (successive prophets; great founders of religions or wisdoms; authors of sacred traditions [*hadîth qudsî*], poets, great artistic creators) towards diverse and necessarily changing *receivers*. The concept of revelatory flow allows us to come back, on a concrete and thus generalizable linguistic, literary, historical and anthropological basis, to that concept of spiritual continuity reflected and claimed for centuries in the three great Closed Official Corpuses, the Bible, the Gospels and the Koran.

These movements of ancient conceptual apparatus towards new spaces of intelligibility, where interpretations are enriched by constant contributions from scientific disciplines that are themselves rapidly evolving, merely run on the cognitive level alongside the re-composition of religious belief and its functions that is taking place in day-to-day life under the action of uncontrolled forces. There remains much to be done in order to provide this subversion with didactic formulations accessible to all and to make operational the lessons of the humanist attitude in all contemporary Islamic contexts. One of the most fruitful aims of this subversive project as applied to a long and rich tradition of thought is to deprive the west of that dialectical contrast that lets it construct Islam as a foothold now available to its claims to rule the world and an easy pretext for its humanist failings. Furthermore, the anthropological goals of the tasks of subversion as applied to Islam will be sure to spread out wider and wider to all religious, philosophical and political traditions that everywhere encourage communities to confront other communities with the same idea of crusade against an absolute Evil, omnipresent but never objectively and impartially identified. Everywhere are paraded the same virtuous aims attributed to the struggles of angry crowds: parties of God, holy war, Justice and Development, Justice and Good, liberation fronts, those for emancipation, national construction, unlimited freedom, etc. In western democracies constitutions do not allow political parties to parade religious allegiances openly, but that does not prevent lobbies from forming whose religiosity or political programs are as far removed from humanist values as in the primitive social settings where religion operates more than ever as the opium of the people.

Discursive journeys do not escape the linguistic constraints of every narrative formed from swarming, complex, tangled reality, which is irreducible to linear, fragmented constructions placed end-to-end. Humanism proves its worth only in the lived manifestations of what the utopian vision of humanity prescribes for human beings in search of perfection. That is why one of the conditions for realizing humanism as conceived, dreamt of, sought after, is constantly, critically to revisit both what is thought, desired and prescribed and what is experienced. The humanist criterion is more relevant than the religious criterion for tracing the ideological divisions between schools of thought that today's political movements and practices claim to represent. Instead of staying within the deceptive framework of a crude opposition between Islam and the west – like the theoreticians of the clash of civilizations –we trace the shifting and necessarily tortuous borders between the battles for a humanist democracy and the militant movements wedded to systems with dual criteria that are cynically used by states which in any case bear heavy historical responsibilities. One of the functions of humanism has always been to control, by constantly providing critical thought, values and legitimating markers, the anarchic changes imposed in human history by policies of the *fait accompli.* This process of following lived history with the claims of a critical humanism was relatively well carried through, as we have seen, during the exceptional phase of classical Islam; it was effective in a more limited, precarious and fragmented way during the long period when anarchic thought and official political thought shared the social spaces for intervention. Democratic humanism, as we conceive of it in this exploration, cannot avoid a critical, constructive, retrospective and prospective return to a tradition of thought that continues to have an important bearing on the directions of history in a period of globalization.

What is Humanism? My Western Response

Friedrich Wilhelm Graf

In the German language, the concept of "Humanismus" is relatively new. The term was coined by the Jena philosopher and educational reformer Friedrich Immanuel Niethammer in 1808 as a counter-concept to the so-called "philanthropinism" of the Enlightenment, with its distinct focus on practical knowledge and skills (Niethammer 1968 [1808]: 79-445). Niethammer developed his concept as an educational ideal that pointedly was not concerned with imparting the utmost of useful knowledge, but, instead, with man's higher, intellectual nature, with the development of an autonomous personality prior to any specified purposes or functional requirements. In this context, Niethammer took recourse to Johann Gottfried Herder's concept of "true human existence", of the "epitome of the perfection of human nature, of all moral, reasonable, and aesthetic development" (Rieks 1967: 15). In the 19th century, there were hopes to find this "true human existence" or "true mankind" above all in Greek antiquity and, to a lesser extent, in ancient Rome. For this reason, a humanist education, the development towards true humanity, was primarily conceived of as the study of the knowledge, aesthetic ideals, and ethical theories of classical antiquity. In 1859, the term "humanism" was applied to a particular historical epoch and intellectual attitude by Georg Voigt (Voigt 1859). It was intended to describe an Early Modern time striving for humanity in accordance with the ideal of the ancients, the Greeks and the Romans. Here, it was especially the Renaissance that was regarded as the age of "humanism", for the predominant view held that at this time the clerical narrow-mindedness of the Middle Ages, which were so decisively affected by theological scholasticism, had been overcome and, with a view to the Greeks and Romans, an ideal of "true human existence", characterized by freedom, self-determination, and autonomy, had been developed. In 1885, the education historian Friedrich Paulsen coined the term "neo-humanism" in an attempt to systematize the widely divergent positions that took recourse to an antiquity idealized as normative (Paulsen 1885). Then, in 1932, Lothar Helbing made use of the term "third humanism" (presumably) for the first time (Helbing 1932). This was a programmatic concept applied to the attempts on the part of German humanities scholars, above all scholars of Greek, to once again convey precise normative ideals onto a modern society sadly experienced as being empty, meaningless, decayed, fragmented, and shapeless. This context of cultural criticism surrounding the use of the term "third humanism" deserves special attention. Since the early 19th century, the term "humanism" has primarily been used when contemporary society were found to be characterized by a fundamental lack of orientation, by a decline in value systems and morals, by materialism and the perversion of "true human existence" to a purely "specialist human life", or to a state of hedonistic self-diversion. The concept of "Humanism" seems to express a reaction to what has been experienced as a cultural crisis. This concept was able to and still can embrace widely divergent content, depending on the specific political and cultural hopes and expectations, which are accordingly – by way of the normative image of true, ideal personality – projected back into the "good old days" of antiquity. The spectrum of the ideals of "true human existence" designed within the framework of the Western discourse on humanism is extremely broad and subtly differentiated, ranging from Roman Catholic anthropology to Marxist conceptions of future society. In any case, the appeal to "humanism" always involved a concept of the heroic, noble, daring, highly moral, genuinely free "person" or "personality", a particular image of human nature regarded as normative. In answering the question "What is humanism?" then, I will proceed as follows: First, I am going to line out classical Western interpretations of man as a "person". Then, I will discuss the problems involved in the contemporary – and, especially in the debate among German scholars, inflationary – use of the term "*Menschenbilder*", or "images of man".

The Freedom of Personhood, or: Thou shalt Respect the Limitations on the Definability of Man

Worldwide, within the past 20 years there have been heated controversies on the concept of "personhood", primarily in the context of bioethical and biopolitical debates. These interpretational controversies have brought various uncertainties about the epistemological status of persons to the forefront. Some moral philosophers define the term "personhood" primarily with reference to psychological concepts; others build on models developed in modern cybernetics. A third group offers a definition in terms of modern neurophysiology. Still others appeal to modern Western moral traditions, according to which a person must be understood as an autonomous human subject, endowed with the ability to engage in self-reflection, with freedom of choice and action, and with the ability to assume responsibility. It is, however, quite difficult to reconcile these various conceptions of personhood with one another, as they relate to widely divergent areas. In this state of nearly hopeless confusion, I think that it may be useful to take recourse to the history of the concept of personhood. In an exemplary fashion, I would like to do this with respect to the metaphysical theories of personhood which were developed within Western Christian theology from the 13th century onwards.

Western concepts of personhood have been immensely influenced by the traditions of Latin Christian theology. The classical debates *de persona Christi* had an especially substantial impact. From the end of the 1st century, Christian theologians attempted to conceive of the human Jesus of Nazareth as being God's Son or God. This made them assume that two natures – human and divine – were both combined in a single person. In doing so, they were especially concerned with the identity of the divine human Jesus Christ and with his being a person. In this sense, the classical Christological debates can be understood as a substantial and productive source for the subsequent conceptions of the dignity of persons.

From the 2nd century, Christian theologians adapted ideas of the Stoic philosophical school about the dignity of the person (also handed down in Cicero) so that they could describe man as *imago dei* (likeness to God) and could mark man's outstanding position with the term *animal rationale*. Yet, for modern Western conceptions of "person", the Christological debates, above all those from the 13th century onwards, were more momentous. In his seminal studies on the history of the theoretical concept of the "person", Theo Kobusch has shown that, in the 13th century, Christian theologians began to develop an ontology of *ens morale* unlike Aristotelian metaphysics (which was oriented primarily to natural objects) in order to come to terms with the phenomenon of human freedom (Kobusch 1997). Alexander of Hales distinguished between *subiectum*, *individuum* and *persona* of Christ. *Subiectum* refers to the order of nature; *individuum* is related to the order of reason, and *persona*, finally, is part of the moral order. A "person" is fundamentally defined by the fact that freedom is an essential quality in a person's make-up. A person has dignity because the person is a free being. On this freedom, the privileged position of persons in comparison to all things and to all other living beings in the world is based. *Libertas inaestimabilis res est.* Since a person is fundamentally defined by freedom, this person, then, is distinguished from all material objects in this world.

The various discourses *de persona Christi* have exercised a profound influence on Western concepts of human rights and of the dignity of persons – concepts developed from the outset of Early Modern time which eventually had decisive legal consequences in the catalogues of human rights in modern liberal democracies. The substance of Immanuel Kant's conception of moral autonomy and of his classical second formulation of the categorical imperative has also been decisively affected by elements of this theological tradition. It is of utmost significance to keep these historical constellations in mind, especially with a view to current debates. The individual, to whom subjective rights are attributed by modern, predominantly Western theories of human rights, must always be understood as *a moral person*. This person can never be conceived of merely as a physical subject or as a psychologically intelligible individual. The idea of the dignity of man only makes sense if it refers to a moral person or to man as a free being.

Many conceptions of personality put forth in current bioethical debates are reductionist in relationship to the classical Western theories. Conceptual difficulties and problems of practical decision-making often arise because no adequate distinctions are made between the various perspectives on human beings. For the majority of more recent bioethical theories, persons are understood as a class of objects characterized by specific qualities. Here, the decisive areas for determining personality are the natural, psychological and physical practices inherent in people's lives. Thus, major characteristics of a moral personality, such as freedom, responsibility, accountability, mutual acknowledgement, competence in self-criticism and self-reflection, are not in the least taken into consideration.

The dignity of a person, the sanctity of life, the infinite value of the human soul, the integrity of the body, etc. – such ideas and concepts are originating in the context of distinct religious traditions. Even where these concepts were transformed into rational philosophical conceptions of the moral autonomy of man (above all, an accomplishment of Immanuel Kant), they maintained a quality of the absoluteness of religious belief. In this way, a significant resultant problem arises for modern ethical, especially bioethical, discourse.

Bioethics is usually conceived of as a branch of applied ethics. Working within the framework of applied ethics, bioethics attempts to put general moral norms into concrete terms with reference to certain conflict situations at the borderlines of human life. In order to do justice to the dignity of the person at the same time, moral philosophers concerned with bioethics search for clearly defined and – this is the decisive point – empirically identifiable criteria of personhood. But is it possible to empirically identify a person at all given that the term "person" actually means the absolute moral autonomy of man? Freedom, in a morally relevant sense, can be empirically established or verified only to a limited extent. To put this into terms that reflect the religious origin of ideas like the dignity of a person or the sanctity of life: precisely for the sake of personal freedom, the person is to be defined as non-definable. The limitations on our ability to define personhood and personal dignity may present a problem to certain philosophers or others concerned with bioethics, particularly if they are inclined to declare their scientistic world view to be the only possible perspective on such issues. Yet, anyone who attempts to do justice to the wealth of humanity's moral traditions in the context of bioethical discourse will have to accept the limitations on the definability of a person. Moral intuitions, moral values, and religious traditions are precious goods that should not simply be sold out at give-away prices. Taking such religious and moral traditions seriously is not to be equated with some form of ethical parochialism. The dignity of the person is not at all an only-Western conception derived from Jewish and Christian traditions. On the contrary, this idea, expressed in other terms and other symbolic languages, is also an element in various different religious traditions and cultures. No group of theorists, including Christian theologians and enlightened Western philosophers, has access to a conclusive, comprehensive definition of the dignity of a person. And this is only logical. It might just be the case that the dignity of the person, that a person's moral freedom, precisely transcends any single, specific definition.

Imago Dei, or:
Thou Shalt not Make Any Image of Man

In the beginning was the image. Jerome, one of the Church fathers, did translate "*logos*" from the prologue of the gospel according to John as "*verbum*", and thus accredited to the spoken and written word a world-creating power which the power of images could only ever fall short of attaining. Yet, thanks to enormous energies spent on their research, scholars of religious history know better now: for the most part, mankind's stories of religious faith began as a form of image-magic. Through their images, the gods acquired vividness, presence, and proximity to everyday life. The devout did not only express grateful respect to the statues of their gods abiding in the temples by reverential proskynesis, bowing, or humble visual contact, but they also kept them in good condition, clothed them and provided them with food offerings.

Image worship was also a formative force in the religious history of the old, pre-exile Yahweh cult. The programmatic, and, in the perspective of the contemporary religious field, unique anti-iconic standpoint of post-exile Judaism reflects stiff religious competition which those devoted to Yahweh attempted to overcome by setting harder logical standards than their rivals. Again and again they contrasted the many "idols" of neighboring faiths with the singularly divine Yahweh, who, as the creator of heaven and earth, was exclusively entitled to being worshipped. For the Jewish faith of antiquity, the demand to be worshipped exclusively on the part of the sole, unique God and the ban on making images in the Second Commandment were closely interconnected. Closer examination of the Hebrew Bible reveals that it contains no general ban on the making of images, but, instead, only a number of "legal texts" that declare the making and use of cult images to be taboo. These texts reflect much craftsman-like knowledge of widespread techniques for the production of images of gods and cult statuettes.

Devotional images of gods made of stone, wood, or precious metals were only "the work of your own hands", as the prophets polemically remarked. Being simple artifacts, they were just as incapable of providing salvation as were Samaria's calf or a snake made of iron. For the sake of the uncontaminated worship of Yahweh, central *topoi* of all later religious criticism were formulated in technicians' language: the dominant images of God were said to be simply poor examples of human workmanship. Furthermore, there was no guarantee at all that they would actually do justice to God's real nature. A demystification based on the logic of production behind the many images of gods was combined with a strictly theological argumentation: with Yahweh's unique transcendence, which was believed to elude any kind of inner-worldly manifestation, with the persisting difference between creator and creature, with the non-sensory, intellectually more abstract character of the specifically Jewish idea of God.

There is, to be sure, no direct path from the bans on images in the Hebrew Bible to the various disputes on images within and between the Christian churches. A concise distinction must also be drawn between the icono-phobia of Muslim clerical elites and the increasingly compromise-oriented discourse on images of the rabbis: If many Jewish religious authorities permitted images that served only as decorations even in sacred rooms, Sunni and Shiite Koran exegetes with especially solemn convictions soon rejected in their pious criticisms of political rulers every illustration of any living being, and especially that of human beings. Nevertheless, this differentiation of perspectives only confirms the fact that in all three major monotheistic religious faiths the disputes on images among the scribes and scholars were carried out with much greater argumentative complexity than has sometimes been suspected within the last few months.

At this point, Hans Belting's argument that "religion offered a true training ground for the use of media, which it occasionally consecrated and sometimes condemned" (Belting 2005: 12), attains a certain significance. Belting maintains that all of the controversial media concepts "dominating current debates are still burdened with the heavy weight of the Christian faith" (Belting 2005: 8) – with the abstract distinctions and argumentative strategies of theologians that had been under dispute for centuries, since in their heated controversies on the Word of God, Holy Scripture, and the sacred aura of images, these theologians had contemplated the power, seductive quality, and credibility of images much more intensely than those engaged in any other scholarly professions.

In 1956, Günther Anders lamented the modern "icono-mania" and explained the "dominant addiction to images in contemporary society" with modern man's inability to cope with his contingent uniqueness (Anders 1956: 56f.). In Anders's view, by the abundance of pictures, the finite individual tries to produce for himself a multiple existence and to attain a visible persistence as a personal triumph over the transitoriness of a particular moment in life, a bit of immortality. Other cultural critics perceived parallels between the contemporary "floods" of images and the great Flood, which only permitted a good life in the small counter-world of Noah's ark. Yet, superficially "updating" atavistic religious myths do justice neither to the fascinating wealth of ideas in the past's theological debates on media nor to the need for the distinctions necessary in the present controversies.

Critical distance to images should relate less to the seemingly endless loop of images presented in the mass media, but, instead, to those conceptual icons we have fixed inside our heads. A Protestant theologian whom the Swiss reformers, in particular, have taught about the irrevocable priority of the sovereign Word of God in comparison to any image-like representations, will not want to participate in the trivial iconoclasm conducted by the victims of the image "floods". It would seem intellectually more intriguing to examine, on the basis of *Begriffsgeschichte*, those new language cults in whose "temples" "models" ("*Vorbilder*") are revered, "personal idols" ("*Leitbilder*") are accorded respect, and "images of man" ("*Menschenbilder*") are acknowledged to have normative authority. Anyone who is aware that every single person is to be conceived of as *imago dei*, will understand the new discursive praise of "images of man" as being, at best, a form of idolatry. I have shown this in detail in my book *Missbrauchte Götter – Zum Menschenbilderstreit in der Moderne* (Graf 2008). We should engage in a new iconographic controversy here, especially in the light of an inflationary use of the formula "Christian image of man".

Particularly in biopolitical discourse, recourse is often taken to this "image of man" to establish a basis for clear guidelines of ethically correct actions. But can images generate norms? Do they indicate ethical imperatives? Who has drawn up a particular "image of man" – and with which political interests or moral intentions? As long as these issues are not debated, taking recourse to the "Christian image of man" amounts to little more than implementing a convenient weapon in the contest of worldviews. But the notoriously obscure phrase is not suitable as a major concept for serious ethical reflection. For how can the origin and validity of this "image of man" be conceived of? Two possible answers can be distinguished: either the "image of man" is produced by a non-human subject, for example, by God, from a specific external point of view on man. Or: We produce this image ourselves through the reflections of our self-contemplation.

Yet, the latter is completely lacking in ethical plausibility. Why should reflectively produced self-images be able to impart some fundamentally new orienting knowledge to us that we are not always already aware of? Either we are always aware of the limitations placed on us or of the norms established for us, or we are lacking in such knowledge and, then, neither can attain it by producing self-images. Moreover, the expectation that we could acquire hitherto unknown ethical insights by means of self-reflection remains an irresolvable quandary because of the obscurity of the "image of man"-concept. How do we know that we portray ourselves adequately in the images we make of ourselves? Who can guarantee the congruence between the person producing the image and the person being depicted?

But reference to the "image of man" remains problematic even if it is not the result of human self-contemplation, but the product of a perception from the outside, a binding human ideal established by God. In its account of God's sovereign creation of His most noble creature, the creation myth of the Hebrew Bible, the Old Testament of the Christians, says that God created man in His own image. In accordance with the Hebrew ban on images, at the same time it is maintained that we creatures cannot form any adequate image of the creator. But if the Creator Himself transcends the limits of pictorial representation, how, then, can we imagine a fixed image of His likeness? Being free creatures, would God the creator identify us with ready-made images?

Thus, also in light of God as an image-producing subject, talk of the "image of man" is ethically meaningless. Every individual is much more than and different from what he or she is able to discern in self-perception. And no one is simply the sum of the images that others have made of him or her. Only at the end of time, in the bright light of Paradise, we will be able to see God face to face. And only then we will be freed from all of those 'image-of-man' idols we have surrounded ourselves with in our illusory mania for security. Only then we will be able to provide a conclusive, definitive answer to the question: "What is humanism?" My own individual response is a very modest one: "humanism" proves itself in the willingness to constrain neither the other – respectively the others – nor oneself to a specific image of man – for the sake of each individual's personal freedom.

(English translation by Thomas La Presti)

Part III: Religious Dimensions

Ideology und Utopia:

Some Brief Remarks on the Relation

between Religion and Humanism

Volkhard Krech

The Terms Humanism, Religion, Ideology, and Utopia

Humanism is a movement that supports a worldview called *humanitarianism*. This worldview focuses on human dignity, on the education of the mind (in German: *Bildung des Geistes*), and on human rights. In European history, humanitarian ideas first arose in Antiquity. As a movement, it originated in the Renaissance and proceeded throughout Modernity up to this day. The humanitarian worldview is based on potentials which are conceived as being inherent in the human being itself, as it is expressed in Pico della Mirandola's phrase *plastes et fictor* in his text *"Oratio de hominis dignitate"* (Pico della Mirandola 1953). Certainly, humanitarian ideas differ within the humanist movement. But they all have in common that the concept of dignity is an axiomatic condition of human existence; human dignity is both the starting point and the purpose of all political and cultural efforts. Historically, but not inevitably systematically, humanism tends to emancipate itself from religion – at least in its institutional form–, since humanism regards religion as patronizing human beings and therefore inhibiting human autonomy.

Religion is also a certain attitude towards life, the world and the self. But in contrast to humanism, the so-called world religions since the Axial Age are based on the distinction between immanence and transcendence (cf. Schwartz 1975: 3ff.). A religious worldview looks upon everything – including relations between human beings – with regard to the Divine.

Finally, I use the terms *ideology* und *utopia* as defined by Karl Mannheim (Mannheim 1936). Ideology does not only depend on a certain perspective – this holds true for every piece of knowledge, attitude or behavior, but it also pretends that an assertion represents reality. Thus, ideology turns regressive. A utopian-minded attitude, on the contrary, is not congruent with existence.

According to Mannheim, a utopian attitude, when guiding human action, leads to a disruption of the existing order.[1]

The Interrelation between Religion, Humanism, Ideology, and Utopia

I will now turn to some considerations on the interrelation between religion, humanism, ideology and utopia. One might assume that religion in general proceeds within a utopian framework. But this is obviously not the case; religious attitudes can be both utopian und ideological. Ideologically-minded religious behavior does not refer to transcendence as a way to look upon life, the world and the self in a different way. On the contrary, it identifies concrete circumstances and issues, e.g. certain political constellations, as expressions of the Divine. An ideological religious attitude is based on the distinction between immanence and transcendence as well, but at the same time it is leveling it. In other words: It legitimates existent circumstances as sacred. In contrast, a utopian-minded religious attitude refers to the distinction between immanence and transcendence in order to question well-known issues and existent circumstances.

With regard to humanitarian ideas, the following problem may and does occur: An ideological religious attitude claims to represent the Divine. Thus, it might not care about a single human being, since every action has only one aim, namely the praise of God. In this perspective, human beings are just perceived as instruments for the Divine mission or, at worst, lacking worth at all – which is the case when it comes to "holy terror." While humanism *historically* might turn anti-religious, religion can *systematically* be anti-humanitarian. In this case, humanism is an essential correction of an ideological religious attitude.

On the other hand, humanism might degenerate into inanity if it is not based on ultimate concerns. I am in doubt as to whether the notion of human dignity itself, especially in its secular form, is strong enough to serve as an ultimate value. Religion has precisely this potential of combining the cognitive, the emotional and the active dimension of human existence. That is the reason why religion is able to provide us with ultimate concerns.[2] Thus, in order to create a commitment to humanitarian convictions, humanism cannot get by without integrating at least some aspects of a utopian religious

---

1 | Cf. Mannheim 1985: 169: "Utopisch ist ein Bewusstsein, das sich mit dem es umgebenden 'Sein' nicht in Deckung befindet. [...] Nur jene 'wirklichkeitsfremde' Orientierung soll von uns als eine utopische angesprochen werden, die, in das Handeln übergehend, die jeweils bestehende Seinsordnung zugleich teilweise oder ganz sprengt."

2 | Cf. Tillich 1957: 1: "Faith is the state of being ultimately concerned: the dynamics of faith are the dynamics of man's ultimate concern." In Tillich's succession cf. Neville 2001.

attitude. Taking the history of humanism into account, it is itself sometimes a kind of a religious worldview; this is the case whenever it is based upon ultimate values.

To my eyes, humanism and a utopian religious worldview are sisters. They share many overlapping ideas, and both traditions can strengthen each other. Already the conviction expressed in the Hebrew Bible that a human being is both God's creation and his portrait supports the idea of human dignity not only by cognitive means, but also emotionally and as a motive for action. This conviction is shared at least by all so-called Abrahamitic religions – and I guess by all religions, therefore they have great potentials for actualizing humanitarian ideas.

Why should humanism rely on religious concepts? Humanism has to deal with the following problem: We all know that we should recognize one another, as Hegel had stated, without reducing him to a purpose of one's own interests, as Kant stated, and as it is also expressed in the "Golden Rule", which appears in the ethical systems of many different cultures (cf. Wattles 1996). I think this is the core of humanitarian ideals. But how can this knowledge lead to proper ethical behavior? Let me put forward the example of three modern thinkers who try to answer this question by combining humanitarian with religious ideas: Namely, the French sociologist Émile Durkheim with his theory of society, the French philosopher Emmanuel Levinas with his considerations on ethics, and the German philosopher and sociologist Georg Simmel with his considerations on the basis of sociality.

It is remarkable, that a hundred years after the French revolution, Émile Durkheim spoke of the sacralization of the person as an indispensable condition of modern society. During the Dreyfus Affair in 1898, Durkheim wrote: "The human person [...] is considered as sacred, in what one might call the ritual sense of the word. It has something of that transcendental majesty which the churches of all times have given to their Gods" (Durkheim 1975a: 61f.). A few lines later he explains the reason for this:

[I]f the dignity of the individual derived from his individual qualities, from those particular characteristics which distinguish him from others, one might fear that he would become enclosed in a sort of moral egoism that would render all social cohesion impossible. But in reality he receives this dignity from a higher source, one which he shares with all men. If he has the right to this religious respect, it is because he has in him something of humanity. It is humanity that is sacred and worthy of respect (Durkheim 1975a: 64).

The sacralization of the person is an integral part of Durkheim's concept of civil religion. Durkheim's theory gives an example of the fact that even a cultivated but secular society – a society that is secular in many ways and for good reasons – is still constrained by religious convictions. Every individual has to be considered sacred; this is the basis for a humanistic society. Thus, the individual is not disposable, it is a human being and a Divine entity at the same time.

In contrast to Émile Durkheim, Emmanuel Levinas looks upon social relationships from the perspective of the individual. According to Levinas, subjectivity means responsibility before it is intentionality. The relation between one individual and another is perceptional and sensual as well as transcendent. There is neither a notion of the other as a human being nor of human dignity, since the Divine dimension arises from the face of the other. Therefore, Levinas suggests understanding religion as the bond between one individual and another (cf. Levinas 1987: 46.) The social relation is an ambivalent process at the border between immanence and transcendence (cf. Levinas 1987: 371). Subjectivity primarily is sensuality, and reflection and action[3] are always related to sensuality.[4] Thus, being humanitarian is not a moral behavior, but a combination of sensual evidence and a utopian religious attitude.

One might locate Georg Simmel's concept of religion somewhere between the two approaches mentioned above (for details see Krech 1998). In his "Excursus on the Problem: How is Society Possible?" that is part of his *Sociology*, Simmel explains the conditions of sociality in the form of the three "sociological a priori". The first a priori consists of the process of constructing types. Because of the fact that every human being achieves only parts of his ideal individuality, "the practice of life [...] is based upon those changes and additions, upon the reconstruction of those given fragments into the generality of a type and into the completeness of this ideal personality." (Simmel 1992: 49 [own translation]). The second a priori covers the fact that "each element of a group is not only a societal part, but beyond that something else [...] that the individual, in certain facts of his personality, is not an element of society" (Simmel 1992: 51 [own translation]). Both sociological a priori combined express "the most common conformation of a basic form of life as such: that the individual soul can never have a position within a relation without standing outside of it at the same time, that it cannot be inserted into an order without finding itself in opposition to that order at the same time" (Simmel 1992: 53 [own translation]).

It is remarkable that Simmel sums up his explication of the "basic form of life as such" by reflecting on the relation between the religious individual and God:

The religious human being feels himself completely encompassed by the Divine Being, as though he was merely a pulse-beat of the Divine life; his own substance is unreservedly, even in mystical amalgam of identity, merged into that of the Ab-solute. And yet, in order to give this melting any meaning at all, the devotee must retain some sort of self-existence, some sort of personal vis-à-vis, a detached ego, to which the dissolution into the Divine All-Being is an endless task, a process only, which would be neither metaphysically possible nor religiously tangible if it did not proceed from a self-being of the person himself: being one with God

---

3 | In the shape of agapé and caritas (and I might add: subjectivity in the shape of the Hindu bakhti and the Buddhist ahimsa).

4 | Cf. Levinas 1987: 170: "Sexuality is the example for the relation that is performed before it is reflected" (own translation).

is conditional in its significance upon being other than God" (Simmel 1992: 54 [own translation]).

Thus, the "basic form of life as such" is the condition for both religious ideas and socialization processes: sociologically speaking, in the form of the individual's double situation, i.e. that it has its setting in the socialization process while at the same time being antithetical to it; within religious semantics as the interrelation between the individual and God.

Religious Humanism and Humanitarian Religion

Today's theories of religion strengthen contingency as the primary function of religion. (cf., e.g., Lübbe 2004; Luhmann 2000). To realize that everything is as it is, but that it could also be different, might lead to a religious interpretation. Religion handles the problem of contingency by translating unfamiliar phenomena into familiar ones. Thus, it reduces the range of possible actions and decisions. Religion broaches the issue of the difference between the human being and society, i.e. the distinction between the finite consciousness and the world that is constituted by communication, and mediates the difference through special semantics. Due to concrete circumstances, religion either balances the processes of socialization and individuation, or it stresses one of them – but always with regard to the other, since the religious core topic consists of the difference between socialization and individuation.

By handling the problem of contingency, religion has special relevance for the constitution of personal and social identity (cf. Hahn 1974). According to Hans Mol (Mol 1976), one might speak of the "sacralization of identity." With regard to personal identity, religion broaches the issue of the individual's difference to socialization processes and encourages the individual to distance himself from societal expectations. In some sense, religion expresses the identity of a human being in a counter-factual way, but at the same time religion mediates the difference between the individual and social entities since identity also covers a collective dimension in the form of identifying with values, worldviews, patterns of behavior, and attitudes (from local communities and nations to the entire humankind). Non-religious worldviews and attitudes may and do lead to social integration, but religious semantics are especially relevant for identity building since it emphasizes the "concern about the human being" in a special manner.

A humanitarian religion must, to some extent, be a personal religion, as preferred, e.g., by William James (James 1982) and Charles Taylor (Taylor 2002). On the other hand, this might lead to a kind of sacralization of personal experience. As Hans Joas puts forward, self-transcendence might be one of the sources of religion, but religion's possibility of emerging out of the experience of self-transcendence is restricted by certain social and societal conditions; not every experience of self-transcendence must lead to religion (Joas 2004). Thus, religion starts with self-transcendence, but at the same time it is a *fait social*, as Durkheim states (Durkheim 1975a). On the other hand, religion may not be reduced to a societal function; this would mean to bind the sacred potentials. Therefore, the individual religious experience and the sacred dignity of the personality (individuality?) of the other have to be considered.

All modern thinkers mentioned above identify the problem of social anomy and an atomistic indifference as well as a holistic, totalitarian sociality. But they look upon those problems from different angles. E.g., while Durkheim stipulates individualism for the sake of society, Levinas claims sociality for the sake of the individual. However, both intellectuals combine humanitarian and religious ideas. If we understand religion as being responsible for mediating the difference between socialization and individuation, if we consider it to be both a social bond and a shelter for individuality, a utopian-minded religiosity protects humanity against degenerating to a sentimental, ineffectual humanitarianism, or against becoming merely one more ideology, as it is expressed in the following section of the book *Die Vertreibung aus der Hölle* (*The Banishment from Hell*) by Robert Menasse:

The Latin teacher Spazierer (Walker) [is described as follows]: His red-shining cheerful face emanated in an exemplary manner a hedonism that couldn't be erased by age, only by death. How Victor had hated him when he had asked especially mean questions at his promotion exam so that Victor failed and had to learn the entire summer to prepare himself for the re-examination. At that time professor Spazierer had said to him: "If you want to pass the examination in a humanistic grammar school, then you ultimately have to recognize: Humanism has nothing to do with being humanitarian! Sit down!"[5]

---

5 | "Professor Spazierer, Latein: Sein rotglänzendes heiteres Gesicht strahlte auf vorbildliche Weise eine Genusssucht aus, die von keinem Alter, sondern erst vom Tod gebrochen werden konnte. Wie hatte Viktor ihn gehasst, als er bei einer Versetzungsprüfung besonders gemeine Fragen stellte, so dass Viktor nicht bestand und die ganzen Sommerferien für eine Nachprüfung lernen musste. Damals hatte Prof. Spazierer zu ihm gesagt: ,Wenn du in einem humanistischen Gymnasium bestehen willst, dann musst du endlich begreifen: Humanismus hat nichts mit human zu tun! Setzen!'" Menasse 2001.

New Wine in Old Bottles?

Reflections on the Scope for a Jewish Voice in a Humanist Intercultural Dialogue

Jonathan Webber

Given the long tradition of Jewish thinking on intercultural matters, as well as the heterogeneity of Jewish voices in today's world, this brief essay cannot purport to be representative of the wide range of approaches needed to tackle this complex subject.[1] There are aspects of the Jewish experience of the whole contemporary debate about multiculturalism which raise major questions about the nature of religious and cultural difference – in particular whether it can or should be transcended. Difference, as the British Chief Rabbi Jonathan Sacks has forcefully argued in a response to Samuel Huntington's thesis of a clash of civilizations, is a distinctively Jewish religious preoccupation: God turned to one people and commanded them to be different – in order to teach humanity the "dignity of difference" (Sacks 2002: 53). The purpose of this essay, however, is not to explore the political consequences of the celebration of difference but rather something more modest – to present some basic data about Jewish views on intercultural dialogue and to consider some of the methodological preliminaries which are required if Judaism, as a religious tradition, is to have a voice in a specifically humanist dialogue. The main emphasis is on religion, although – in the spirit of proposing a contribution to intercultural dialogue – religion is understood here not necessarily as a self-contained category of its own but rather, in anthropological perspective, as an intrinsic part of culture.

---

1 | I am grateful to Prof. Jörn Rüsen for the invitation to offer a Jewish voice at the conference on humanism he convened at the Kulturwissenschaftliches Institut, Essen, in July 2006. The text here, which has benefited from the many important contributions made by others to that conference, is a revised version of the paper I originally presented there. The primary and secondary literature on nearly all the topics presented here is extremely extensive; to avoid unnecessary overload I have limited myself to citing simply a handful of representative sources.

1.

Seen from a distance, Jewish religious culture offers the distinct profile of a universalist vision of humanity, proposing itself as a podium from which the divine message should spread to all the world. Brotherly love is a key part of this: the very first prayer mentioned in the Hebrew Bible is that of Abraham, trying to intercede with God to save the people of Sodom from destruction.[2] The religion of the Hebrew Bible, which opens with the concept of Adam and Eve as the parents of all human beings, is without a doubt deeply preoccupied with the physical and spiritual welfare of the individual person and of all humanity.[3] It is true that God developed a special relationship with Abraham, and from him to his family, and from there to a people or nation of which Abraham was the ancestor; but this people was chosen not at all for its own sake but explicitly for the purpose of making a strong universalist impression on the nations of the world. For example, the plagues that afflicted Egypt are repeatedly presented in the book of Exodus as an opportunity for the *Egyptians* to learn about the existence of the one God.[4] The concern of the Hebrew Bible with the welfare of the world generally, and the Israelite role in maintaining this, is unquestionably central to the culture; King Solomon, for example, is described as seeing the Temple he built in Jerusalem as the religious centre for all humanity, not just the Hebrews.[5]

---

2 | Gen. 18: 20-33. Reference to this episode was a favorite theme of the late Shlomo Carlebach (1925-94), an outstanding religious song-writer of Jewish spiritual music, who was fond of impressing audiences at his public concerts with Judaism's fundamental concern with universal brotherly love.

3 | The Talmud is perfectly specific on this: "The Bible says that God created Adam as the father of all mankind. This teaches us that to destroy a single life is to destroy a whole world, even as to save a single life is to save a whole world. That all people have a common ancestor should make for peace since no one can say to anyone else 'My father was greater than your father'" (Mishnah Sanhedrin 4: 5). The statement about saving or destroying a whole world follows on from the observation (ibid.) of the curious use of the plural in the Hebrew word "blood" at Gen. 4: 10 (after the murder of Abel, God says to Cain "the voice of the bloods [*sic*] of your brother cry out to me from the ground"). The Mishnah explains that Cain had taken not only one human life but also all his potential offspring (for an English-language version of the Mishnah, see Herbert Danby, transl. and ed., *The Mishnah* [London 1933]; for ease of comprehension, the translations of Bible, Mishnah, and Talmud sources given in this chapter are given in paraphrase).

4 | See, for example, Exodus 7: 5; 8: 6, 18; 9: 14, 29; 14: 4, 18. Later in the narrative, after the Israelites had left Egypt but then turned to the worship of a golden calf and in consequence were threatened with total destruction because of their disobedience, Moses successfully intercedes with God – specifically using the argument that to wipe out the nation would make a bad impression on the Egyptians (Exodus 32: 12).

5 | I Kings 8. The theme is carried through in the prophetic books of the Hebrew Bible, most notably in the well-known phrase of Isaiah (56: 7), that "my house shall

Post-biblical, rabbinic Judaism built very consciously on these foundations. In the literature of the Talmud the sentiment is clearly expressed that righteous people of all nations have what was called a "share in the world to come," i.e. God's blessing in the heavenly sphere. There was certainly nothing at all in rabbinic Judaism equivalent to the Christian idea of *extra ecclesiam nulla salus*, that outside the Church there is no salvation. On the contrary, it became perfectly normal for Jewish teachers to respect the intrinsic value of other religions – even if the rabbis also declared the objective truth of the Torah as superior to other faiths. There was no pressure here towards relativism: members of other faiths can certainly know God, even if what they believe in is not absolutely true in Jewish terms. It was not an issue of truth claims at all; what was important was correct behavior – social justice, disinterested acts of kindness, the dignity of man, humility – these things were what God wanted from humanity, as the biblical prophet Micah had written.[6] One does not need esoteric knowledge in order to achieve salvation, not even belief. Basing themselves on the laws given to Noah after the flood in Genesis 9, the rabbis of the Talmud elaborated seven principles that were applicable universally, what we would perhaps call natural law: the need to establish courts of justice, and to forbid idolatry, blasphemy, murder, sexual immorality, theft, and cruelty to animals. This cluster of laws, known in the literature as the Noahide laws, the seven principles for the descendants of Noah (that is to say, the entire human race), defined the Jewish vision of universal social justice. They were given detailed elaboration in the talmudic literature, and as such constitute to this day the universal Jewish charter, clearly indicating a Jewish ethical and moral concern for the world at large.

It is important to note that belief in God is not one of these seven principles of universal social justice: Judaism was interested in correct behavior, not in metaphysics or truth claims. Certainly the other monotheistic faiths were good for the world, and in the opinion of some rabbinical scholars help to pave the way for the coming of the messiah; but the Jewish view of its own place in the world was based on the idea that God had put the Jews there in order to make their own distinctive contribution to humanity in general, through the principles of *tikkun olam* (helping to repair the world of its defects), *darkhei shalom* (promoting peace in the world), and *kiddush hashem* (setting standards of moral behavior in Jewish dealings with non-Jews in order to proclaim the greatness of the monotheistic ideal). In short, it is not difficult to argue that from the beginning, Jews have always had a sense of mission to the world and the improvement of mankind.[7]

---

be a house of prayer for all the peoples." The brief examples given in this and the following paragraph are merely for the purpose of illustration and (as will become clear in the course of the argument that follows) do not represent a comprehensive theory.

6 | Micah 6: 8. Note that the appeal in that verse is to "man" in general.

7 | For the talmudic references, together with a concise and accessible scholarly survey of this material (on which the above two paragraphs are largely based), see

Thus far, then, the basic biblical and talmudic principles which constitute the essential starting-point for a Jewish voice to the inter-religious dialogue. But it would be simplistic to rely on these features from the Jewish cultural reservoir as being typical of the entire system. In fact they constitute only a highly selective, monothematic reading of the subject – for it is perfectly possible from within the Jewish tradition to present a much more nuanced picture. "The Lord protects all those who love him," to quote a predictable, non-controversial passage in the book of Psalms (145: 20); however, the verse continues with an important complementary statement: "but all the wicked he will destroy." Protection of the good seems to imply the destruction of the wicked, following the classic principle of reward and punishment: what hope, then, for followers of other religions and societies? One well-known suggestion from the book of Ecclesiastes is that peace in the world may therefore be subject to the context and the circumstances: "[There is] a time to love and a time to hate, a time for war and a time for peace."[8] Certainly there are passages in the Hebrew Bible where even state-sponsored genocide is clearly envisaged: "In the cities of those nations whose land the Lord your God is giving you as an inheritance, you shall not leave any creature alive. You should annihilate them [...] as the Lord your God commanded you" (Deut. 20: 16–17).

It should be emphasized that the Jewish ethics of war cannot be read directly from isolated fragments such as this, given the considerable range

---

Solomon 1991: 209–244. The Jewish understanding of mission does not mean proselytisation, even though there were periods when this did happen; converts would be welcomed, and Jews wanted the world to admire Judaism, but there was never any coherent strategy for active proselytisation. When times were bad for the Jews (religious persecution, whether or not accompanied by pogroms), the dream of world peace and the universal acceptance of the monotheistic ideal could be directed into speculation about a messianic future; and so relatively little attention was paid to the Noahide laws. In modern times, however, a greater interest in them has resurfaced, most notably by Elia Benamozegh (1823-1900), rabbi of Livorno, who tried to persuade a would-be convert to Judaism to adopt Noahism rather than Judaism; and more recently Rabbi Menachem Mendel Schneerson (1902-94), who as the Lubavitcher rebbe became an exceptionally active figure in Jewish spiritual outreach worldwide, commonly referred to the seven laws of Noah as defining the Jewish mission to the world. For a detailed study of the Noahide laws see for example Lichtenstein 1981, Novak 1983).

8 | Ecclesiastes 3: 8. A surface reading of this well-known passage would suggest that the author is simply saying that it is wise to make good decisions and to do the right thing at the right time. But it is likely that this is not the author's meaning: the passage opens with the statement "A time to be born, and a time to die" – i.e. referring to the beginning and end of life which (normally speaking) are outside the ordinary control of human beings, governed by conditions not of their own making. Everything is (pre)ordained, the author seems to say – war and peace, just as birth and death.

of post-biblical opinions; in particular, the Israelite military conquest of the biblical land of Canaan and the attack on its indigenous tribes later on came to be historicized in rabbinic thinking – it was understood as being set within a context of the monotheistic attack on idolatry in ancient times and could not be used to promote or justify militarism at any other time or place. Still, the point does need to be made that Judaism has no commitment to pacifism as such; violence is certainly permissible if used in self-defense.[9] Self-defense may be understood metaphorically – whether as the need for the individual to put up spiritual resistance against the temptation to wrongdoing, or for the Jewish community in diaspora to put up cultural barriers so as to resist what is regarded as the pernicious influence of a morally polluted world and thereby to preserve the coherence of their own spiritual enclave. This view of the world – typical of what today is called fundamentalist – prioritizes the need for Jews to *separate* themselves from wider society in order to preserve their own spiritual purity, rather than contribute what they have to offer to humanity in general; non-Jews are simply not to be trusted (Heilman 2006: 25, 51, 56, 81–84).

If hatred is indeed a valid emotion, so too is it permitted to engage in a just war. "Pour out your anger on the nations that do not know you," it says in the book of Psalms; "Pour out your anger over them, and let the fire of your indignation overtake them" (79: 6, 69: 25). There are sufficient resources, in other words, to justify a distinctly oppositional, antagonistic, aggressive, bigoted Judaism; and those who follow events in the Middle East nowadays will have no difficulty identifying instances of this.[10]

In reviewing these two very contradictory positions summarized very briefly above it needs to be concluded that neither of them is adequate, taken on its own. Each of them is in that sense a simplistic reading of a highly complex cultural picture; more accurate would be to say that both these positions need to be read together. In attempting to characterize the history of the Jewish tradition over four thousand years from the time of Abraham (c. 2000 BCE), one solution could be (following Solomon 1991: 223) to propose a periodization in which one particular style has tended to dominate in a given historical period – for example, (a) the polemic against idolatry in the Hebrew Bible, followed by (b) a more defensive attitude by the rabbis of the Talmud in a hostile, largely pagan world; then (c) the struggle to survive in the Middle Ages in the context of the missionising power

---

9 | Thus, for example, the law (Exodus 22: 1) regarding the killing of a thief found breaking into a private home, formalized into the rabbinic principle that "if someone comes to kill you, act first and kill him" (see the commentary of Rashi on this verse and the Talmud at *Sanhedrin* 72a).

10 | The latter two verses from Psalms occur together (alongside a similar sentiment from Lamentations 3: 66) in the domestic Passover liturgy known as the Haggadah. In this context it is to be understood not as a call for vengeance but rather a prayer for divine justice, given that it was added in to the Haggadah in the Middle Ages, during the period of anti-Jewish persecution following the First Crusade of 1095. See Sacks 2003: 68–69.

and zeal of Christianity and Islam; and finally (d) new challenges for inter-religious relations in the modern world, in particular the sense of solidarity with other faiths in an increasingly secularized, disbelieving world. Such a periodization is certainly one way of acknowledging and conceptualizing the shifts of emphasis within what is a very long and convoluted history for which generalizations can be deeply misleading.

But the difficulty with a unilinear, chronological approach, based on a sequence of historical periods, is that it overlooks the simultaneities. The truth is that both Bible and Talmud give out contradictory messages; and for the scholars of the Middle Ages, let alone for the diaspora and Israeli Jews of the contemporary Jewish world, all the literary sources, complete with their internal contradictions, are simultaneously available. In practice, therefore, what can perhaps best be taken to characterize the Jewish world seen in a long view is not a predefined position but rather a struggle – a struggle between the sense of mission and that of rejectionism, a struggle between universalism and particularism, a struggle between the desire to assimilate and the desire to retain a distinctive identity, a struggle between the search for an intercultural discourse and its abandonment altogether.[11] By putting it this way, and emphasizing the whole concept of inter-religious relations not as a predetermined, pre-packaged "solution" to a major theological and sociological problem but rather as a continuing struggle between competing mythologized visions of reality, the Jewish case is probably closer to certain other religious particularizes than is commonly thought, and as such may provide a useful model for much wider application in the contemporary general debate about the scope and nature of intercultural humanism.

---

11 | One particularly important example of the struggle, within the Jewish tradition, is the (otherwise remarkable) story in the book of Exodus about how the ancient Israelites were enslaved, as an entire people, by the Egyptians. Why would the memory of having been in slavery need to be insisted on in this founding text? Why should the people forever need to be reminded about such a humiliating past? The text gives a decisive answer – that God intervened and brought them out of slavery to become their redeeming God; and it proceeds to build a very substantial part of the entire cultural system around it, working in rationales for many of the ritual duties as mnemonic devices specifically to recall both the slavery and the redemption. Even the observance of the sabbath is explained as a recollection of the emergence from slavery, i.e. from materialism (Deut. 5: 15). In this sense the struggle between monotheistic Israel and idolatrous Egypt, between materialism and spirituality (between slavery and freedom, as it is put), is a model of a struggle that is to be reenacted in the life and the consciousness of each individual. Some would conclude that the message here is that universal spirituality can be achieved by Jews only through their rejection of foreign cultures; others might put the emphasis differently and say that dialogue – to be "a light unto the nations" (e.g. Isaiah 49: 6) and, thereby, to spread the monotheistic ideal and the unity of humanity – is the key objective.

2.

If there is a struggle between these two competing standpoints – for heuristic reasons I have so far expressed them in binary terms, but nothing is of course that simple – one obvious question that arises is how the choice between them, or the mobilization of resources from the cultural reservoir, is actually made. There is clearly a strongly pragmatic aspect to this, even if (by definition) ideological justifications can be provided that make the rhetoric that is used seem timely and even self-evident. For example, at a time of peace, where the government of a multicultural, multifaith society is secular and does not favor any one faith community over another, the scope for reaching out cross-culturally through interfaith dialogue and communication is immense – invoking such notions as "common ground," or the contribution of religion to harmony, tranquility, human dignity, ethical behavior, the ideals of peace and reconciliation, and so on. The rhetorical appeal, capable of drawing on a rich range of resources of the type noted above, can typically include warm memories of a golden age when minority communities lived peacefully and productively with majority society. At a time of war, however (including of course the presence of terrorist activities, but more typically during times of state-sponsored repression, persecution and violence against minority groups), interfaith communication is of course under great pressure and usually does not function well. Where there is intercommunal violence, cultural difference and particularist belonging are obviously exaggerated, and the boundaries dividing groups from each other are commonly essentialized. In such contexts, the rhetorical appeal is often made to an imagined past characterized principally by ancient ethnic hatreds – and to account for those periods or contexts where violence did not occur, it is deemed to have been present "just below the surface".

There is no single historical memory here: it depends on the context. The violence experienced by minority communities can be understood and explained either as characteristic of difficult and troubled relations over a long period of time – or, alternatively, as the arrival of "politics" from the outside, disturbing a long period of calm between local peoples. Other agendas will determine which historiography is used in practice; both kinds of memory are simultaneously available, and of course memories of war are often invoked anachronistically during ordinary peacetime.[12] To put that point another way, the present-day obsession with antisemitism or Islamophobia, whether real or imagined, clearly has the effect of reinforcing community members with a sense of belonging and to discourage them from attributing any major significance to intercultural humanist discourse and interfaith dialogue. Certainly the Jewish community leadership finds the fear of post-Holocaust antisemitism a convenient and appealing strategy to mobilize group cohesion in an otherwise deeply fractured modern Jewish world.

---

12 | For a recent ethnographic study in Bosnia, concerning the personal and political dynamics of how memory creates and sustains hostility, see Sorabji 2006: 1-18.

These fears, open to challenge as they may be, should however not be minimized. References to the universality of antisemitism in prewar Poland, a ubiquitous ingredient of the popular Jewish understanding of how the Holocaust could have happened,[13] would seem to be part of the way ordinary Jews make sense of their diaspora history. Such a view links seamlessly with, and is perhaps encouraged by, the classic Zionist approach to the European Jewish past – dominated by anti-Jewish stereotype and pogroms, offering little optimism for the future, and thus presupposing the need for an independent Jewish state. The massive Jewish migrations from the former Soviet Union to Israel in the 1990s[14] was initially triggered by the widespread belief that major anti-Jewish violence was imminent, based on the idea (as in Yugoslavia) that serious intercommunal unrest would erupt after strong central government, which had hitherto succeeded in repressing latent ethnic tensions, had lost control. Even if such anxieties prove groundless (which in some cases, as in Yugoslavia, was not at all true), the very language of the hopes and fears of minority communities, based on indigenous readings of their own histories, form an essential part of the ethnography and need to be taken seriously.

But even here the actual evidence on the ground can point both ways, and generalizations are difficult. There is an unmistakable increase in recent years of quite high-level Christian–Jewish and Muslim–Jewish consultations, involving leading rabbis, priests, and imams; there are new proposals to include courses on attitudes to other religions in the training of rabbis; and there is even a proposal to establish a permanent inter-religious assembly at the United Nations, specifically to encourage an ethical, moral, and religious input to debates otherwise dominated by political and economic affairs. I myself am involved in a UNESCO initiative to bring together university scholars of religion and consider the role of universities in exposing students from diverse faith communities to universalist approaches.[15] Education is

---

13 | The negative Jewish stereotype of the antisemitic Pole and its linkage with a belief in Polish co-responsibility for the Holocaust as it unfolded in Poland (home to the largest Jewish community in prewar Europe and the setting for the six main death camps) has been discussed at length by both Jewish and Polish scholars. For two useful recent collections of papers surveying this subject see Zimmerman 2003 and Biskupski/Polonsky 2007, especially the introduction and the chapters by Engel, Polonsky, and Pawlikowski.

14 | By January 2007 the total figure for Jewish immigrants to Israel from the FSU had reached one million, equivalent to approx. 18% of the total Jewish population (5.6m) and equivalent also to one-third of the total number of immigrants to Israel since the state was founded in 1948. This wave of immigration from the FSU has now, however, substantially declined, to approx. 9,000 persons per year (figures from the Jewish Agency, the Israeli statutory body that oversees immigration, as quoted in the *Ha'aretz* newspaper, 30 December 2006).

15 | For a good recent example of the inter-religious work being undertaken by UNESCO, see UNESCO 2006, the proceedings of a conference published by UNESCO which debated how far the French concept of *laïcité* (secularism) helps or

commonly seen in fact as the principal arena (other than the media) in which stereotyped anxieties that exist between different cultures can be countered, and there is a growing new awareness of the need radically to reorganize teacher training and curriculum development in European schools so as to address the realities of present-day cultural diversity. Perhaps the notion of European citizenship is a new humanist concept, still in its infancy; but concrete proposals are emerging to consider ways in which school curricula can combat stereotypes, question the "strangeness" of the Other, and demonstrate the interconnections, socio-cultural exchanges, and mutual influences that at least the three Abrahamic religions have experienced together in Europe.[16] Parallel trends at grassroots level are also observable. But my colleagues in Jerusalem tell me that attendance at such grassroots meetings between Jews and Arabs falls off very sharply each time there is a terrorist attack. It seems that universalism is very fragile, a luxury in peacetime for those with little else to concern them – somewhat reminiscent, perhaps, of the lukewarm reception in Eastern Europe during the height of the Cold War to middle-class Western preoccupations with the rights of women. The revival and respecification of a humanism that would speak to contemporary issues will evidently be a slow and tortuous process – especially because there is no universal peace today; far from it.

3.

Reference has already been made above to the language of inter-religious dialogue. In fact the assumptions that are brought into that discourse are equally problematic. For example, should the emphasis be on a stable narrative, smoothing out the inconsistencies between a religion's historical legacy of both universalism and particularism, masking out the uncertainties, and altogether presenting a sense of theological coherence

---

hinders dialogue, how far religions themselves work towards dialogue, and a survey of current initiatives favoring a culture of dialogue. The United Nations has also agreed to encourage its member states to develop educational programs "to inculcate future generations with the lessons of the Holocaust in order to prevent future acts of genocide" (42nd plenary meeting of 1 November 2005) and has designated 27 January (the anniversary of the liberation of Auschwitz in 1945) as an annual International Day of Commemoration in memory of the victims of the Holocaust (ibid.), a lead which many European states have already taken up. In such contexts the "lessons of the Holocaust" are conventionally construed in universalist terms ("a warning to all people of the dangers of hatred, bigotry, racism, and prejudice," to cite the U.N. text).

16 | A very thorough survey is presented in Kaul-Seidman/Nielsen/Vinzent 2003, demonstrating point by point how school curricula and textbooks seriously lag behind the changed cultural, political, and demographic European realities, and proposing a series of detailed recommendations.

and robust commitment to a general concept of humanity? Or should the strategy rather be to be open and honest about the internal contradictions, to acknowledge incoherence, to acknowledge and indeed to struggle with the doubts and hesitations within one's own faith tradition? Most of the time, it seems, people in a dialogue situation prefer the soft option and make the universalist claim that their tradition has all along emphasized nothing else but a love of humanity; and of course the rhetoric is available for them to pull out a selection of biblical quotations to prove it. But the preference for platitudes of this kind, which probably dominates far too much of the inter-religious dialogue, is a distortion – in the sense that it is not a representation of the whole truth.

The preference for platitudes may not really be traditionally Jewish either. The whole structure and content of the Talmud stress the basic idea that any statement in the biblical text has *multiple* layers of meaning and thus contains *multiple* truths – for example, both its plain meaning and its allegorical meaning, as well as mystical and homiletic meanings. The job of the talmudic scholar is precisely to struggle with this multivocality; there is no one correct reading of any biblical text. The Jewish view is that spiritual meanings may be hidden within the text and can be brought to light only when compared and contrasted with other passages in the text. The very awareness of this intertextual multivocality within the Hebrew Bible, through the close study and contemplation of the divine word, is in this sense treated as extremely fruitful in spiritual terms. What this hints at is an important aspect of Jewish culture – the retention within the system of contradictions and differences of opinion. There is no quiet smoothing out of inconsistencies here; multivocality is built into the whole structure of the enterprise.[17]

---

17 | Many of the textual difficulties that eventually gave rise in modern biblical scholarship to the "documentary hypothesis," i.e. that the Five Books of Moses in particular are not one single document in origin but rather a compilation from different sources, were noted long ago in the talmudic literature, and meanings and explanations were provided for these apparent discrepancies. Following Psalms 62: 12 ("God spoke one utterance but we heard two"), Jewish tradition proposed precisely that this is in the very nature of divine revelation to humanity – and that this is why (to take just one example) the two versions of the Ten Commandments given in the text (Exodus 20 and Deuteronomy 5) are not identical. On the contrary, the differences between them (such as "Remember the sabbath day," in the former version, and "Observe the sabbath day," in the latter) are not only "normal" discrepancies typical of the supernatural transmission process but also carry important intrinsic meaning. The verse from Psalms quoted here is briefly expounded in an interesting passage in the Talmud (*Sanhedrin* 34a) where a further verse is brought into the discussion: "Is not my word like a fire, says the Lord, and like a hammer that breaks a rock into pieces?" (Jeremiah 23: 29). One medieval commentator (whose notes appear in the standard editions) suggests that the Talmud may here be reinterpreting this verse from Jeremiah to mean that it is the hammer itself that is split when striking a very

There, then, is at least one answer to the question. The stable narratives and positive-sounding, monothematic platitudes, as a representation of Jewish religion in dialogue situations, do little more than offer a conditioned response to specific circumstances and in that sense is not a typical representation of how Jews deal with difficult issues.[18] In other contexts, as is well known, everyday Jewish life may be highly politicized and include strong doses of argument, debate, disagreement, interruptions, telling jokes. Certainly in the Jewish case (though applicable also very much more widely), "religion" is not a self-contained, tightly bounded philosophical system of belief and thinking; it is a cultural system, heavily dependent on the use of socially meaningful symbols and symbolic behavior, and profoundly integrated within a very wide range of socially situated events and circumstances.[19] "Religious views" cannot thus be neatly summarized without much wider cultural reference. This is a particularly important point to bear in mind when considering Jewish views on a specific subject, especially given that Jews have historically thought of themselves as a people, not as a "religion" as such, which is many ways is an outsider's construction.[20]

Furthermore, like any minority group, diaspora Jews possess multiple identities in terms of their sense of belonging to the majority societies in which they live, the need to learn how to "dwell" wherever they happen to be. They collectively hold multiple models in their heads, and especially so as regards their attitudes to other cultures – not to mention the controversies

---

hard object, i.e. that any biblical verse, when subjected to the scrutiny of a keen intellect, splits into different meanings so as to convey many different teachings (for an English-language version of the sources from the Babylonian Talmud cited in this chapter, see Epstein 1961).

18 | To give a rather striking example from criminal law: the Talmud records the view of one eminent sage that an accused person is automatically acquitted if the judges unanimously agree that he is guilty (*Sanhedrin* 17a; I am grateful to Rabbi Shlomo Freshwater of London for drawing my attention to this passage).

19 | In understanding "religion" in this way I am following the anthropological view of Clifford Geertz (see for example his "Religion as a Cultural System," in Geertz 1966), though the approach is well established within academic Jewish studies also: see for example Neusner 1983, which in the attempt to provide a theoretical basis for comparative work specifically related the study of Judaism as a religion to the history of its social settings)

20 | The biblical term for the Jewish collectivity is *edah* or *am* ("community" or "people"); certainly today *am yisrael* ("the people of Israel") is probably the most commonly used Hebrew-language term, to refer to Jews worldwide (not just the Jewish citizens of the State of Israel). "Religion" or "ethnic group" (or, more recently, "faith community") are, however, the common terms used in English to refer to the Jews; in interpreting Jewish identity they clearly relate to conceptualisations and categorisations of Jews relevant in wider society, rather than being based on a reading of indigenous Jewish ideas. The subject is explored in more detail in Webber 1997: 257-79.

and wide differences of opinion over the appeal of many beckoning sociocultural strategies deriving (wholly or in part) from those other cultures, including assimilation (in its many different forms), secularism, socialism, and Zionism, alongside the desire to remain within traditional Orthodoxy or adapt to modernized, reformist interpretations of that tradition. Today's Jewish world is essentially characterized by considerable cultural heterogeneity, with the result that one cannot say that all individuals who regard themselves as Jewish would necessarily think of themselves primarily as "religious", or even "religious" at all. Indeed, their sense of belonging to the Jewish community at all may be only partial or intermittent; in that sense, ordinary Jewish identity (and especially that element of it which relates to a positioning vis-à-vis other cultures) is often something that is struggled with, rather than fixed, immutable, or self-evident.

This is an additional reason why the presentation of a stable narrative would not do justice to the facts. In practice, what all this means is that the theology can be presented in many different ways, emphasizing the positive attitudes to others, the negative attitudes, or (more honestly) the entanglement of ideas, the multiple readings, the ambiguities, the paradoxes. The possibilities are numerous, and today's multiculturalism and identity politics have added yet further dimensions to Jewish self-definitions. The choice that is made about what is actually said will largely depend on the circumstances, especially the identities of those taking part in the discussion. But it ought to be said that, in general, Jewish historical consciousness tends to tug Jews to look inward: even if Jews in an interfaith context are able to show the theological space that they theoretically can make available for other religions, they feel they have inherited a deep suspicion of other societies and nowadays often find it difficult to avoid thinking in terms of their negative historical experiences – especially after the Holocaust and, furthermore, after decades of Arab denial of Israel's right to exist.[21] On the other hand, and by the same token, this sensitivity to social realities past or present can facilitate a passionate engagement with universalist social justice when circumstances permit, as indeed Jews did, for example, in large numbers during the American *Civil Rights Movement* in the 1960s. It can be done again nowadays, through the communicational possibilities of the internet, where a globalized cyberspace permits new forms of religious expression and the (re)construction of

---

21 | This is, of course, not at all the same thing as how Jews may be seen by others (even if that, in turn, may influence how Jews see themselves). The identity of victimhood has given way, in some contexts, to Jews being seen as part of the new establishment – especially amongst those anti-Zionists who see Israel as having followed a trajectory from an embattled, overwhelmed, rescued fragment of post-Holocaust European Jewry to "super-Jew" and racist arch-villain. Given the wide range of Jewish self-positioning and celebrating difference in the context of numerous modern ideologies, there are many tales to be told about the negotiation and performance of Jewish identity in a multicultural world. See for example Gilmour 2006.

religious identities online, without the need for physical contact with synagogue or rabbi. In that sense there is room here for optimism – but only a cautious optimism. This is because the challenge and the opportunities for developing effective skills in intercultural communication in today's world are completely new; just because of globalization such communication is a daily reality. Today's questions are thus not really the ones which were asked by the Jewish scholars and philosophers in early modern times, let alone in medieval times: even if Jews can draw on the cultural reservoir to try and answer them, there are no ready-made, off-the-shelf, clear-cut answers. The whole project has to be done creatively, with a lot of imagination, looking backward at the inherited tradition as well as forward into the future.

4.

Even so, organic social and ideological change has of course taken place within Jewish society over many centuries. Accommodating change within any cultural system – pouring new wine into old bottles – is however not always straightforward to conceptualize. Theologically speaking (at least in terms understood by Orthodox Jews), the Jews of today are the same people as those that stood at the revelation on Mount Sinai more than three thousand years ago. They are the descendants of those people, but the covenant that was made there was explicitly intended for their biological descendants. Nothing, in the theological sense, has changed; the text of the Bible read in the synagogue today is (or at least is deemed to be) still the same text it always has been. This belief in sharing a common culture and common origins is the major unifying feature of Jews, both today and across the centuries.

The sociological realities, however, are utterly different. From earliest times the history of the Jews has been one of migrations, and Jewish culture has always been the product of the intense interactions with the new cultures of the non-Jewish majority in which the Jews found themselves. The significance of this cannot be overestimated: Jewish culture constantly underwent change, whether in the field of law, language, art, food, or music – and even certain theological ideas as well. It was precisely in their engagement with the cultures of their environment that Jews constructed their own distinctive identities, conditioned by how majority society saw them (defining them as a religion, for example) and also by how the Jews both adopted and at the same time resisted the majority culture's definition of them. As is normal for any minority group, Jewish identity was thus constantly being culturally negotiated and re-negotiated, in somewhat syncretistic fashion, place by place, generation by generation. It also means, by definition, that Jewish identity was not fixed or immutable; it changed as the cultural context changed. One should therefore really speak about Jewish cultures, in the plural, as well as Jewish identities, in the plural.[22] But all the

22 | This view is presupposed in a collection of papers I edited in Webber 1994,

while the theology provided the sense of continuity: nothing had changed at all – or to put it another way, cultural change was merely an illusion. It may be new wine, but because the bottles are old bottles, the new wine is not necessarily perceived as new after all.

The Jewish experience thus offers an interesting and useful model here. It is certainly possible to innovate very dramatically in religion, especially in the field of intercultural relations, whilst retaining a strong sense of continuity and particularism. But, once again, it is not so simple. Until very recently, the history of the cultural innovations of the Jews in diaspora for two thousand years remained very largely hidden; the rabbis had no particular interest or motive in recording it and certainly not in historicizing it. Culturally speaking, time stood still while the Jews were in exile from their homeland and awaiting the final messianic redemption. It was only in the nineteenth century, as a function of the Jewish Enlightenment and Jewish political emancipation that the first secularizing European Jewish scholars, principally in Germany, came to believe that this social history was a better guide and source of inspiration for Jewish identity than traditional Jewish law. What happened in effect was that history became one of the key intellectual starting-points for the journey out of the world of religion and Jewish ritual observance. As university education became available to Jews for the first time, new patterns of community leadership emerged; the Orthodox rabbis ceased to hold a monopoly of knowledge and thus of power. And so it was that Reform and Progressive Judaism came into existence, which fundamentally understood that change, not timeless eternity, was the true reality. It was a powerful idea, enabling lapsed or lapsing Jews to historicize themselves, as Jews, in the newly secularizing European environment. If Jews had adapted themselves in the past, they could equally well adapt their lifestyles to the habits of modern civilization. Judaism thus became redefined as "the evolving culture of the Jewish people," to quote the slogan of the new movement. The willingness to innovate became a new Jewish value

The key discovery here, still being uncovered today, was cultural pluralism and the fundamentally hybrid nature of Jewish culture. Here we have moved beyond simply the intertextual multivocality of the Hebrew Bible. Jewish history is now understood as having included nationalists and chauvinists, humanists stressing moral virtue and social justice as more important than religious ritual, Hellenist Jews who sought assimilation with Hellenist culture, the presence of both mystical and rational philosophical trends within Judaism, and of course Jewish contributions to the arts and

---

entitled *Jewish Identities in the New Europe*. David Biale's monumental, 1200-page edited collection, which argues programmatically for a new interpretation of the totality of Jewish history along these lines, is indeed specifically entitled *Cultures of the Jews* (Biale 2002). The "cacophony" of voices preserved in the Bible (the complaints of the people as well as the admonitions of Moses) truly resembles the state of Jewish culture today; despite the world of difference between the modern age and the ancient, the problems of Jewish identity remain startlingly similar, he says (1150).

sciences in wider society. What this perspective leads to is that if Judaism is essentially an ethnic culture, it is by definition *interdependent* with other cultures and cannot really be understood without reference to them. This is why it can indeed be argued that there is scope for cautious optimism about a Jewish voice with regard to today's intercultural questions. Cultural differences, in this approach, can certainly be operationalized positively, in a non-oppositional frame of reference, even if the very idea of an ethnic culture places man at the centre, not God or a revealed religion. But the argument is that this is part of what Jewish society has always done, whether or not its activities in this field were acknowledged at the time by the community's religious leaders.

Interestingly enough, the term "humanism" has been explicitly appropriated by Jews who have begun to turn these ideas into an institutionalized secularist Jewish movement of their own. For example, the *Society for Humanistic Judaism* was founded in the USA in 1986 and claims to have about fifty congregations affiliated to it; there are a few such groups in Europe, most notably the *Centre Communautaire Laic Juif* in Brussels, and the movement is certainly growing in Israel, with a college in Jerusalem significantly named the *College of Pluralist Judaism*. But the agenda of these humanist Jews is largely inward-looking, viz. to help provide Jews with "an alternative to conventional Judaism" (as they put it), for example by creating secular rituals for the celebration of the sabbath and traditional Jewish festivals. There is still very little here of a more sophisticated contribution to inter-religious relations, probably because of the commitment to an old-fashioned nineteenth-century humanism that is militantly atheist, strongly secularist and anticlerical. A new Jewish universalism, less oppositional to its own past, is yet to arise.

5.

Is there in fact scope for a *religious* Jewish humanism which by being anchored in traditional religious faith and religious values but with an ethic of service to humanity could speak with legitimacy to other religions? Certainly some contemporary Orthodox Jewish scholars believe this to be perfectly possible and indeed highly desirable, although they still represent a harassed minority view within their own traditionalist circles.[23] On that evidence it

---

23 | One particularly celebrated case concerns the work cited above of the British Chief Rabbi, Jonathan Sacks. His book *The Dignity of Difference* (2002) was fiercely condemned by other Orthodox rabbis on the grounds that it suggested that no one faith has a monopoly on spiritual truth, that God is only partially comprehended by any one faith, and that God has spoken to mankind in many languages and traditions. Sacks's purpose in putting forward these ideas was (in part) to articulate a Jewish voice to address the problem of religious violence, to plead for tolerance in an age of extremism, and that people should feel enlarged – not threatened – by

is very likely that the Orthodox Jewish religious establishment would have great difficulty with the overtly "humanist" approach of such bodies as the *Sea of Faith Network*, founded in the 1980s. But the *Network*, which includes a substantial range of opinions, does demonstrate that religious humanism is not necessarily a contradiction in terms, but merely that it acknowledges the human aspect of making meaning in religion and of course the contribution of religion to the community spirit in comforting the lonely and helping people navigate difficult moral decisions and other challenges of ordinary life. There is thus no need to take up a humanist battle against all forms of religious expression or to insist on an irreconcilable binary opposition between religion and humanism; on the contrary, humanism has to take religious realities into account and be tolerant of them. The two approaches may in any case well be able to live together.[24]

The purpose of this brief essay has been to present some of the methodological and cultural issues in considering the scope for a "Jewish voice" to the contemporary intercultural debate. My argument is fundamentally optimistic, despite many reservations. Certainly there is scope for a Jewish voice in today's intercultural dialogue, and indeed some aspects of the Jewish experience could be useful as a model. The notion of religious humanism, inasmuch as it appears to be a contradiction in terms, signposts the difficulties. As a form of cultural self-awareness, religious humanism hovers between two different states of mind, or (at the very least) encourages sensitivity to a wide spectrum of possibilities that may inhere in a given context. In that sense it a good example of a double consciousness – something which is in

---

difference (see the second edition of Sacks 2003). His rabbinical critics had expressed their horror at the thought that Judaism could be only a partial truth (they even took out an advertisement in the Jewish press stating that this was a heretical teaching and that the book should not be in a Jewish home) and had thus forced the Chief Rabbi to issue a second edition in which the offending ideas were (as he put it, ibid.) "redrafted [...] so as to circumnavigate" the contested issues. For an important recent sociological survey of contestation between accommodationist modern Orthodoxy and particularist, traditionalist (*haredi*) Orthodoxy in the United States, see Heilman 2006. Reform Judaism, however, has historically been far more accommodating and imaginative as regards the challenges of interfaith dialogue, at least with Abrahamic partners; for an excellent, detailed presentation of the issues, by a Reform rabbi with considerable experience of such encounters, see Magonet 2003).

24 | The Jewish liturgy, a cultural text of considerable intrinsic interest for its inclusiveness of a wide range of literary sources and encompassing a similarly wide range of moods and emotions (see for example note 10 above), does occasionally betray (and transcend) the duality. To give an illustration of this: one paragraph in the sabbath service praises God for making the sabbath holy, but a sentence or two earlier in this liturgy refers to the *Jewish people* who sanctify the Sabbath (*am mekadeshei shevi'i*). Holiness, one might say (following Durkheim), is a social creation but is attributed (metaphorically, in a religious humanist perspective) to its divine source. At any rate, both ideas are simultaneously present in the liturgical text.

any case well known to diaspora Jews, who as minority communities have been familiar for centuries with double consciousness (even if the term itself is new). It has been an integral part of helping Jews to navigate their environment and, in effect, to be able to create radically new ways of being in the world.

On the other hand, we must be aware of the difficulties. Multicultural and inter-religious dialogue needs to be understood as a new language, where the key words that are used are either neutral terms that do not really resonate in the tradition (multivocality, for example), or else they are imposed by one of the partners in the debate. The understanding of these terms may be far more culture-specific than is generally realized. If we are going to do "global theology" we need to be aware that basic concepts like holiness or salvation or covenant (even, perhaps, love and forgiveness) do not necessarily mean the same things in all religions, not even in the Abrahamic religions. Intercultural dialogue means, almost literally, developing and learning a new language, and it is not clear where the cultural resources for that could come from. It means finding neutral cultural territory, and it is not clear where *that* could be located. Above all, dialogue, like religious humanism, is a *constructed* relationship. It will depend on the energy, the insight, and the creativity given by the parties to the dialogue just how to sustain and manage such relationships – fragile, delicate, and subject to change as they necessarily are, and requiring the need to nurture feelings both of connectedness and of respect for the other's autonomy.

But even if such relationships are built on a historical background of considerable tension, it is also true that they may thereby be profoundly transformational. Hence despite the operational difficulties these are enriching ventures of enormous promise. They remind the participants to become aware of their fundamental interdependence and, in their search for the commonalities and interdependencies that link them together, to know that reality ultimately depends on the imagination; that all social identities are composite and malleable, multiple and not fixed;[25] that we *become* who we are; that there can always be movement and the opportunity to reach out to the open horizon of a universal consciousness; and that we therefore have the power to attribute to dialogue something that can change the world. It has to be done; it is a Jewish duty arising from its common mission with other religions and indeed with all humanity.

---

25 | For a good recent study of this well-established anthropological view, see Hastrup 2007.

"Who Observes Religions?"
Negotiating Faith, Reason and the
Idea of Humanism in an "Era of Terrorism"

Georg Essen

1. A Clash of Cultures
   and the Ambivalence of Religion

For just a brief while people in the Western hemisphere could bask in a pleasant glow, believing they had reached the "end of history" because of the success of liberal democracy and the free market economy. But appearances were deceptive. Today the intellectual debate is dominated, not by Francis Fukuyama's thesis of the end of history, but by Samuel Huntington's prognosis that a clash of civilizations looms on the horizon (cf. Fukuyama 1992; Huntington 1997). Industrial society as we know it, in its classical format, has gradually evolved into a new kind of society governed by globalization and multiculturalism, as a result of which we are witnessing, and sometimes experiencing, a growing insecurity and disorientation. The manifest failure of old ideologies has triggered a search for some sort of foothold, which we hope to find in a "cultural turn": people are looking for identity through reappraising their cultures. Ultimately that seems to be the explanation for the multitude of potential conflicts lurking behind this reappraisal.

Cultural differences arise from processes in which people differentiate between what they identify with and what they differ from, leading to individual and collective identity construction. That identity in its turn may fall prey to the normative asymmetry of ethnocentrism, the logic of which runs as follows: my culture or myself believes it can only maintain its identity by attaching less value to the otherness of others. Hence it seems justifiable to speak of a clash of cultures when an increasingly intimate global dialogue evokes a similar asymmetrical response in others, so that cultural diversity is experienced as a direct reality which occasionally erupts into violence (cf. Essbach 2000; Ackermann/Müller 2002).

No wonder that Huntington himself propounds a dialectical escape route to avert the impending cultural conflict he fears: on the one hand he advocates reinforcement of Euro-American culture, on the other he calls for a politics of cultural coexistence (cf. Huntington 1997: 301-321). This option, however, seems hopelessly naive – which cannot be blamed entirely on the new strategic initiatives of the present U.S. American government that seems to perpetuate the hypothetical universality of Western culture through its own imperialistic foreign policy (cf. Brezinski 1997). A scrupulously honest view of globalization, such as that of Dieter Senghaas, leads to the conclusion that economic globalization effectively results in the expansion of just one cultural type; economic hegemony, being the Western cultural model. The outcome will be that Western universal culture will assume a dramatically more homogeneous form and impose cultural change willy-nilly. This form of globalization culminates in "civilization, like it or not", because Western culture represents "universal culture" as such and, one way or another, has reached that level of universality well ahead of all others – for the latter all that remains is a "catching up" operation in order not to lose out in the race for cultural interconnectivity. Thus globalization processes appear to destroy the very foundation of the right to cultural diversity, because the trends towards a uniform "global culture" create pressure to avoid political and economic isolation (cf. Senghaas 1998; Kaufmann 2001; Virt 2002).

There is something to be said for the theory that the growth of religious fundamentalism is expressive of unassimilated experiences of crisis in the midst of globalization processes, inasmuch as they increasingly undermine traditional life-worlds and whittle down existing links with religious foundations and values. In apparent contradiction of their universalistic claims to meaning, under certain societal conditions religions tend to support anti-globalistic trends that are intent on new forms of particularity. Is this attributable to the fact that the construction of religious notions of identity leads to true-false binary interpretations, hence run the risk of becoming a religious variant of ethnocentrism? Apparently such interpretations which are typical of monotheism, give rise to a world view fraught not only with significance, cults of identity and orientation, but also with conflict, intolerance and violence (cf. Assmann 2001; Essen 2007). From this point of view religious approaches that lay claim to exclusiveness can be used as instruments to compensate people for what they experience as cultural marginalization.

It has been recognized for some time that the peculiarities of modern life do not cause religions to disappear, but far rather generate new forms of religious communication. Neither is it surprising that modernization should offer fertile soil for religious radicalism. But nobody could have foreseen how violently the tension between modernity and religious traditions would explode on 11 September 2001, when 19 Islamist fundamentalists, motivated by their own notions of pious rage, using commercial airliners as missiles, flew into the Twin Towers of Manhattan – symbols to them of the cultural/ economic hegemony embodied by the "Great Satan". 2,974 people, not counting the assassins, died in the attack, including the citizens of ninety nations. In the context of globalization emerging in the wake of accelerated modernization and heralding total uprooting, a problem that secular society believed it had solved once and for all has inadvertently been put back on the religio-political agenda: in frighteningly unambiguous symbolic language 9/11 triggered a search for strategies to restore the always delicate balance between religion, politics and violence (cf. Wils 2004).

2. Religious Conflict as Challenge to Modern Societies: Notes for a Religio-Political Agenda

While it is always risky to point out historical parallels, I must nonetheless venture to attempt just this. A comparison of the situation outlined above to the horrors of internecine civil warfare across 17th century Europe should seem obvious for various reasons. In response to these wars basic strategies and mechanisms were developed to terminate the bloody religious conflicts that still direct history. Here one must emphasize, that *first* and foremost among these strategies, is the separation of church and state. The intention was that religion should no longer be an essential ingredient of the political order but should be left solely to private conscience, within the domain of civil society. This divorce of politics from religion, of church from the state, is the basis of all modern constitutional states: where it concerns worldview the state is neutral and is no longer fundamentally tied to religion.

Secondly, it should be noted that the Enlightenment ushered in a radically different interpretation of morality and justice. Structures, rules and laws, virtue, ethics and morality were not explicitly abolished, but instead were anchored in human reason, which is a law unto itself and grounds the binding nature of moral obligation in its own autonomy. It follows that principles of justice and morality would henceforth be secular. The premises of the modern constitutional state are based on the disjunction of religion and politics, while justice and ethics are grounded in secular morality: these two facts are absolute conditions for peace in pluralistic societies. The separation of government from religious influence means that all legal decisions which affect the public must have a secular basis, since that is the only way in which all citizens can have a say in them. These principles culminate in liberal constitutions that guarantee equal subjective rights for all and assure citizens of personal autonomy which is shared by everyone. That is the true meaning of egalitarian universalism, the yardstick being that every person deserves unconditional legal backing and is recognized as an end in his or her own right. For the sake of freedom the disjunction of religion and state does not entail proposals for a lifestyle that would be normative for everyone. In this sense it is certainly anything but incumbent upon the constitutional state to suppress the diversity of cultural and religious values in civil society. On the contrary, the constitutionally enshrined basic rights are there to protect those values. These universalistic norms must ensure that cultural and religious differences are treated strictly in compliance with the principle of equality and the mandate of tolerance. A fundamental requirement, however, is that in a pluralistic society these norms are universal and ensure freedom only inasmuch as they are based on secular premises. After all, the fact that universally binding ethical pronouncements are possible in a political community is grounded in acknowledgment of a moral obligation, which can be shown to be binding and unconditionally mandatory even within a pluralistic society.

A *third* comment concerns the project known as the European Enlightenment; a project designed to counteract the mystical mind-set which had prevailed for centuries by means of rational modes of thought. Those in the forefront of this project saw themselves as autonomous thinkers critical of religion, who demanded that faith be answerable to reason by way of these humanistic processes brought about by Enlightenment thinking. This process – one could call it the taming of religion by rationality – was supposed to protect people against what Kant called dogmatism: authoritarian thinking bound up with moralistic codes, and that of the individual's conscience, similarly bound up with those codes is legitimized vis-à-vis a long established ecclesiastical orthodoxy that "reduces the natural principles of morality to side issues" (Kant) (cf. Essen 2006a). To this end autonomous philosophy declared truth to be indivisible and insisted that public attestations of truth be subjected to rational criteria, for instance by determining how consistent religious claims are and how well they can be substantiated. The ever more advanced methodology of such research in its turn became the basis for the authority of science, to which modern societies have accorded a monopoly of knowledge about the world (cf. Habermas 2001: 41).

The historical background I have sketched is meant to show that justice, morality and the Enlightenment as fundamental principles of the political culture of European civil societies are historical achievements, which could make it possible – in a manner of speaking – to "civilise" religion. The legal phraseology of this process derives from the painful experience that Christianity – in spite of a proclaimed faith in the God of Jesus Christ – has proved incapable of resolving sectarian conflicts in a non-violent manner. In this sense, to put it bluntly, it has become quite natural to be mistrustful of faith-based truth claims in the public political realm of non-secular constitutional states as we know them today. The principles of a secular judicial order, secular morality and autonomous reason are reflected in the normative mechanisms and instruments of European modernity that are in place to regulate the role religion plays in secular civil society. However, when we analyze the strategies employed by religious authoritarians to situate their various belief systems within heterogeneous society, these essential Enlightenment principles, which define progressive, modern European thought, can induce "cognitive dissonances". It is for religious institutions and communities to take the opportunity, if they hope to maintain a presence in secular civil society, to venture further cognitive leaps regarding their own reflexive attitudes on any number of issues (cf. Habermas 2001: 40-42).

Firstly, it must be accepted that one's own religious consciousness must digest the experience that living in a pluralistic world presents; alternative versions of religious meaning that cannot simply be incorporated into one's own faith-derived context. For apparently contradictory reasons, this experience could be a product of globalization: growing communication in a globalised world goes hand in hand with the experience that there is a diversified supply of cultural and religious meaning. At the same time globalization gives rise to a plurality of religions and cultures that are inevitably interlinked.

Secondly, in a modern society one would expect public proclamations of truth-claims to be submitted to a scientific scrutiny of their premises. Such testing happens mainly at universities. A *université sans conditions* (cf. Derrida 2001), in which such academic studies are conducted, require religions to account for their claims of possessing true knowledge to scientific criticism and to have the reliability of such claims tested according to prevailing methodological standards.

Thirdly, religious consciousness must investigate the premises of a constitutional state based upon secular morality (cf. Habermas 2001). The current European debate on civil law shows that pluralistic, multireligious societies will have to base their democratic, rational common sense beliefs mainly on the secular decision-making principles laid down in modern constitutions. Current moves – still in the early stages – to enact international law indicate that a politically structured global community will have to develop a legal system oriented to the Enlightenment principles of a rational world order if it is to regulate religious and cultural diversity peaceably.

Considering the European experience of religious politics, one cannot overemphasize the fact that the strategies that helped to civilize the various forms of Christendom ultimately had to be imposed, even enforced, on the churches from outside (cf. Essen 2004). It is flagrantly obvious, as extensively recorded in Catholic history over the past two centuries, that anti-modernist religious resentments both within the sects and in society at large create a highly precarious, even explosive situation that can easily unleash them in a *Kulturkampf.* Hence it would seem that the position religious institutions and communities adopt in the processes of modernity are determined by the anything but incidental issue of the conditions under which a religious sect believes itself capable of critically balancing its own basic truths with the principles and core beliefs of modern civil societies and, more especially, to engage constructively with a socio-historical situation characterized by the processes of secularization. To this should be added that the plurality of faith-based notions of truth definitely does not oblige anybody to give up the absolute claim to truth which any religious faction feels committed to in practical life. What religions must do is open themselves to the question of what *they* can contribute to an ethos of recognition which civil society requires if it is to handle the burning issues of cultural diversity on both a short and long term basis. For it is quite clear: if in our day and age religious elements in particular turn cultural diversity into a problem in urgent need of attention, should not the religiously committed display some impulse towards recognizing this? Religious thought, with its capacity for pluralism should manifestly go beyond a policy of harmony and a mandate of tolerance – that seems to function more like a truce in the theological battle between exactingly phrased claims to universality (cf. Rüsen 2007a; Essen 2006b).

The point I want to make is the following. The return of religious conflict to world politics, including horrific sectarian-motivated violence, indicates that the history of religious thought in modern Europe could – and should provide an instructive example for a global society that is threatening to get out of hand. At the same time one surmises that pluralistic societies in any case have no political and legal mechanisms apart from the aforementioned basic principles of European modernity with which to resolve cultural and religious differences (cf. Forst 2000; id. 2000a). However, the secular "civilianization" of religion that has to be effected in this manner is stymied by a structurally infrangible barrier: To maintain the liberal dimension of modern societies the state is obliged to base public acknowledgement and acceptance of religious diversity on its own criteria of civil law. But because the law, by its very nature, must be enforced, it follows that it can only regulate people's outward behavior, not their inner belief systems. This is the only way for the state to respect the priority of freedom for its citizens over any and all political considerations. Hence the flip side of this jurisprudential premise is that it makes a free, democratic state manifestly vulnerable, for it is ideologically firmly committed to its citizens' sense of liberty, upon which their free assent to the legal system itself depends.

This dialectics has far-reaching implications. The worst case scenario would be that of a modern society faced with the dilemma that in which devout individuals, as well as its religious communities, are no longer prepared to observe the moral/judicial principles on which the legal harmony of a social/political community depends, or might simply disregard them in practice. On the other hand acceptance of these principles can be effectively stimulated and enforced, as evidenced by the success of modern legal culture in achieving far-reaching constraints on the power of the Catholic Church within civil society. However, there are limits as to what is legally enforceable; therefore acceptance can ultimately only result from free assent.

This structurally infrangible autonomy confronts free, organized societies with the fact that religions, from their own motives arising from self-generated (hence freely arrived at) insights, must effectively handle the cognitive dissonances that are the inescapable products of ongoing modernization/globalization. Otherwise such reflexive transformations will not form part of an expanded religious consciousness, and the necessary reconstruction of religious identity will not be intrinsically stimulated. This sounds as dramatic as I intended it should: if theological bodies persist in refusing to take the reflective leap into that domain where they are competent, they would then appear to have a destructive potential in context of the present global community that with respect to interactivity, has become more complex and much smaller. Clearly, maintaining prevailing law by way of officially legitimized coercive measures has only limited utility in this area, since it can result in merely neutralizing sectarian inspired violence (cf. Romus 2007). Such a measure is confined to reactionary violence, and will moreover give the overall spiral of violence further impetus – in all events, this is not the way to establish universally applicable minimum standards for dealing with cultural and religious differences, since it would permanently impair every form of religious freedom that people lay claim to – and without their assent any curtailment of religious particularity and civil/societal universality cannot succeed.

3. Exclusive and Inclusive Elements in Western Humanism – Re-reading European Traditions

Samuel Huntington's provocative phrase "the Clash of Civilizations" – to strikingly underline the problem again – poses the unavoidable question of how to cope with cultural and religious differences in the age of globalization. Standardizing trends leading towards a "world culture" evidently come with the attendant pressures to fall into step and homogenize, which accelerate the decline of traditional modes of life and erode religiously founded bonds and value systems. In any case, there is a growing need for intercultural communication and functional expertise, as cultural notions of identity have come under a constantly escalating barrage of media communications. Against this backdrop, the importance of a project for a "New Humanism" seems greater than ever, because it is obviously anticipated of such a project to provide new impulses for a hermeneutics of intercultural communication. Renewed interest in humanist philosophy could also have been sparked by the fact that, within man's notions about himself and the world, truth-claims are applied to the development of cultural identities. This in turn makes identities seem rather fragile on all levels; for the individual, for groups, for communities and for societies. In other words, in the intercultural realm, cultures are, by their structure, highly ambivalent symbolic organizations.

As far as cultural difference may be considered to be a matter of, and indeed can be experienced as, cognitive dissonance, the problem on which I have just elucidated may also be viewed in a theoretical light. When dealing with the conflicting truth-claims of various world views, validity and reliability become problematic issues, as alternative concepts of meaning question the validity of one's own convictions and value systems which had so far been deemed reliable. After all, the question of what is true springs from an original interest in maintaining a reliable orientation in life – in fact, it is a fundamental human issue. The question "what is truth?" is one of the basic inquiries we as a species have undertaken, into our self-identities, systems of thought – the total of that which we can reliably know about ourselves and the world. Things are true when they are held to be valid, reliable, and most importantly, immutable. This explicit view of truth becomes problematic when validity and reliability are called into question: Reliability rests entirely on validity. One can only rely on something that is valid; to do other would to invite instability.

Humanist theory and philosophy take special interest in problems like this in the ongoing search for a reliable orientation in life amidst the encroaching processes of globalization. Among other things, seeking to analyze the risk of meddling with cultural identities of individuals, groups, and institutions in view of a weakening of the unique position of identity – cultural and other – which have become detached from all certainties within the scope of the world-at-large, from which many cultures and identities feel threatened with increasing alienation and isolation.

Any contribution that a theory of humanity might make toward a humanist interpretation of globalization processes cannot be limited, however, to becoming little more than an advocate for cultural diversity, possibly to the point of divergence from the cause of universal ethics, emerging concepts of meaning and existential orientations (cf. Straub/Weidemann/Weidemann 2007). It could well be argued that the present dilemmas of *culturality* cannot be separated from those processes which will evidently lead to an interactive global population capable of surmounting any cultural differences. The fact that culture-based identities are increasingly confronted with experiencing alternative ways of being defined, and that these definitions cannot be easily integrated into their own cultural milieu, seems to be caused by contradictory worldwide trends: the exponential growth of information technology which is now globally available, further complicated by a bewildering array of identity concepts. Yet, at the same time, this phenomenon of globalization entails the unavoidable fusion of the multiplicity of formerly sovereign cultural worlds. Both of these factors should be considered any persons attempting a more unified theory of the human identity: on the one hand a dialectics of global universality and cultural specificity, and on the other, the internalization of plurality within a culture as a result of globalizing influences. The sensitivities that the Humanist scholar brings to the study of cultural diversity should, at all costs, be prevented from devolving into ethnocentric-leaning interpretations, if only to salvage the question at issue from the ideological backwaters: What will constitute the solidarity, the essence of this still developing planetary community?

Those of us attempting to lay claim to a universal truth, as we have just seen, and who also happen to be of western European origins, as I am, will soon find themselves under ideological scrutiny. Universalisms originating from Europe have all too often born the ugly countenance of colonialism: Peoples were subjected, nations were robbed – not least of their autonomy; ethnic groups were uprooted and followers of indigenous religious were forcibly converted. Moreover, this repressive species of universalism implemented a capitalist economy with its well-known ecological and social consequences. As a result, the current processes of globalization are often perceived as the imposition of the western model of modernization.

As is well-known, Max Weber saw European modernization as part of the process of the disenchantment of the world, and he also pointed out the interconnectedness of certain aspects (Weber 2000). Societies which modernize themselves will transform and finally dispel those theologically-based world views that can no longer provide a meaningful outlook on life. The downfall of traditional worldviews stems from a rationalization of culture, which leads to individualization/privatization of *comprehensive doctrines*, as John Rawls put it (Rawls 1999). According to Max Weber, these processes of individualization are driven by a combination of the administrative state and capitalist society. This will lead not just to a general differentiation of state and economy, but in the end to a differentiation of all aspects of life in modern societies. This, in turn, is followed by intermittent jolts towards individualization, gradually freeing people from the social forms of industrial society – class, estate, family etc. The results are ambivalent, however. On the one hand, this emancipation of the individual leads to better chances at freedom, and offers new possibilities for self-determination, liberation from the constraints of authoritarian social environments, culturally determined modes of life and groups based on certain world views. At the same time, functionally differentiated societies, in which complex and independent processes are purpose-driven, are of necessity post-traditional societies that have broken free from the motivational foundations of the previous cultural world views. As a consequence, the individual has almost lost the option of falling back on tradition-based knowledge as to what constitutes a good and meaningful life. Cultural reserves of knowledge and meaning appear to have been exhausted, and the forces that once held together modern society seem to have lost their cohesive strength, making it even harder to take an autonomous direction and the planning of one's life into one's own hands, and by this route making meaningful decisions on the individual level. Modern societies are societies founded on risk-taking, in which the process of finding one's identity is very often a patchwork affair, in which identities are constitutionally susceptible to any and all winds of change.

My main interest however is not in the empirical observation and descriptive grasp of these processes of modernization. Instead, I would like to level some necessary criticism by putting into question the basic assumptions surrounding the de facto imposition of western modernity – a criticism that, from a European's perspective, should rightfully be a form of self-criticism.

My thesis, in which will, I hope, indicate the complex character of this paradox, is stated as follows: European criticism, including self-criticism, of modernization as it is in fact, imposed around the world, find their arguments lodged in exactly those main categories which have come under the suspicion of having become ideologically subsumed within the dialectic of intercultural unity: universality and reason, subjectivity and autonomous freedom. Against this backdrop, we now need to look at one of the most pressing problems a hermeneutics of intercultural communication is faced with. I would like to return to the tasks anticipated earlier in this article: the development of an objective model of humanity as intercultural endeavor.

The goal I propose is to suggest a route through the cognitive dissonances existing between the outer and inner pluralities of several disparate cultures. From the point of view of system theory, this is done in such a way that the experiencing of cultural diversity is integrated into one's own system, thereby successfully preventing any determinate of a cultural self-description through the externalization of cultural differences. The decisive challenge will be for an interculturally sound model of humanity to provide a cultural recognition of the difference between a system and the world around it. It formulates the compulsory conditions for a hermeneutics that will be able to reduce any given culture's idea of uniqueness within the multitude of cultures to the inner coherence of its convictions.

This reflection on the limits between "inside" and "outside" perspectives necessarily starts from the idea that the way towards a well thought-out self-awareness of cultural praxis can only be reached in a roundabout way through relations with the outside world. The "outside world" may appear as the "other" in this system, but the native positions can be determined in the decision-making processes. This means that the realization of the self can only gain its particularity in the mirror of the other. The outer world will appear as the horizon of meaning within which self-realization will determine its place and find its cultural anchorage. These attempts at orientation will also cause the native perspective on foreign culture to become a foreign perspective on the native culture. From a hermeneutical point of view, the essential realization should be the normative insight that the reflection of the native in the foreign cannot take place without recognizing the native value of the culturally foreign.

This final thought is essential, for it does not merely affirm the hermeneutical insight that any understanding is inclusive by nature – though admittedly, those native aspects that warrant being held on to also include this aspect of a methodical approach to self-understanding based in intercultural hermeneutics. Any attempt, therefore, at a comprehension which aims toward integration, constitute a universal – that is, unifying interpretive context – mutual comprehension guarantees mutuality in cultural otherness (!) The question remains, however, whether exclusivist concepts of universalism are really capable of recognizing real otherness and therefore comprehending diversity. Attempts at forming an all-inclusive understanding tend to regard the exotic merely as a hermeneutical challenge, to be reduced to that which is already known. An inclusivist style of universalism, in spite of all good intentions to the contrary, will base its conditional recognition on the cunning hermeneutical presumption of sameness, and will therefore remain blind to the other in its otherness. This would amount to cultural isolation based on a subtly chauvinistic concern for the other, which in the balance, would then sidestep the issues of cross-border, trans-cultural communication.

There are reasons, however, to doubt whether there actually is a form of humanism that is not inclusivist. By inclusivist I mean to ascribe the ideals I believe are connected to being human to any human being regardless of their state of alterity. The questions is, however, whether this inclusivism has a built-in exclusivist agenda and whether this humanism, if it is inclusive, is really only concerned with a reductionist translation of the unknown into the known. The latter is most certainly not the case, as humanism expressly regards itself as a moral universalism, as is clear from Kant's philosophy of history, for example. A moral universalism does however presuppose recognition of the freedom of others as a basic principle of the legal order proposed, because in its production and codification of a rule of law, it ties this same rule to the idea of freedom and installs autonomy as the essential element of this rule of law. It must mean, however, that the inclusivist pretensions of my humanism are regulated and oriented by the principle of reciprocal recognition. In other words: it is founded on the recognition of the freedom of others, expressly recognizing the otherness of others. The type of inclusion we see here is, to use a distinction Jürgen Habermas has made, not based in the hermeneutical assimilation of the other, but rather on taking it into account. The latter is of course subject to the free consent of the other, and will therefore have to unconditionally respect and recognize the self-determination it hopes to retain for itself. That is why a moral universalism which aims for the recognition of the freedom of others can be supplemented with a hermeneutics of intercultural communication, enabling inclusions that do allow for differences.

Considering the all-to-real imposition of the European model upon the rest of humanity, this moral universalism would again be an ethical criterion to be critically applied to our own history, explicitly taking a self-critical approach to any imperial claims as its main focus, as it were. If this program is taken seriously, then the old charge of eurocentrism can finally be laid to rest.

Man in the Light of God:

An Essay on Humanism in Islam

HASSAN HANAFI

Prejudices or Anachronism?

Stereotypical imagery is very detrimental to socio-cultural analysis; Western culture considering itself as the only culture, which invented notions of Man as the center of the universe instead of God; substituting anthropocentrism for theocentrism as did Socrates, Augustine, Descartes, Kant and Feuerbach, has been a predisposition of long standing among the thinkers of the West. Every culture has its version of humanism with the axis centered on the name of Man: Confucius in China, Buddha in India, Mazdek in Persia, Amenhotep in Egypt, Socrates in Greece, al-Farabi, Miskaweh and the Islamic mystics, etc. Every culture passes through this portal from God to man, from the I Ching to Confucius, from Hinduism to Buddhism, from Zoroastra to Mazdek, etc.

This misjudgment or misperception stems from a lack of universal consciousness which could place cultures within one global synopsis. Not all cultures live the same historical moment. In each period of universal history there was a dominant culture: In more remote times the empires of China, India, Persia, Mesopotamia, Egypt, Classical Greece, Rome and Classical Islam. Nowadays Western culture dominates in its own western modern times. However, given the alarming signals from many contemporary western philosophers, proclaimed with headlines like: The Decline of the West (Spengler), The Crisis of European Science, Loss of the Lived, Bankruptcy of Philosophy (Husserl), Values Turned Upside Down (M. Scheler), Crisis of European Consciousness (P. Hazard), Western Civilization on Trial (Toynbee), etc., it may be that the course of historical cultures is about to change. Euro-centrism ends and Asia-centrism begins. Westwind ends and Eastwind begins (J. Needham).

Every culture has its own periodization. Western culture has its famous triadic division: classical, mediaeval and modern. Given the centrality of Western culture nowadays, Euro-centric periodization has become that of all other cultures. Greco-Roman culture is in the classical period, Islamic and Jewish cultures are located in the mediaeval period. Only the western culture is alive in the modern period, and yet this is sheer anachronism. Each culture has its own historical course, identical or different from other cultural courses. For instance, Islamic culture is not a part of Western mediaeval culture but is located rather in its own classical and golden age. After this era comes the mediaeval period after Ibn Khaldun which corresponds in western temporality to modern times. Contemporary Islamic culture is entering into a third phase, the new classical renaissance since reformation and first renaissance in the last two hundred years, which corresponds to the closing stages of western modern times, post-modernism, deconstructionism, nihilism, skepticism, agnosticism, the death of God, the death of man, *L'écriture au point zero*, etc.[1]

A meaningful comparison has to be made between two cultures existing within the same historical space, for instance the comparison between Islamic culture in its classical period with Western culture in its mediaeval phase; the comparison of Islamic culture in its mediaeval post-Khaldunian era with Western culture in its modern sense. Islamic culture now is positioned at the beginning of the 15th century (1427 H.) the time before M. Luther and G. Bruno, the time of the Inquisition. Humanist thought as represented by Erasmus (1469-1536) did not appear until the end of the 15th century AD. Islam as a religion is located at the beginning of its 16th century. Humanism appeared in the West at the end of the middle ages and at the dawn of its modern period. However, the comparison between Islamic classical culture and modern Western culture is a necessity, since the West has become the frame of reference for the Rest.

"Islam and Humanism" is not a dialectical matter, a negative assessment by the West and a positive one in Islam. It is a matter of research, neutral and disinterested. Apologetism, negative or positive, is not science.

Theology or Anthropology (*Homo Loquax*)?

It is easy to find the roots of humanism in Islamic culture by digging into classical theology, philosophy, jurisprudence, mysticism and scriptural sciences, all retained in traditional form and garb, screened off behind theocentrism and scripturalism. Time however is capable of unveiling these obscurities to uncover the humanism lying buried underneath layers of traditional scholasticism.

Theology is still centered on the theory of Essence, Attributes and Acts. The Essence is: Being, Everlasting, Self Subsistence, Transcendent and One; this the description of pure consciousness, *cogito ergo sum*. Being is the primary description of Essence. This being has no beginning in time and has no end. Being is born in time as a continuous flux. Life existed

---

1 | This is what H. Nakamura called: Parallel development.

before creation and survives after death. Pure consciousness exists per se, independent of relations with others or with things. The Essence is pure, Transcendent, Invisible not anthropomorphic. The essence of the human being cannot be described or formulated. Finally, the Essence is one given the unity of human consciousness.

The Attributes are Omniscience, Omnipotence, Life, Hear, Say, Speech and Will. This is the ideal type of the perfect man, idealized in Heaven, incapable of being realized on Earth. The relative is pushed to the absolute. Only Feuerbach was able to reconstruct Theology as anthropology turned upside down: Man self-deified, sanctified his ideals and exteriorized his essence. It is easy to end with this alienation and to bring back the essence of humanity to humanity. God is not a reified idol but a τελος, progress in mankind and throughout history.

The acts of God such as word by sending revelation through prophets to guide human knowledge and Grace to help and to strengthen human action are reflected in man but *à rebours*. The issue is not to defend the rights of God and the duties of man but to defend the rights of man and the duties of God. If God is Omniscient man also has his own reasons for understanding and to interpreting the word of God according to his own reason. Reason is a natural light. Clarity and evidence are criteria of truth. Man has his reason. He can distinguish between right and wrong, good and evil, even before revelation. Revelation confirms what reason conceives.

If God is Omnipotent man also is capable of doing. He has his *liberum arbitrium*. He can decide freely without any intervention of Divine will. If his actions are determined, there will be no accountability. Islamic Theodicy requires reason and free will of man to be responsible for his acts. Divine Justice certainly means justice for man.

The ninety-nine Names of God, if put in clusters denote pure self-consciousness, consciousness of the world and consciousness of man through three major types of human reason: Pure reason, practical reason and the faculty of judgment as enumerated by Kant. Self consciousness appears in Names such as: Rich, Saint, Peace, Greatness, Dignity, Sublime, etc. The consciousness of the world appears in Names such as: Creator, etc. Consciousness, when manifested in humankind as theoretical reason is recognizable in names such as: Expert, Witness, Wise, True etc. Names denoting practical reason are: Giver, Gracious, Charitable, Generous, Maintainer, Preserver, Useful etc. Names of the faculty of judgment are: Just, Observer, Merciful, Compassionate, Docile, Forgiver etc. Divine Names are indeed the hopes of man, the ideal man, man as he should be. Since he cannot realize them all he keeps them as ideals. With time they become sanctified, worshiped and identified with God. This is the model of the *Homo Loquax* of dogmatic theology. The discourse of God is indeed the discourse of man.

Ontology or Psychology (*Homo Sapiens*)?

Ontology is theology on the metaphysical level. God is the Necessary Being. He has the same Attributes, Acts and Names as in theology though without personification. God is the ειν ὄν. Is it God or man in his ecstasy? Can the Noûs feel His presence and realizes that He is a part of Him, never separated from Him? Meister Eckhart in his ontology interprets in full depth the theology of Thomas of Acquinas. Theosophy is the work of the heart while theology is the work of dialectical reason. There is more significance in Jacob Boehme's *Mysterium Magnum* than in *Summa Theologica*. The Abstract Ontology of N. Hartman is indeed an experience of the heart in a metaphysical language. Being is shared by God and man alike. To distinguish between the Absolute Being and the relative is the mark of modesty.

The relation between God and the world is not as plus is to minus in an oppositional duality as in theology, as stated in the famous theory *Creatio ex Nihilo*. God and the world are One Entity with the difference being of degree not of kind, as is the case with the theory of creation. Graduation means continuity and discontinuity alike. It is discontinuous as in the example of creation and continuous where, like the concept of the eternity of the world, God and the world are identical without the polarization of a negative vs. positive, and without graduation. This is a vision of the human beatified, the unity of all things experienced through love.

This unity of the world reflects itself in the unity of the self, the harmony of psychological triadic powers as Plato categorized them: volition, anger, and reason. Every power has its virtue. The virtuous aspect of anger is courage. The virtue of reason is wisdom. The harmony between the three powers is justice. The good will always aims at the *sumum bonum* as in Aristotle. Virtue is the medium between two extremes, the golden mean. Any metaphysical system generates its own ethics. Theory of creation generates ethics of action. Theory of emanation generates an ethics of mediation. The eternity of the world is itself is metaphysics and ethics. Being in the world generates situational ethics.

Man is the self-consciousness of the Ideal and the Real of this unity between God and the world. Through intellect he can conceive God, communicate with Him, directly without the intervention of prophets. A philosopher has the same powers of cognition as a prophet, for both, philosophy and prophecy arise from the same source. The prophet utilizes imagery in order to stimulate the imagination of his listeners while the philosopher uses logic and hypothetical concepts. A prophet requires an exterior cult following, while a philosopher is satisfied with a more interior following of the mind. A prophet speaks to the masses, while a philosopher speaks to the elite. This is the model of *Homo Sapiens*. Revelation is mute without human understanding. The tablets of Moses are only forms carved onto stone. They become alive only by human assimilation and realization. God communicates to man. He created man to be known by Him. What is the value of an "Object" if not seen and recognized by a Subject?

Man needs to be an autonomous unity not split in two: Soul and body. Soul is eternal with God. The body is perishable with the world. This duality in man made him prefer the eternal nature of the soul over the contingent nature of the body. He became through this soul half-angel, and through the body half-beast. The pure soul distinct from the body is an aspiration, a hope for the future and a personification of the ideal. The revolt against dualism since Descartes is one of the major factors in the development of contemporary thinking. The body has lost, thanks to existential philosophy, it dreadful aspect The *Cogito* is as Sartre showed in *La Transcendence de l'Ego*, a mere illusion, a vacuum. The body described by M. Merleau-Ponty as an instrument of intrusion in the word, being-in-the-world, through language, movement, conflict, and love is almost a glorious body. It is a puritanical or Cathar-esque concept of man which is responsible solely for this dualism. Human consciousness is the third way between soul and body.

Jurisprudence or Human Rights (*Homo Faber*)?

Classical Islamic jurisprudence has until recently, been dominated by a legalistic and punitive approach, a certain kind of deontic logic, of what ought to be done. Revelation came in to direct and to orient. Revelation as it is used here means God's intention or plan for man. Jurisprudence kept this intention as it is without reversing it and making it an intention of man to God as in dogmatic theology. Jurisprudence does not even use the word "God", substituting the term "Legislator"; such terminology being oriented towards legal practice. The authenticity of the narrative followed by its linguistic interpretation is finally realized in the world through human action. This is the model of *Homo Faber*. If revelation is to be implemented, it will be through a call for action, not for theory. It assigns the minimum of rational certitude to prevent partial points of view and to concentrate on human action by a certain kind of economy of time.

Revelation is invoked to maintain five pillars of the law: The preservation of life, reason, norms of conduct, dignity/honor, and public wealth. These pillars combine individual and collective human rights. Life is an absolute value irrespective of who is living, a Jew, a Christian, a Muslim, a Hindu, a believer or a non-believer, a human being, an animal, vegetation etc. Life is one of the three major attributes of the Divine, the condition of omniscience and of omnipotence. These five pillars relate specifically to man and community. They are not centered alone on the individual's rights as is the case with the famous "Universal Declaration of Human Rights", declared twice in the west, during the French Revolution and after the Second World War, based on a radically individualist concept of the human: absolute freedom, including sovereign rights over one's own body and extended to encompass the subject areas of nudity, abortion and homosexuality.

These universal intentions are realized in practice through human action, according to another five levels of behavior: That which is obligatory as opposed to obligatory inaction, non-obligatory action, non-obligatory inaction and, finally, primitive innocence. The obligatory is an imperative to act because of the benefits resulting from the action. The obligatory inaction is a prohibition; that which one must not do because of the damage and the injuries which might result from the action. This obligation or necessity is not determined by God but by human nature and the spontaneous will to action or inaction arising therefrom. That which is optional or non-obligatory is the manifestation of human freedom. The descending revelation is equal to the ascending nature. Finally primitive innocence is nature, itself equal to its own legality. Nature is good. Revelation motivates human action towards natural goodness. There is no imposition, punition or reward if one implements or does not implement these spontaneous modes of natural behavior.

The Islamic penal code, usually considered harsh and severe, is force-as-dissuasion not unlike the logic behind the proliferation of the atom bomb: Ideally, never to be used – *except as a deterrence*. Mercy prevails upon/over punishment. Actual physical punishment is a rarity. Capital punishment has an ambiguous status in the philosophy of law. Within the legal systems of certain nation-states it is permitted, yet is prohibited in others. Can an error such as killing be corrected by another error of the same kind – that is – physical liquidation? The killer can be sentenced to life imprisonment in order to protect society from his evils. The severing of bodily members, for instance chopping off the hands of a thief, is contrary to human rights. Man owns his body. He *is* his body according to Gabriel Marcel, exchanging the idea of *having* a body to b*e*ing one. Among the (more obvious) injunctions raised against decapitation is that it is contravenes human dignity. Stoning was the definitive punishment enforced by rabbinical authority which Christ famously refused to apply, preferring forgiveness. The law of the talion aims only at deterring the committing of any crime against the body. Banishment is a more subtle, though also, extreme form of punishment in that the individual is physically removed and isolated from his community and homeland. Additionally, there exists many devices by which these harsh penalties can be excused and/or suspended such as, clemency, lack of evidence, necessity, human weakness, self-defense, attenuating circumstances etc.

The Perfect Man (*Homo Patheticus*)

Mystics preferred existential experience as a method for gaining know-ledge, not the dialectics of theologians, nor the reasoning of philosophers, nor the casual experimentation of the jurists. It is through existential experience that knowledge can be asserted more directly. Truth reveals itself in living experience by intuition. Phenomenology is a theory that comes very close to this. Here, Islamic humanism appears very clearly. Human experience is similar everywhere. It is as universal as human reason is to the enlightenment.

Spiritual experiences are needed for initiations to the mystical path. It begins by repentance on the spot, by a sudden μέτανοια. Through individual effort the mystic goes through different stages, seven, eleven or thirteen, always a prime number signifying the non-divisible unity of God. The stages can be compared to steps in a stairway to mount, such as poverty, asceticism, acceptance, resignation, reliance, gratitude, love etc. These are all human passions, pacified and reversed, out of which the perfect man is forged. In reformist movements, these passive reversals become more activist in practice, for example: resistance, revolution, protest, opposition, rejection, negation, and renunciation.

Ascending from one step to another some transitional psychological states appear as a sign of completion of the previous step and the forthcoming of future ones. They are signs of encouragements that the mystic is taking the right path. These binary states are like traffic lights, green and red – green to pass, red to halt. Signs are also binary, possessing a positive and negative dialectic. The negative precedes the positive, such as: Drunkenness/awareness, fear/hope; estrangement/familiarity, absence/presence, distance/intimacy; nothingness/existence; self-affirmation/self-annihilation. In reformist movements once again the passive states are reversed to more active ones such as regression/progress, underdevelopment/development; war/peace, conflict/dialogue, etc.

Humanism appears also in mysticism in the reciprocity of consciousness between master and disciple. Human actions are made by face to face relations. Learning is done through guidance. Knowing is possible through dialogue. Bookish knowledge is dead. It cannot go through from a dead man to a living man. God is alive and man, whether a master or a disciple, is also alive. The humanism of knowledge is transmitted directly from heart to heart not indirectly by intermediary narrators. Mutual love between the master and the disciple depicts in *miniature,* the mutual love between man and God.

Man in the World (*Homo Mundi*)?

Man is a generic term used here to denote the average worldling, the mass of humanity, the ordinary, simple human being, not the ideal described in theology, philosophy or mysticism nor the human reality described in jurisprudence but worldly mankind in the role of vocational hero. Man is fragile. He can be sick, handicapped, and he dies.[2] He comes into the world and he leaves it. He is contingent. However, he learns and understands the meanings of words and things. He also speaks and communicates. He has a fragile psychology: carelessness and impulsiveness, weakness, negligence, slackness, backward-looking. Often ruled by fear, he is emotional, helpless; by turns either a supplicant or demanding, anguished, hopeful or pessimistic, joyful then sad, accepting and rejecting, thankful and an ingrate,

---

2 | Man Insane is mentioned in the Quran 65 times.

remembering only to forget, violent, antagonistic, authoritarian, dictatorial, questioning, doubting, ignorant, dialectical etc. This is what Pascal called *la misère de l'homme.*

However, Man also is great. He is the recipient of revelation, the partner with God in dialogue. He is the center of the universe. Everything is made according to his stature and measure. God is human. The world is human. He is the vice-regent of God on earth. He assumes the responsibility of realizing the word of God as an ideal structure of the world. He can be immortal through his work and his impact in the world is similar to that of artists, thinkers, writers, and leaders.

He is challenged by many obstacles. The world is resistant to his will. The powers of opposition and oppression refuse to recognize his value, dignity and rights. They want to destroy his powers and deny his whole existence. Man accepts all these acrimonious challenges. He is also reasonable, courageous, resilient, loving, innovative, self-sacrificing and creative, powerful, etc. This is what Pascal referred to as *La grandeur de l'homme.*

However man assumes his responsibility, he uses his reason and his free will to implement the message he has received, as the vice-regent of God on earth, not though as a political ruler, or the ruler of a theocracy, or *Hakimiya*, which means the sovereignty of God on earth through the law, but through individual work and individual responsibility. He is merely the carrier the message, which is his vocation on earth. Man in Arabic, *Insan*, has no plural to denote this individual responsibility. None have sinned for him and none can save him. He must save himself by himself. This is what Pascal called *Le Noeud*, with Jesus Christ and the church as two external saviors.

Man is the measure of all things, but the question that must be asked is: which man, the particular, individual man of Protagoras, or the universal Man of Socrates?

Islamic Humanism bears more similarities to Socrates, than to Protagoras. Man as the image of God and God as the image of man. This is also one of the highest meanings of incarnation on the phenomenological level. God became man as man becomes God. Thus the twofold advancement of *Aller et Retour* is identical.

Part IV: Perspectives of Interpretation

Feminism as Integral to the History of Humanism

Gianna Pomata

One very Gracious Form of Human Relation

In 1936 Margery Fry, Principal of Somerville College at Oxford, wrote an essay in honor of Gilbert Murray, the Oxford Professor of Greek and long time Chairman of the League of Nations, a great humanist as well as an outstanding supporter of both pacifism and feminism. Gratefully commemorating Murray's generous contribution to Somerville and to the cause of women's education, Fry also paid a moving tribute to the very special relationship that had existed between the men and the women committed to the feminist cause before the advent of women's suffrage. After this victory, she noted, that special relationship was bound to disappear. "The weapons of education and enfranchisement are in the hands of women. So far as they still have special battles, they can fight with the weapons of ordinary citizenship. And as they can never again have quite such need of help, so there will be no new-comers to one very special place in their regard and affection, no renewal of *one very gracious form of human relation*" (Fry 1936: 49-61).[1]

Fry was at loss to find words to define this form of human relation – a male-female partnership that defied the most deeply rooted assumptions on Victorian gender roles.

In the earlier days of the Women's Movement [...] the attitude of the general public towards the new ideas was simply one of amused contempt. So there grew up a very special, and in many ways, a very beautiful, relation between the women who were claiming 'the right of every human soul to enter, unhindered except by the limitation of its own power and desires, into the full spiritual heritage of the race' [she quoted here Murray's words in *Religio Grammatici*] and those generous men who joined the battle on their side [...].

---

1 | At p. 49: emphasis added.

How must we describe the motive which led such men as Arthur and Henry Sidgwick, T.H. Green, Bishop Talbot, Professor Pelham, and Gilbert Murray to devote themselves, with infinite patience, to the foundation and management of women's colleges? It is tempting to call it "chivalry" [...]. Yet, looked at more closely, it is the very antithesis of chivalry. The woman of the nineteenth century had had her fill of chivalry. She was tired of offering, by virtue of her weakness, a pale occasion for protective valour [...]. It was the sense of being believed in, valued, and wanted for their potential help in the life of the community, in the endless struggle against cruelty and ignorance and needless suffering, which roused a peculiarly cordial gratitude in the women of the emancipation movement.

There was no patronizing element in Murray's feminism, Fry concluded. His main motive was simply his belief in women's contribution to social and educational progress. His was not "the *credo* of a knight-errant" – rather it was that of a "a man who can offer help without attributing helplessness."

This deeply felt tribute from woman to man, from a feminist to a humanist, may be used as the starting point for raising an issue that cuts across centuries of European intellectual history. What, if any, is the relationship between feminism and humanism? Is there a positive or a negative correlation between feminist and humanist values? Much recent feminist theory, especially in the field of literary studies, has vehemently denounced humanism as a form of ideology that has falsely universalized male experience, by making it the paradigm of human experience in general (for instance Moi 1985: 8; for similar views cf. Jardine 1985; Butler 1990; Braidotti 2002: 158-180). It has been argued that in presenting the case for a universal notion of humanity, humanism has been all too often, in fact, only a disguised form of "masculinism." What's more, some feminist theorists have joined Foucault and other proponents of postmodernism in the project of "deconstructing" Western humanism. They have espoused the postmodernist repudiation of a central tenet of humanism, the notion of the human subject as an autonomous moral agent. As a result, they have argued that humanism is flawed not only because it has privileged male experience and devalued women's perspective, but also because it relies on an illusion, the notion of an autonomous and universal self. From this standpoint, consequently, feminism looks strongly opposed to humanism.[2]

These critics use a very sweeping and vaguely defined notion of human-ism. They see humanism as an abstract set of ideas that they posit at the core Western modern philosophy. They are not interested in humanism as a specific historical phenomenon, related to specific social and cultural conditions. And yet I would argue that when we consider the social and cultural

---

2 | Such views have been so widespread in the 1980s and '90s that Pauline Johnson has spoken of "the hegemony of anti-humanist sentiment within contemporary feminism" (Johnson 1994).

history of humanism,[3] as it developed in Europe in the early modern period, the opposition between humanism and feminism dissolves. On the contrary, we discover that throughout European history, as I will argue in this essay, feminism and humanism have often been intimately and positively related – that feminism, indeed, is part and parcel of the history of humanism from its late medieval development to the current effort by international feminism to affirm women's rights as human rights. Seen in this perspective, the history of feminism is not just the history of the women who fought for women's emancipation; it is also the history of those men who seconded that struggle because of their inclusive vision of humanist values. It is also the history of that "very gracious form of human relation" which developed between women and men in their joint pursuit of the feminist cause – a relation that can be traced at various times and places in European history in spite of the prevailing hierarchical pattern of European gender roles.

Are Women Human?

"Are women human?" asked in 1938 Dorothy Sayers, an Oxford-trained scholar and committed humanist, as well as the author of some of the first feminist mystery novels (Sayers 1971).[4] In this provocative pamphlet, Sayers denounced the persistence of a deeply ingrained stereotype of woman as "the Human Not-Quite-Human," noting that it was based on the denial of single women's individuality. This was a much debated topic in turn-of-the- century European culture. Even late Victorian men admitted, on occasion, how deeply rooted was male inability to see the individual woman. The novelist George Meredith, whose works described the dilemmas of the "new woman" and the search for new gender models, wittily made this point in *The Egoist* (1879), a novel that famously captured the egotism of Victorian men. "It is the habit of the sportive gentleman of easy life, bewildered as he would otherwise be by the tricks, twists, and windings of the hunted sex, to parcel out fair women into classes; and some are flyers and some are runners; these birds are wild on the wing, those exposed their bosom to the shot. For him there is no individual woman. He grants her a characteristic only to enroll her in a class. He is our immortal dunce at learning to distinguish her as a personal variety, of a separate growth" (Meredith 1968: 230).[5]

---

3 | On the variety of definitions of humanism see Southern 1995.

4 | A student of the medievalist Mildred Katherine Pope at Oxford, Sayers translated Dante's *Divine Comedy* and the *Chanson de Roland*. She combined the independent pursuit of scholarship with a successful career as writer of a series of mystery novels based on the egalitarian partnership of the investigating duo, Lord Peter Wimsey and Harriet Vane. See Brunsdale 2005: 423-439.

5 | Sayers does not mention Meredith but quotes a similar pronouncement by D. H. Lawrence (*Assorted Articles*): "Man is willing to accept woman as an equal, as a man in skirts, as an angel, a devil, a baby-face, a machine, an instrument, a bosom,

Confronted with this attitude, turn of the century feminists asked for women the fundamental right to be categorized and treated as individuals – no more, no less. Sayers repeated this claim: "What we ask is to be human individuals, however peculiar and unexpected" (Sayers 1971: 29.

The demand for full humanity and individuality was central to the 19th century suffrage movement. While advancing the request of the vote for women as a class, suffragists were acutely conscious of the need to anchor this request in the right of every human being to individuality and self-determination, as Elizabeth Cady Stanton made plain in her extraordinarily eloquent plea *Solitude of Self* (1892).

The strongest reason for giving woman all the opportunities for higher education, for the full development of her faculties, her forces of mind and body, for giving her the most enlarged freedom of thought and action; a complete emancipation from all forms of bondage, of custom, dependence, superstition; from all the crippling influences of fear – is the solitude and personal responsibility of her own individual life. The strongest reason why we ask for woman a voice in the government under which she lives, in the religion she is asked to believe [...] a place in the trades and professions, where she may earn her bread, is because of her birthright to self-sovereignty, because as a individual she must rely on herself.[6]

Though expressed in its strongest terms by 19th and early 20th century feminism, this claim of women to full humanity and individuality was not new. Already in late medieval and early modern Europe women had faced being classified, in even stronger terms, as "the human not quite human," and had tried to answer the question "Are women human?" with a persuasive yes. Starting in the early 15th century we find, in European learned culture, writings by male and female authors that centre on the defense of women from the misogynist slander that had been heaped upon them. This debate, which was called the *Querelle des femmes,* was fuelled by a persistent outpouring of misogyny that kept questioning whether women were actually of the same species as men. "Women are not human beings" stated, for instance, the title of an anonymous treatise that appeared in Germany in 1595 and quickly circulated throughout Europe, prompting among others the vigorous rejoinders of two Venetian writers, a lay woman, Lucrezia Marinella, and a nun, Arcangela Tarabotti, who both wrote to extol "the nobility and excellence of women" and to argue that women were indeed of the same species as man (Acidalius 2006 [1595]; Marinella 1600, English transl. 1999; Tarabotti 1651, English transl. 1998).

a womb, a pair of legs, a servant, an encyclopaedia, an ideal or an obscenity; the one thing he won't accept her as is a human being, a real human being of the feminine sex" (Sayers 1971: 33).

6 | Address before the United States Committee on Woman Suffrage, Feb. 20 1892, in Stanton 2001: 4.

An Event of Greater Significance than the Crusades

What was the intellectual and social context of the *Querelle des femmes?* The defense of women developed as a humanist genre. It was associated from the beginning with the social phenomenon of humanism, namely the creation of a new culture outside the monastic institutions, where learning had been confined in the middle ages, and the formation of a new type of intellectual – a scholar who rejected celibacy and retreat from the world as the preconditions of the intellectual life. This new notion of culture had momentous consequences for women. Already in 15th century humanism we find the earliest emergence of that phenomenon which, Virginia Woolf said, she would describe, if she were rewriting history, "more fully and think of greater importance than the Crusades or the Wars of the Roses. The middle-class woman began to write." (Woolf 1929: 97) This did not happen for the first time towards the end of the 18th century, as Virginia Woolf herself assumed, but much earlier, in the early days of humanism when women writers like Christine de Pisan and Hélisenne de Crenne (Willard 1984; Wood 2000) in France, or Laura Cereta and Isotta Nogarola in Italy (see King 2005), mastered humanist erudition and used it to articulate for the first time a self-conscious vision of women's role and value in society and culture.

At the beginning of the 15th century, Christine de Pizan (1365-1431) portrayed herself as a scholar in her study. In the first chapter of her main work, the *City of Ladies* (1405), she described herself sitting in her *celle*, surrounded by books, engaged in "the regular habit of the study of letters," which she called "the practice of my life." Christine began her career as a humanist author only after she had become a widow, when she found herself obliged to support her mother, children and niece, and to combine making a living as a scholar with the task of overseeing her household – a double challenge that in her *Livre de la mutacion de fortune* she described as dramatic as being transformed from woman into man (Pisan 1959-1966; Zühlke 1994).

It is in the households of some humanist scholars of the Renaissance that we find the first cases of the inclusion of women – daughters more commonly, but occasionally also wives – in the life of learning, the life that in the Middle Ages had been strongly associated with male celibacy and the creation of the universities as "a world without women." (Noble 1992). Until the 15th century, celibacy was the rule among Christian European scholars (more strongly among philosophers and theologians than lawyers and physicians). An established tradition connected the scholar's identity with the monastic ideal, often flavored with a strong element of misogyny and contempt for family life. The scholar's social prestige was intimately bound up with the avoidance of the web of reciprocal obligations associated with family ties. In the famous interchange between Abelard and Heloise, reported in Abelard's twelfth-century *Historia calamitatum,* the life of the mind had been defined as completely incompatible with family life. The scholarly persona was not only male, but also unencumbered by duties to women and family. Christine was unusual in assuming the persona of the scholar, though a woman, but was even more unusual in doing so without dropping family responsibilities and cares.

With humanism traditional prohibitions against the marriage of scholars started to erode – a process that gained emphasis with the Reformation's rejection of clerical celibacy (but the overall trend had started well before the Reformation). Some humanists tried to do precisely what had been declared impossible, that is, combining the pursuit of learning and higher knowledge with family life (Algazi 2003: 9-42). In a few rare cases this involved husband and wife jointly cultivating learning within marriage: this is the case of Thomas More's first marriage with Jane Colt (1488-1511) or the relationship of Conrad Peutinger (1465-1547) and Margarete Welser (1481-1552) (Hess 1988: 113-148).[7] But the scholarly habitus only very rarely included wives: it was more often transmitted from fathers to daughters: Christine had been taught by her father, and this is the pattern we find for other women humanists such as, for instance, the Italian Caterina Caldiera and Lucrezia Marinella, or the French Nicole Liébault, all daughters of humanist physicians (King/Rabil 1983: 18-19 [for Caldiera]).[8] Much more rarely, as can be expected, do we encounter a matrilineal transmission of the scholarly habitus within the family, as in the exceptional case of les Dames des Roches, Madeleine and Catherine, mother and daughter, both celebrated protagonists of French humanism.[9]

The inclusion of women in scholarly and literary pursuits was also favoured by another feature of Renaissance humanism, the shift of the site of learning from the universities – a world without women – to the courts, where women were present as powerful patrons and where they could occasionally carve out a role for themselves among the court literati, as Christine did. Different from the universities and the monasteries, which were based either on the total exclusion of women or on the rigid segregation of the sexes, the Renaissance courts were places where men and women could to some extent meet and interact in the pursuit of a new culture, based on the re-appropriation of the cultural heritage of antiquity. Women humanists claimed a share in this heritage. Like their male counterparts, who used classical learning to find alternatives to the narrow mindset of medieval Scholasticism, these women creatively selected from ancient culture those elements that could be used to argue for the advancement of women's status and the broadening of women's sphere. Today for us classical culture, with its

---

7 | But see also Cousins 2004: 213-230 on the ambiguities of More's view of women's education.

8 | Lucrezia Marinella was the daughter of Giovanni Marinello, author of a treatise on women's diseases; Nicole Liébault was the daughter of the physician and anatomist Charles Étienne, and the wife of the physician Jean Liébault, also the author of a text on women's illnesses.

9 | Madeleine des Roches (ca.1520-1587) personally supervised the education of her daughter Catherine, instead of sending her to be educated in a convent, as was customary. See Roches/Roches 2006.

undeniably elitist connotations, is precisely the culture from which women were excluded. But listen to a fifteenth-century Italian woman humanist, Laura Cereta (1469-99) as she replies to a scholar who had praised her as an exceptional woman:

You pretend to admire me as a female prodigy, but there lurks sugared deceit in your adulation [...] I would have been silent, believe me, if that savage old enmity of yours had attacked me alone [...] but I cannot tolerate your having attacked my entire sex [...] With just cause I am moved to demonstrate how great a reputation for learning and virtue women have won by their inborn excellence, manifested in every age as knowledge, the (purveyor) of honor. Certain, indeed, and legitimate is our possession of this inheritance, come to us from a long eternity of ages past.[10]

Cereta goes on to list a long series of learned women from ancient history, including two celebrated women humanists of her time (Isotta Nogarola and Cassandra Fedele). "All of history – she claims confidently – is full of examples such as these." For Cereta, classical culture provided a way to affirm her literary vocation. Reading the female authors in the *Querelle des femmes*, we repeatedly find that they used the classical tradition as a repertoire of stories that celebrated positive, even glorious forms of feminine transgression. An example is the story of Telesill (from Plutarch's *Mulierum Virtutes*) – the woman from Argos who was healed of a disease after making a vow to dedicate herself to the Muses. With this story in mind, Catherine des Roches, in the *Dialogue d'Iris et Pasithée* (1583) argued that a woman can legitimately refuse marriage in order to devote herself to learning. Another example is the story of Agnodice (from Igynus's *Fabulae*), the Athenian girl who disguised herself as a man to learn the art of medicine, which was forbidden to women. Catherine des Roches developed this story into a plea for the right of women to education, to the "glory that comes from serving the Muses, daughters of Memory" (Larsen 1987: 250-56).

Male Feminism and Anti-Scholasticism

Though few in numbers, women humanists provided an important precedent for the argument in favor of women's right to education – an argument that would be made increasingly from the 17th century on. But equally important for the future history of feminism would be the presence of male voices among the defenders of the cause of women. In strong contrast with the traditional misogyny of the medieval scholar, a new attitude of philogyny is displayed in the texts of the men who contributed to the humanist *Querelle des femmes*. Why did these men rally to the defense of women? Partly, it

---

10 | Laura Cereta to Bibulus Sempronius: Defense of the Liberal Instruction of Women, in King/Rabil 1983: 81-82.

can be argued that their goal was to court the favor of women rulers in the competition for patronage – a vital necessity for the humanists, who were often in search for a position at some princely court. But the new attitude was also fostered by the humanist rejection of the old persona of the medieval cleric with its appendages of celibacy and misogyny. The humanists criticized the traditional clerical disparagement of matrimony, and some of them even raised their voice to denounce women's oppression in marriage. So for instance, the great humanist physician Antonio Musa Brasavola, drawing on Erasmus's *Colloquia*, strongly condemned the brutal treatment of wives by traditional husbands, advocating a more humane attitude.[11] Such brutality Brasavola implied, went hand in hand with the narrow and prejudiced habits of mind that were produced by Scholastic training.

Indeed, the most distinctive trait of the humanists' defense of women was the attack on Scholastic culture and its philosophical cornerstone, Aristotelianism. From Agrippa of Nettersheim in the early 16th century to Poullain de la Barre in the late 17th, anti-Aristotelianism was a long-term feature of the *Querelle des femmes*. The main feminist argument of the humanists was to question the Aristotelian-Scholastic view of woman as "error of nature," a failed male, an imperfect version of the male paradigm. Already Agrippa in the *Ur-text* of the *Querelle, De nobilitate et praecellentia foeminei sexus* (1509, pub. 1529) had dismissed the Aristotelian notion of woman as an error of Nature, proposing instead a new appreciation of the female body as *"miraculum naturae,"* a wonder of nature, the masterpiece of nature's virtuosity (Agrippa 1996: 59-61). This was indeed a daringly new view, which reversed the conventional notion of male superiority. The form of the argument in the *Querelle des femmes* of the first half of the 16th century was often the paradox, the figure of speech that introduced unheard-of ideas by turning the received view upside down.[12] This strategy of argumentation indicates how difficult it must have been to advance new ideas about women in a context that was still dominated by the Scholastic emphasis on the authority principle and the compliance with tradition. The paradox of women's superiority may have been argued by some humanists simply as a way to display virtuosity in the art of debate, without real belief in the substance of the argument. Thus for instance, the mysterious physician (and probably heretic) Ortensio Lando in his *Paradoxes* (1544) amused himself and his readers by arguing that "Woman is more excellent than man" and that "Aristotle was not only an ignoramus but also the most wicked man of his times" (Lando 1544: 78v-85v; 94r-95r). This may have been tongue in cheek – nothing more than an intellectual joke. But by the end of the 16th century the argument against the Aristotelian-Scholastic view of woman had gained real weight and gravity. The late-Renaissance physician Andrè du Laurens, writing in 1593, was dead serious in rejecting the Aristotelian notion of woman as

---

11 | Antonio Musa Brasavola, *Examen omnium syruporum* (Venice 1538), 1r-3v; see Bacchelli 2004: 93-100, especially 97-98.

12 | Colie 1966: 102ff. on the use of paradox in the *Querelle des femmes*.

"primum monstrum naturae, animal mutilum, occasionatum": "We do not approve of this opinion of Galen and Aristotle. We believe instead that Nature intends to generate both female and male. Saying that woman is an error or slip of nature is a "barbaric" notion, unworthy of a philosopher" (Laurens 1595: 280). As Ian Maclean showed in his book *The Renaissance Notion of Woman*, in the second half of the 16th century the Aristotelian/Scholastic view of woman as "imperfect male" and "error of Nature" was rejected by several doctors and replaced with the argument that each sex is perfect in its own terms and according to its own function. The female sex was no longer thought to be the imperfect and incomplete version of the male. (Maclean 1980: 28-46). At the end of the 16th century even a woman was confident enough to attack the greatest philosopher of antiquity. Strengthened by her humanist education, the Venetian Lucrezia Marinella, daughter and sister of physicians, upbraided Aristotle as the main slanderer of women and opposed his views to those of Plato and Plutarch in her contribution to the *Querelle*, once more a treatise *On the excellence and nobility of women* (1600). (Acidalius [1595] 2006; Marinella [1600] 1999; Tarabotti [1651] 1998).

The most enduring contribution of Renaissance humanism to the long-term history of feminism may well have been the association of a negative view of women with the irrational prejudice and blind obedience to authority attributed to the Aristotelian-Scholastic mindset. In 1674 the Cartesian philosopher and feminist Poullain de la Barre, arguing for the mental equality of the sexes and for women's right to education, candidly confessed that, as an ex-Jesuit, he had to shake off a lot of Scholastic baggage before he could adopt a rational view of women. "When I was a Scholastic, I considered (women) scholastically, that is to say, as monsters, as beings inferior to men, because Aristotle and some theologians whom I had read, considered them so." (Poullain de la Barre 1674: 327, 331-34).[13] The inequality of the sexes, Poullain stressed, was simply a prejudice – "of all prejudices, the most remarkable" – an irrational belief that the true philosopher was bound in honor to confute and combat wherever he met it. This conviction was a lasting legacy of humanist feminism to the feminism of later centuries. The 19th century men who, like Gilbert Murray, supported the cause of women's education and suffrage, were motivated, among other things, by the humanist ethos that required the rejection of irrational prejudice.

Feminism with a Human Face

The proto-feminism of the European Renaissance was definitely a minority trend, but it did open up new possibilities. The participation of women in the pursuit of learning, newly viewed as the highest form of cultivating humanity, was a cultural revolution of far-reaching consequences. It involved

---

13 | Poullain's *De l'égalité des deux sexes* (1673) was translated into English as *The Woman as Good as Man, or the Equality of Both Sexes*, London 1677.

a new understanding of women's capabilities within a broader, more inclusive redefinition of humanity. It involved granting women, in European history so often disqualified and dispossessed in matters of material inheritance, some share at least of the spiritual heritage of the past. Women's claim to humanist culture long predated their claim to civil and political rights, but the latter cannot be understood without the former. The humanist feminism of the early modern period paved the way for the "first wave" of the women's movement of the 19th century, which asked for women the rights to education, property, and citizenship.

And in spite of the anti-humanist stance of some post-modern feminist critics, there is plenty of evidence that also the "second wave" of the women's movement in the 1970s started with an understanding of feminism strongly associated with humanist values. Some feminist leaders of the '70s such as Betty Friedan and Gloria Steinem clearly articulated this view (see for instance Steinem 1987: 11-15). More recently, several feminist theorists have argued against the hegemony of anti-humanist sentiment within contemporary feminism (Johnson 1994. See also Soper 1990: 11-16; Benhabib 1992). Indeed, forgetting or eradicating these humanist roots would be a disaster for feminism, as it would cut the link to a line of critical thought that has renewed significance and potential in our difficult times. Faced with a mounting tide of irrational fundamentalism at home and abroad, Western feminists may well need to go back for inspiration and sustenance to the intellectual and moral tradition of humanism, with its firm commitment to rational inquiry and to the rejection of prejudice. Even more importantly perhaps, the humanist roots of European feminism acquire new relevance today, when feminism is more and more based on international dialogue across cultures, in the pursuit of a multi-cultural definition of human rights. The assertion of women's rights as human rights (Bunch 1990: 486 -498; Tomasevski 1993; Peters/Wolper 1995; and especially the theoretical framework for cross-cultural norms of justice, equality and rights for women provided by Nussbaum 2000) necessarily implies a feminist redefinition of humanity, while also positing, at the same time, a feminism closely allied with humanism – a feminism with a human face.

A feminism with a human face must not necessarily be however, a feminism with a European face. The humanist roots of Western feminism are not something to denigrate but neither are they part of a dogmatic definition of feminism to impose on all cultures. More modestly, they provide historical evidence of the connection between the pursuit of a critical mindset and a more inclusive, non-hierarchical vision of humanity. They invite research and reflection on comparable cases of this connection in other cultures. They invite us to inquire, in other cultures, which intellectual and social contexts have fostered or hindered a clearer perception of women's humanity. A feminism with a human face will require a new humanism, forged in a new dialogue within and across cultures.

Humanism and the Literary Imagination

Erhard Reckwitz

In 1945 Jean-Paul Sartre defined the philosophical school of existentialism as the ultimate form of humanism: "L'existentialisme est un humanisme." The same could be said about literature: "Literature is a humanism." In the following I shall give a short account of why I consider this equation to be justified. I shall invoke numerous sources in support of my claim, which accounts for the high degree of intertextuality of the ensuing argument in the way it is presented.

1.

In the concluding paragraph of his comprehensive survey of almost five hundred years of French thought on what determines selfhood and otherness, Tzvetan Todorov sums up the merits and demerits of the universalist as well as relativist approaches in this debate, all the ramifications of which he analyzes within the space of more than five hundred pages. The universalist pretensions, especially those propounded by Europe over centuries of colonialism in the course of which the Europeans have been claiming to bring the light of civilization to the benighted inferior races, has become unmasked as a narrow ethnocentrism: What passes for universal values amounts to nothing but the articulation of specific European prejudices and interests. This culminates in the emphatic charge: "Universalism is imperialism" (Todorov 1989: 510).[1]

The natural consequence of this would be to resort to a more enlightened or liberal relativism, following the insight that "all our judgments are relative to a time, a place, a context" (Todorov 1989: 510).[2] This would lead to a modern egalitarianism, both in historical and synchronic terms that takes the following form: "The value of today is not the one of yesterday,

---

1 | "L'universalisme, c'est l'impérialisme". The English translations of German or French quotations are my own.

2 | "[...] tous les jugements sont relatifs: à un temps, à un lieu, à un contexte."

and everybody is a barbarian in the eyes of their neighbor" (Todorov 1989: 510).[3] This kind of thinking, although it seemingly presents a solution to the more glaring problems posed by universalism, leads to a few obvious difficulties: Apart from the fact that relativism thus formulated is tantamount to making another absolute truth claim, which leads to the obvious logical contradictions, there is one fundamental danger inherent in this line of thought: "the relativist foregoes the unity of mankind" (Todorov 1989: 510).[4] Once that unity has been given up cultural and/or racial discrimination, which was thought to be the exclusive province of universalism, comes in by the back door: "The absence of unity permits exclusion, which can lead to extermination" (Todorov 1989: 510)[5]

Furthermore, relativism leads to the conundrum of its proponents being incapable of denouncing any kind of injustice or act of violence for the simple reason that it proceeds from a culture other than their own. Todorov therefore postulates a new humanism which, because of the inviability of both universalist and relativist definitions of humanity, can only be "a critical humanism" (Todorov 1989: 513).[6]

Wherein, then, does this consist? He does align himself with relativism in so far as to concede that human beings are subject to historical and social conditioning factors, but then he makes his bid for his kind of universalism: "What every human being has in common with all others is the capacity for refusing such determining forces. [...] freedom is the distinctive feature of mankind" (Todorov 1989: 513)[7]

2.

The human capacity for transcending the here and now thanks to the gift of imagination forms an essential part of the freedom from any kind of determinism or programming that, for instance, animals are prone to. According to Sartre the imagination is capable of intellectually freeing human beings from the constraints of reality via "the negation of the world" (Sartre 1986: 371)[8]

This "irrealizing function" (Sartre 1986: 13)[9] takes the form of negating

---

3 | "Le bien d'aujourd'hui n'est pas celui d'hier, et chacun est barbare aux yeux de son voisin."

4 | "[...] le relativiste renonce à l'unité de l'espèce humaine."

5 | "L'absence d'unité permet l'exclusion, laquelle peut conduire à l'extermination."

6 | Emphasis in the original: "*un humanisme critiqueç*"

7 | "Ce que chaque être humain a en commun avec tous les autres, c'est la capacité de refuser ces determinations, [...] la liberté est le trait distinctif de l'espèce humine."

8 | "[...] la néantisation du monde."

9 | "[...] fonction irréalisante."

what is given, or as Bachelard has put it, "by searching in reality for that which contradicts our previous knowledge, the new experience says no to the old experience [...]" (Bachelard 1988: 9).[10]

This negation of commonly held assumptions about reality is what literature is all about, and it is my contention that literature is the most relevant manifestation of the anthropological need human beings have for exceeding the limitations of their circumstances. The confrontation of the institutionalized positiveness of the world such as it is with the essential negativity of literature is achieved through what Hans Robert Jauss has termed aesthetic experience, which suspends our pragmatic involvement with the world especially with regard to the temporal dimensions of present, past and future: "It [aesthetic experience] permits us to 'see anew', and due to this unveiling function it grants us the enjoyment of fulfilled presence, it leads us into the realm of fantasy and thereby suspends the constraints of time; it anticipates future experiences and thus opens up new possibilities of action; it allows us to recognize that which has passed or been repressed, in the process preserving time that had been lost." (Jauss 1984: 39-40).[11]

By confronting everyday experience with its other, aesthetic experience has the power "to transfigure the everyday and transgress the admitted norms" (Ricoeur 1985: 258).[12] The implicit offer made by literary texts of adopting or at least playfully trying out imaginary roles leads to what Helmut Plessner has designated as an "increase in anthropological dimensionality." This makes literature into an ideal testing ground for experimenting with alternative modes of reality without running the risk of colliding with pragmatic constraints, or as Paul Ricoeur states: "it is the function of fiction [...] to serve as a laboratory of thought-experiences unlimited in number." (Ricoeur 1985: vol. 3, 258).[13] Literature, like any other art form, thereby confronts our shared and commonly accepted version of reality with another one that causes the former to appear as utterly contingent and consequently as devoid of its seemingly unchangeable solidity: "Art lets the world appear in the world" (Luhmann 1986: 620-672, 624),[14] i.e. there are more worlds than just the one we inhabit. Consequently, the study of literature, given the malleability or plasticity of human nature that literature seems to be so

---

10 | "[...] en cherchant dans le reel ce qui contredit des connaissances antérieures [...] l'expérience nouvelle dit non à l'expérience ancienne [...]."

11 | "Sie [die ästhetische Erfahrung] lässt ‚neu sehen' und bereitet mit dieser entdeckenden Funktion den Genuss erfüllter Gegenwart, sie führt in andere Welten der Phantasie und hebt damit den Zwang der Zeit in der Zeit auf; sie greift vor auf zukünftige Erfahrung und öffnet damit den Spielraum möglichen Handelns; sie lässt Vergangenes oder Verdrängtes wieder erkennen und bewahrt so die verlorene Zeit."

12 | "[...] de transfigurer le quotidien et d'en transgresser les normes admises."

13 | "[...] la fonction de la fiction [...] est de server de laboratoire pour des expériences de pensée en nombre illimité."

14 | "Die Kunst lässt die Welt in der Welt erscheinen."

ideally suited to embody as well as promote, is extremely worthwhile: "If literature permits us to see that the plasticity of mankind causes it to strive for fulfilling a potential which does not enclose it within its actual realization it should be able to provide considerable insights in anthropological terms" (Iser 1991: 12).[15] Other critics have equally emphasized the potential for utopian wish fulfillment in and through literature, such as Gert Ueding who maintains that way beyond utopian writings in the strict generic sense all literature amounts to a "planned and imaginative discovery as well as activation of the creative capacity of mankind for critically rejecting the constraints of reality through aesthetic projections" (Ueding 1978: 7-14, 10).[16] This is borne out by the fact that, within their semantic universe, in most literary works there occurs a clash between what certain characters wish for and the obstacles that stands in their way, which in the terminology of modal logic as applied to narratology can be expressed as a conflict between the wish-world of the protagonists and the ordinary world or obligation-world thwarting or counteracting their desires (cf. Ryan 1991).

In a similar measure Franz Koppe sees what he calls aesthetic discourse as determined by the articulation of human needs and requirements over and beyond their formulation in ordinary pragmatic discourse. Very importantly he steers the utopian potential of literature away from pure contentism by emphasizing the relevance of aesthetic form and its connotative processes whereby the otherwise contingent material of language is made semiotically meaningful and relevant on the semantic, phonetic and syntagmatic levels (cf. Koppe 1983: 135). This is commonly referred to as the meaning of form and it should be emphasized that the innovative potential of literature should manifest itself not only in *what* it says but, most importantly, in *how* it says what it wants in formal terms. Certain literary modes such as realism strive to ensure a sense of "verisimilitude" ("vraisemblance") (Genette 1971: 71-100). by offering the reader a recognisable phenomenal world that he can relate to, but no matter how critical of reality such texts may be in terms of their thematic concern, they still tend to "enforce upon us a sense of the unalterable solidity of the world" (Eagleton 1996: 162). This can only be counteracted by administering an aesthetic jolt through introducing formal innovations that force the reader out of his complicity with the world as it is, thereby making him look at it with new eyes. The dialectic interplay of form and content is best summarized by the opposing statements of "everything in the literary work is form" (Viktor Sklovsky) and "everything in the literary work is content" (Jan Mukarovsky), both of which are justified because in literature there is no content that has not been subjected to formal procedures

---

15 | "Wenn Literatur zu erkennen gibt, dass die Plastizität des Menschen nach Vergegenwärtigung drängt, die nicht zum Einsperren in die Vergegenständlichungen führt, dann dürfte ihr anthropologischer Aufschlusswert nicht unerheblich sein."

16 | "[...] planvoll phantasiereiches Entdecken und Aktivieren des schöpferischen Vermögens des Menschen im ästhetischen Bild und kritische Absage an eine hemmende Wirklichkeit."

of presentation, just as much as only by applying such procedures can the aesthetic content be, as it were, shaped into existence. Paul Ricoeur has emphasized the absolute necessity of a literary work of art breaking with the conventional notion of mimesis as a faithful reproduction of reality: "It is precisely when a work of art breaks with this kind of verisimilitude that it truly fulfils its mimetic function" (Ricoeur 1985: vol. 3, 278).[17]

3.

Perhaps more than any other art form literature is ideally suited for mimetically projecting other worlds if we take the literal meaning of mimesis in the sense of "making the absent present." (See "Representation." In: Cooper 1995: 364-369, 365.) This is due to the notational system of language that is literature's material with its in-built capacity for what in linguistic terminology goes by the name of displacement, which denotes that "It is possible to talk about events remote in space or time from the situation of the speaker (unlike most animal cries, which reflect immediate environmental stimuli)" (Crystal 1987: 397). This implies, of course, that not only does literature embody the imaginative processes of an author, but it also gives rise to a corresponding imaginative response in the mind of the recipient. However, in order for the alternative world to be understandable it cannot possibly be a total departure from the known world. According to Wolfgang Iser, the diffused quality of the imaginary has to be translated into the more concrete pseudo-real world of fiction, which thereby acts as an intermediary between the known and the unknown. This, as Iser points out, causes the old ontological dichotomy of reality and fiction to be collapsed because fiction is not the total other of the real but, in spite of all irrealisation or transgression of the latter, its continuation (Iser 1991: 23). For the unknown to be thinkable at all it has to, at least to some degree, invoke the known.

Hence all the fictional text does is to de- and re-contextualize the familiar elements of reality it has incorporated into its internal context in order to project its own version of the world. In the process, it has to a large extent to rely on the linguistic and encyclopedic competence of the recipient because otherwise it would have to invent a totally new language: "No reference could be made, for example, to a 'woman' or a 'battle' without defining the referents in full" (Elam 1980: 104). Even when developing a new meaning of "woman" or "battle," literary fiction relies on our general knowledge of what these concepts signify because language could never hope to be entirely devoid of meaning, and the novel meaning can only come into existence because of the de-pragmatization of language in fiction. Hence literature presents us with what Karlheinz Stierle calls a "linking world that connects our world with the realm of the imaginary in its own specific manner, while at the same time

---

17 | "C'est précisément lorsqu'une oeuvre d'art rompt avec cette sorte de vraisemblance qu'elle déploie sa veritable fonction mimétique."

signaling its transitional status." (Stierle 1983: 173-182, 176).[18] In other words, even the boldest imaginings always refer back to the real conditions which stimulated them, because negation is a relational operation that inevitably bears the imprint of what it strives to transcend, or as Gérard Genette, quoting Valéry, puts it: "Just like the lion is almost [...] nothing but digested mutton literature is almost nothing but fictionalized reality" (Genette 1991: 60).[19] This comes very close to the Joycean injunction to "disentangle and recompose the known world" that sums up his modernist aesthetics of creating a new vision of reality.

4.

Roland Barthes, in one of his beautifully apt statements that sound almost poetical, has summed up the ultimately humanist concern of literature: "Science is crude, life is subtle, and it is in overcoming this gap that the importance of literature lies. On the other hand the knowledge that it imparts is never an ultimate whole; literature does not claim to know something but that it knows *about* something; or better: that it knows some of it – that it knows a lot about people" (Barthes 1978: 12).[20]

To the generalizing world of concepts literature opposes the singularity and incommensurability of the individual case. What Ricoeur refers to as the individuation of the literary text along with its illusion of actual presence enables fiction to create its effect of "'depicting' and 'putting in front of our eyes'" (Ricoeur 1985: vol. 3, 274).[21] This is precisely what makes literature so powerful in pragmatic terms because it invites our identification both with what is admirable and horrible. The example Ricoeur adduces in order to substantiate his claim is the literature of the holocaust which, far beyond our purely intellectual knowledge and ethical condemnation of the atrocities committed, moves us when it presents us with the fate of human individuals "like you and me." The literary text thereby invites our identification with the individual cases presented while at the same time cautioning us to maintain our "critical distance" (Ricoeur 1985: vol. 3, 275).[22] in order to avoid taking the fictional for the real and being oblivious to the way it has been contrived in

---

18 | "Anschlusswelt, die unsere Welt in je spezifischer Weise ins Imaginäre fortführt, doch so, daß die Übergänglichkeit selbst erkennbar ist."

19 | "Comme le lion n'est guère [...] que du mouton digéré, la fiction n'est guère que du réel fictionalisé."

20 | Emphasis in the Original: "La science est grossière, la vie est subtile, et c'est pour corriger cette distance que la littérature nous importe. D'autre part, le savoir qu'elle mobilise n'est jamais entier ni dernier; la littérature ne dit pas qu'elle sait quelque chose, mais qu'elle sait *de* quelque chose; on mieux: quelle en sait quelque chose--qu'elle en sait long sur les hommes."

21 | "[...], dépeindre' en 'mettant sous les yeux'."

22 | "[...] distanciation critique."

order to enlist our empathy. The French semiotician Algirdas J. Greimas has exemplified this principle of individuation by showing how, in the process of production, the *"parcours sémiotique"* of a narrative text takes as its starting point the "deep" semantic structure of opposing concepts, which are then set in motion *("mise en branle")* until, after having undergone a process of "actoralisation, spatialisation et temporalisation," they have been transcoded into "un faire antropomorphe" of human beings acting out the underlying semantic deep structure as protagonists or antagonists, as helpers or opponents etc (cf. Greimas 1970: 157-183). The individuation effected by the telling of a story therefore invariably involves the naming of somebody who did something: "A history that is told names the person who acted" (Ricoeur 1985: vol. 3, 355).[23] The reading process corresponding with this progression from conceptual abstraction to the more concrete level of recognizable individuals acting out their fates would be the very reverse one, i.e. penetrating through the visible surface to the invisible deep structures (cf. Greimas 1970: 157-183), a reading strategy Seymour Chatman has referred to as "reading out" as opposed to a mere reading that remains trapped within the particulars of the story narrated while being oblivious of the more fundamental issues underlying its semantic universe (cf. Chatman 1976: 41-42).

Conversely, narrative has the effect of reconverting the monothetic concepts that have congealed as experience into the polythetic linearity of their formation that remains somewhat blurred and leaves the concepts correspondingly indistinct because they have become tainted by their exposure to the way "real" people, albeit invented ones, behave (cf. Gumbrecht 1986: 202-217). This is due to the fact that one of the most important features of the novel as narrative resides in its ability of at least partially being able to eschew unattractive structural or ideological alternatives by either achieving a compromise on the actantial level or by the narrator leaving the issue unresolved (Pfeiffer 1985: 265-282). This implies that literature is capable of challenging "our allegiance to systematic thought" by couching insights in "a language at odds with the discourse of deadening truth, of discipline". Ultimately, literature thus has the "power to challenge established ways of seeing and saying things in the interest of something potentially better [...]." (Edmundson 1995: 239).

5.

All the insights concerning the liberating force of the literary imagination formulated so far are imbued with a humanist thinking whose ideology can be summarized as follows:

The grounding assumptions of humanism presuppose that experience is prior to its expression in language and conceive of language as a mere tool used to express

---

23 | "L'histoire racontée dit le qui de l'action."

the way that experience is felt and interpreted by the unique individual. The existence of the unique individual is the cornerstone of the humanist ideology [...] inscribed in this ideology is the notion that literature is the product of especially gifted individuals who are capable to capture the elusive universal and timeless truths of the human condition through the sensuous and sensitive use of the tool of language (Rice/Waugh 1989: 1-4, 3).

It would seem that postmodernist and poststructuralist thought has put paid to this notion of individuality and that of individual expression going along with it. Where the subject is seen as dominated by codes beyond its control it is no longer capable of being the Cartesian or Sartrean subject freely exercising its choice of identity or of free agency: As a "*sujet assujetti,*" as Louis Althusser posits it, it is only given the illusion of being a free agent while in reality being integrated into the social practices of ideological state apparatuses that make it into a truly subjected *subiectum.* Therefore it is a "*sujet décentré*" which, following Jacques Lacan, is only capable of uttering its needs by being integrated into the alienating "*ordre symbolique*" of language, the symbolic system of the "*grand Autre*" that is something other than itself. For the purpose of literary expression this means that in the face of the dominance of what Roland Barthes calls "*écriture,*" i.e. the socially and collectively enabling conditions of creating meaning, "*les conditions de contenu,*" the individual author becomes nothing but "*un 'monsieur' parmi d'autres*". The end of the private ownership of the word therefore rings in "*la mort de l'auteur*" because the author is nothing but, according to Barthes, "*le sujet d'une pratique*" who is at the mercy of the intertexts reverberating inside his mind. This amounts to the author not engaging with and transcending the world as a free agent and on his own terms, as postulated above, but as a passive, code-ridden *subiectum* (cf. Reckwitz 1990: 121-156, 126).

Where, then does the much-vaunted imaginative freedom of literature reside if "the alleged decentring of the subject corresponds to the supposed triumph of objectivity, the supposed victory of structural forces which totally destroy the sense of the unity of the individual"? (Larrain 1994: 153). This is the dire problem posed by Jorge Larrain, and he goes on to supply the answer: "But to accept this is to accept the final loss of agency and purpose, the inability of the subject to attempt to change the circumstances, its inability to posit any rational alternative future." (Larrain 1994: 153.) Let us remind ourselves that this flies in the face of everything we have stated so far about the power of the imagination in general and of literature in particular. Is there, then, no way out of the prisonhouse of language and the codes predetermining each and every one of our utterances, thereby making it impossible to go beyond the self-alienating disciplinary forces implanted inside us (cf. Jameson 1972)? This problem is exacerbated by the fact that with the advent of the modern and particularly the postmodern age all the traditional linguistic, cultural and literary encodings of the world are no longer felt to be adequate. How, then, does literature, given modernism's epistemological and postmodernism's ontological doubt concerning the solidity of the world (cf. McHale 1987: 3-25, on this distinction), manage somehow to twist the iron-bars of the codes it is constrained by?

Not all is lost, however, because the cognitive shift from the paradigm of consciousness to the paradigm of language or, as it has come to be called, "the linguistic turn" that seems so entirely to disempower all human consciousness and agency, can be turned against itself. Quite obviously the established literary code – if we single out narrative for this purpose – with its trias of character, action and milieu has been changed dramatically after having undergone the modernist shift away from the 'objective' representation of the world to its constitution in and by the subjective mind, and in postmodernism narrative time has given way to a spatial arrangement of situations, to put it in a somewhat simplified way. This can be seen as an indication that all codes like all systems are not totally monadic *vis-à-vis* their environment. On the contrary, to put it in the language of system theory, they are constantly engaged in observations of, and negotiations with, their environment, in the course of which they incorporate new elements into their internal structure. Language change is a case in point, because language constantly has to adapt itself to new circumstances in order to remain functional. This is not an evolutionary process but the system's response to new referential requirements, i.e. it is a response to a changing world (cf. Coseriu 1974: 245-246).

This begs the question of how the apparent immutability of the codes can be altered: Due to the fact that any code is not a closed but an open system, it can function as a system of "possibilities, of coordinates that indicate the paths that are open and those that are closed ... ." (Coseriu 1974: 47 - Coseriu is referring to Hjelmslev in this instance).[24] Accordingly, Umberto Eco defines a code as follows: "A code is not only a rule that *closes*, but it is also a rule that *opens*. It does not only say 'you must,' but it also says 'you can' or 'it would be possible to do this or that'" (Eco 1985: 275).[25] This openness is made possible because any message is, however slightly, capable of disfiguring or displacing the code because of its being bound to a certain context that lends a specific coloring to each message that the code has not made provision for. Jonathan Culler has described this phenomenon as something that is caused by the interplay of "boundless context and context-bound meaning" (Culler 1983: 196). This is exactly where individual intention that the linguistic turn seemingly had expelled manifests itself again: Even though we may constantly reiterate certain pre-established linguistic or discursive types there is a process of differentiation at work that renders each token, i.e. each individual enunciation, into something that slips beyond the control of the code. This is why signs can escape the fetters of codification (cf. Frank

---

24 | "Möglichkeiten, von Koordinaten, die die offenen und die versperrten Wege angeben [...] ."

25 | Emphasis in the original: "Ein Code ist nicht nur eine Regel, die *schließt*, sondern auch eine Regel die *öffnet*. Er sagt nicht nur 'du musst', er sagt auch 'du kannst' oder 'es wäre auch möglich, jenes zu tun'."

1984: 513). Accordingly Anthony Giddens maintains that "the theme of the decentering of the subject should not lead to the disappearance of the self as agents." (Giddens 1993: 159-174; 165). Although he basically accepts the critique of subjectivism developed by structuralism and post-structuralism he does insist on "the significance of practical consciousness in human day-to-day affairs. Intentions and reasons which agents have for what they do are sometimes capable of being expressed in what they can say about the conditions of their actions" (Giddens 1993: 159-174; 165). Such a constant process of "reflexive monitoring" provides "a context of intentionality and practice" (Giddens 1993: 171) that no code could possibly foresee. Tzvetan Todorov is applying a similar insight to the secondary code of literary genres when he states "A work of art [...] cannot be presented as the simple product of a preexisting combination; it is also that, but at the same time it transforms this combinatory [i.e. code], it develops a new code of which it is (the only) message" (Todorov 1987: 103).[26]

This is particularly the case with what Umberto Eco designates as "serial thinking" with its open and polyvalent structure that is capable of putting each code into question. The main purpose and intent of serial thinking consists in both confirming and upsetting the established codes in order to generate new modes of communication. Serial thinking has the aim of exposing codes to the winds of historical change instead of having them endlessly repeating themselves in their timeless original structure (Eco 1972: 381-382). This is why Jacques Derrida is right in saying that "everything is possible against the police of language – for example 'literatures' or 'revolutions' still without precedence." (Derrida 1977: 82.)[27]

Exactly at this point human agency asserts its rights, in spite of the potentially dehumanizing influence of supra-individual codes and intertexts, and this is when the writing of literature becomes the expression of human individuality: "Writing perhaps is the bringing to light of those workings of the unconscious, of selecting the whispering voices, to invoke the tribes and secret idioms from whom I extract something that I can call Me" (Deleuze/Guattari 1980: 107).[28] At precisely this point the linguistic turn can be turned to the advantage of humanism: If we are controlled by language, and given the inherent mutability of language, it is only necessary to change language in order to maintain our humanity as well as agency: "'Change the language,' a Mallarmean statement, is concomitant with 'change the world,' a Marxist

---

26 | "Une oeuvre d'art [...] ne peut pas être présentée comme le simple produit d'une combinaison préexistante; elle est cela aussi, mais en même temps elle transforme cette combinatoire, elle instaure un nouveau code dont elle est le premier (le seul) message."

27 | "[...] tout est possible contre la police du langage--par example des 'littératures' ou des 'révolutions' encore sans modèle."

28 | "Ecrire, c'est peut-être amener au jour cet agencement de l'inconscient, sélectionner les voix chuchotantes, convoquer les tribus et les idiomes sécrets, d'ou j'extrais quelque chose que j'appelle Moi."

statement." (Barthes 1978: 17).[29] The South African poet Breyten Breytenbach has expressed a similar sentiment more drastically in describing his poetical practice which basically consists in subverting the conventionalized practical or communicative function of language by introducing additional aesthetic structures or devices that cut across its linearity, thereby creating an excess of the signifier. The desemanticisation that results from suspending the codified relations between signifier and signified is the enabling condition for creating new meanings from old ones: "Yes, if there is nothing beyond the organic reality of patterns and repetition and illusion and rhyme and rhythm, then the idea of breaking a structure becomes exciting. The concept of the fuck-up is a liberating idea. Freedom is accepting unfreedom, denying that they are opposites, reading one in the other, and going beyond" (Breytenbach 1984: 87).

Code-dominated and code-dominating – that seems to be the dialectic we find ourselves caught up in, and this also implies that the idea of a monological concept of ready-made truth has to give way to a dialogical one that is open for revision. As far as the reception and critical processing of literature is concerned this means: "we ourselves [have to] come to grips with objects whose complexity resist easy structurations, conceptualisations and interpretations [...]." (Gumbrecht 2003: 134).[30] This enjoins upon the reader an attitude that is the true mark of our humanity, or as Patricia Waugh puts it with regard to the non-closure of postmodernist literature: "maturity is the ability to live with ambiguity, hesitation, contradiction and paradox and still be capable of belief" (Waugh 1992: 164). Literature can thus make us aware of what Clément Rosset has termed *"l'idiotie du réel"* (Rosset 1977: 40), i.e., the irreduceable particularity of the world and the people living in it, thereby teaching us to respect their alterity or Otherness that is no longer perceived as an extension of our own self-image.

---

29 | "'Changer la langue,' mot mallarméen, est concomitant de, 'changer le monde' mot marxien."

30 | "[...] wir selbst [müssen] uns [...] mit Objekten auseinandersetzen, deren Komplexität sich einer bequemen Strukturierung, begrifflichen Einordnung und Interpretation widersetzt [...]."

Humanism and the Social:

An Unclarified Relationship

Bo Stråth

This article deals with some critical remarks on what very generally can be understood as a Western version of humanism and an unsettled relationship implicit in that version.

Humanism as a program contains several unsettled relationships and inherent tensions as it emerged in the philosophies of the Renaissance and Enlightenment. One of these unsettled relationships deals with religion. Humanism emerged as a program with the human being as the centre of the universe and the measure of everything. Man replaced in several respects God. Karl Löwith in his impressive *Meaning in History* in 1949 (Löwith 1949) described the quest for the perfect and the absolute when Man replaced God as the motor of modernity. This quest constituted a kind of secular version of monotheism, and it quite obviously conflicted with the Enlightenment arguments for moderation and tolerance. Löwith's secularization thesis was based on a strong philosophical trend in the nineteenth and early 20th century, with names like Emile Durkheim, Karl Marx and Max Weber as protagonists. They all saw religion as disappearing, residual. This philosophical trend has remained strong until today, although it is an embarrassing fact that it does not provide any explanations for the religious revivalism of recent decades. In some cases like Islam, where rather than a revival, the trend is more of a reaffirmation of its identity as an official state religion as opposed to the West, where a private, individual religious experience, not circumscribed by church institutions and hierarchies prevails.

Reinhart Koselleck (Koselleck 1979; cf. Olson 2006); has drawn our attention to another consequence of the secularized quest for the perfect outlined by Karl Löwith. Enlightenment concepts like "human" and "humanity", and their dichotomous opposites "inhuman" and "sub-human" (*unmenschlich* and *untermenschlich*) substituted earlier dichotomies such as Hellenic/barbarian, Christian-Heathen. The question of how to define what is human brought classification of human beings. The Enlightenment obsession with classification had a long pre-history. Classification through opposing

190 | Bo Stråth

concepts undermined at the end the possibility of mutual recognition and respect between political groups. Koselleck saw the extreme consequences of this conceptual development in the Nazi ideological hijacking of humanity and rationality through which euthanasia and genocide were seen as logical extensions of modernity. Here he comes close to Zygmunt Bauman's pessimistic view of modernity as being in the end, an inhuman project in the name of humanity, pregnant with the Holocaust, and with Theodor W. Adorno's and Max Horkheimer's views on the contradictory nature of the Enlightenment and modernity projects in their *Dialectics of Enlightenment* (Bauman 1989; Adorno/Horkheimer 1947 [1944]. Cf. Kaye/Stråth 2000).

The focus of this article is on a third unsettled dimension of the concept of humanism: the relationships between humanism and "the social". The term "the social" conveys some kind of *collective solidarity*. Humanism in its Western version on the other hand, was basically in its Renaissance origins an individual-focused program. Humanism was *individual autonomy* and mastery of the world; human perfection conceived of in the minds of individual geniuses, the renaissance masters, and after them, the Enlightenment philosophers. As is the case with the relationship between humanism and religion, so the relationships between humanism and "the social" are viewed as a matter of balance in academic and political rhetoric. The obvious conflicts between the concepts are concealed under the discourse on autonomy and not thematized or problematized. Humanism is autonomy and solidarity, and with this equation everything seems clear.

In the motto of the French Revolution – *liberté, egalité, fraternité* – the two concepts – humanism and the social – were kept together in *one* utopian (as it later proved to be) *Denkfigur*, humanism standing for individual emancipation (liberty) and the social for collective emancipation (equality and brotherhood). The humanist program was proclaimed in the revolutionary declaration of the human rights. The idea of citizenship connoted individual rights and the fiction of the nation a collective autonomy of equals.

The revolutionary *Denkfigur* proved to be utopian, because, as we now know, its three concepts in perfect balance soon split up and were transformed into two competing with other conflicting ideologies, liberalism and socialism. They both maintained that they incorporated a dimension of the other, but the tension and opposition was nevertheless clear. These two ideologies certainly also contained an over-lapping element of mutual support. They should not be seen as long cohesive chains of thought throughout history. The semantic field created during the French Revolution should be seen rather as a depository of arguments which could be mobilized and used in widely different combinations contingent upon context and situation. However, as an arsenal of arguments put together in a variety of combinations, the tension between and the contradictions within these various versions and their conceptual underpinnings (liberty-equality) became obvious.

In the Western tradition, the strongest link emerged between liberalism and humanism, with the focus toward individual-oriented liberalism, although the liberal pretensions seeking to define the nation and its autonomy contained a clear collective dimension. The liberal ideal of individual sovereignty had to come to terms with the fact that modern societies exist by maintaining firmly structured hierarchical organizations. The image of individual mastery of the world was translated into the fiction of the nation as the locus of mastery and autonomy. This was the liberal nationalism borne of the French Revolution.

The revolution brought generally in the (Western) Europe of the nineteenth century a transfer of power from the monarchy to the people, irrespective of whether an absolute sovereign reigned or as a ruler controlled through constitutional checks and balances, as Montesquieu formulated it in his program for stability. This power transfer contained a potential of violence, as the events of the French Revolution had recently demonstrated. The fiction of the nation and the image of a sovereign people contained the germ of homogenizing politics, which were anything but humane.

The credo of the human potential of mastery and autonomy, and the shift of loadstar from Hobbes' absolute monarch to Rousseau's will of a sovereign people contained its opposite when free individuals with democratic ideals were subordinated to the fiction of the general will in the incarnation of a strong leader. Montesquieu and de Tocqueville were among those who warned of this development and argued for moderation, reason and tolerance.

One trajectory of humanism in its guise of autonomy and individual sovereignty, emerging in attempts to reduce the friction between individual and collective ideals as the locus of autonomy, ended up in the transformation of nationalism from liberal versions into more holistically oriented ones. Fichte and his colleagues developed the idea of human emancipation in the wake of the French Revolution, toward a collective emancipation based on ethnicity. *Volk* became a key concept. The individual became lost in the fiction of the *Volksgemeinschaft* and so did the social question of equality. Everybody was seen as equal within the nation, but what this meant in terms of relationships between unequal citizens was scarcely considered. Fichte could of course not know how his conceptualization of autonomy and freedom would be manipulated, as was the case with Rousseau, in how his term *volonté générale* would be abused.

A case in point is Giovanni Gentile's philosophy of action. He became possibly the most significant intellectual of the Italian fascist movement the 1920s. Gentile emphasized the humanist inheritance from the Renaissance and translated this into the view on Risorgimento, literally the return of the gushing spring, as a continuation of that original Italian cultural movement which had inspired throughout European a great moral and intellectual revitalization (Gentile 1923). The humanism of the Renaissance was seen as a purifying influence that had provided the foundation for the rebirth of the nation half a millennium later. It is clear that this particular national trajectory was an extreme case, although it was far from the only one of its kind in the deployment of extreme nationalism, and there were as we know, many more such instances, both contemporaneous, and to follow.

All projects of liberal nationalism did not end up going into extreme reverse, but those that did it were far from exceptional cases. In general terms 1848 represented a check of the expansion of liberal national projects in Europe. The liberal rhetoric underpinning them, having arisen amidst the particular conditions of the long economic depression, had evolved, by the 1870's into a more reactionary and aggressive rhetoric. Still in 1871 Gustav Schöneberg, a founding member of the *Verein für Sozialpolitik*, argued: "With the conclusion of the national question the so-called social question is now perhaps the most important of the future" (Wagner 1990: 79-85). As we know Schöneberg erred in his assumption that the national question had been solved with the creation of the German *Kaiserreich*. There are good arguments for the view that the social question is still awaiting a solution at the beginning of the twenty-first century. Of lasting interests is the linkage of the national and with social questions that Schöneberg made. At first sight he merely appears to suggest a temporal sequence of political considerations with respect to two different questions. However, his statement probably makes more sense, as Wagner and Zimmermann have argued, if one assumes, like many of his colleagues of the *Verein für Sozialpolitik*, the founding of which followed immediately upon the creation of the German nation state, that he saw the building of the nation state as the precondition for the successful handling of the social question. The nation, in his view, establishes the framework for the organization of social solidarity. If the liberal-democratic understanding of the nation appeared to guarantee civic and political citizenship, the debate around the social question indicated the search for a yet unattained social citizenship (Wagner/Zimmermann 2004);[1] From their conservative/liberal reform perspective Schöneberg and his colleagues saw the nation state as the arena of social problem solving based on reason and empirical pragmatism. This was an optimistic view at a time just before the long economic depression lasting from 1873 until the 1890s gave the social question renewed significance. One important solution to the economic depression was that from the 1890s on, an arms race accompanied by accelerating nationalism and protectionism had supplanted the philosophy of free trade. The social question was absorbed by the social Darwinism of a nationalist rhetoric, which advocated a struggle among nations where only the strongest would survive. The road to 1914 was thus paved. After the war Gentile continued with his theme of national integration through national strength and rejuvenation. Somewhat later, a romanticist/holistic versions of *Volksgemeinschaft* recurred as a suggestion of how to solve the social question, while National Socialism developed and refined fascism into its most extreme manifestation.

Only in retrospect does the distinction between the various versions of how to cope with the social question in democratic and humanistic forms appear. *Front populaire* in France, red-green worker-farmer coalitions in Scandinavia, The New Deal in the USA, fascism in Italy and National Socialism in Germany; these were all attempts at dealing with the same

---

1 | For the term social citizenship, see Marshall 1992 (1950) and Magnusson/ Stråth 2004.

problem of social integration under conditions of economic crisis and unemployment. Roosevelt sent delegations to Mussolini's Italy to investigate what could be learnt from the Italian way of coping with the crisis which threatened the future of world capitalism (Schivelbusch 2005). Only Italian colonialism in Abyssinia made him wary. Stalin's collectivization policy in the Soviet Union was still another theory in the attempts to unify the social with the national. In the 1930s the social question and its connection to the question of autonomy became the main problem all over Europe and in the USA, as we know.

There was a widespread belief that the social as well as the national question had been solved within the framework of the Western welfare states in the 1950s and 1960s, in the vein of Schöneberg. However, the image of the final solution (!) in those years was based on a sharp demarcation between the Western experience in unifying nation states (the trinity of the liberal, the social and the democratic), and the image of a Communist threat where the social was linked to dictatorship and totalitarianism. Whereas John Maynard Keynes became the icon of the Western model based on virtues and fictions such as the rational management of the economy and strong beliefs in social engineering, Karl Marx was the icon of the Eastern approach to modernity and mastery.

Karl Marx had rediscovered the social when he saw a specter walking around in Europe instead of sovereign peoples, and invented the term class for a new form of collective autonomy. We know today how his theoretical attempt to change the world ("the problem is not primarily how to understand the world but how to change it") ended. The political implementation of the interpretation of his philosophy as an action philosophy ended in disaster, although in the early 1920s much hope was still invested in the Soviet experiment as an alternative to the implosion of the old regimes in the aftermath of World War I.

The New Man as re-imagined in the Soviet manipulation of humanist ideals described individuals subjugating themselves under the self-appointed representatives of the collective, masculine hard working *stachanovits* appeared like bees in an order where every individual was subordinated the fiction of an emancipated totality. Socialism during the Cold War was seen as more or less analogous with communism and in opposition to the humanist program. The brief counter-image was of the Western balance between the social and the democratic, the social and the market (*soziale Marktwirtschaft*, mixed economy), economic growth and political provision of social welfare, a balance where social organization was based on beliefs in the mastery of nature under human conditions.

Reinhart Koselleck was an early observer who also saw long-term problems in the Western approach to human modernity. Furthermore, the Western version had developed pathological forms through the separation of morals and politics, which had been unified under Hobbesian absolute regimes, and through the dynamics of Enlightenment critique and crisis

(Koselleck 1988 [1954/1959]). This was the pathogenesis of the *bürgerliche* society as Koselleck formulated it.

The Keynesian belief in a manageable future evaporated in the West during the 1970s. The international order established after World War II in Bretton Woods collapsed in 1971 when the Dollar could no longer fulfill its role as the universal currency. The oil crisis of 1973 served to underpin changing global power relationships under the label of post-colonialism as much as did the American capitulation in the Vietnam War. The US American attempt to combine social welfare politics through the Great Society Program with global military power through containment of communism failed on the most fundamental levels. The recurrence of mass unemployment was another dimension of the failure of functionalist modernization theories describing a manageable future under democratic conditions based on humanist ideals.

Through processes of critique and crisis the first attempts in Western Europe to stabilize the economies were through massive public spending programs which in a few years undermined the financial capacity of the states. A new wave of critique paved the way for neo-liberal market rhetoric. When the Eastern abuse of humanist ideals had come to the end of the road in 1989, the counter-figure of the Soviet New Man emerged rapidly: the liberal version of the New Man, incorporating the ideals of autonomy and freedom were now based on the individual instead of any kind of imagined collective. The Liberal New Man was as strong and as utopian as his Eastern predecessor. The flexible all-arounder is highly adaptable to new challenges, creative and innovative. He or she is independent and emancipated from all restraining social bonds. From the self-realization of the New Flexible Man is postulated the emergence of a new and better society, although the tension between adaptability and creativity is still not addressed. Thus a critical question arises as to how creative and innovative the remote-controlled flexible New Man really is. Does not his or her ability to roll with the punches make him r her an achievement-oriented fellow with little political loyalty rather than a socially stable character? Utopian and fundamentalist invocations of the New Man have been historically dangerous and there is no good reason why we should judge the liberal model differently (Stråth 2000).

Taken together, these two versions of the New Man (humanist ideals about human perfection and human autonomy aside) means that we must judge the twentieth century in terms of a big deficit in humanism.

Today the confidence in the neo-liberal version of the New Man seems to be eroding. The social question seems to be coming back. The expectations invested in human autonomy are once again ever more implicated with some form of collectivity where ethnicity and nationalism are probably the most conspicuous points of reference. We do not learn from history. This is the indictment of the Enlightenment belief in progress rather than cyclical recurrence. According to the notion of time-as-progress, the future is ever new and cannot be repeated from past experiences. However, history tells us how dangerous these points of reference are when they are used in order to come to terms with the social question. Marx's specter may still be walking around, this time not only in Europe but globally, and the risk is no less than if the specter incarnates in the name of the nation or in the name of class.

My concluding thoughts on the historical oscillation between different forms of autonomy is that the connection between humanism and autonomy based on a set of human rights is too simplistic and too easily manipulated. Humanism, in order to be viable, must also maintain a tradition of human duties and commitments, a thematization of social solidarity and social responsibility. The civic dimension is not only a matter of individual citizen rights, but should also be linked to the republican tradition of rights, duties and commitments for communities transgressing individual horizons. The connection between humanism and social solidarity and responsibility must be addressed in more pragmatic and less spectacular forms than in the French Revolution. The war for human rights against state reason in Kosovo and the War on Evil in Iraq demonstrate how dangerous the situation is if we use the term humanism in an un-reflective way. This conclusion goes far beyond the European point of reference for the concept of humanism. The problem is truly global.

One of the things that "globalization" augurs is the end of the "social" (which is to say, the corporate) mode of organization. Making "social history" the center of the discipline of history – in an attempt to go beyond the cultural turn of the discipline – would be a sign of conscious recognition that this mode of organization is coming to an end. Certainly the effort to conceptualize or imagine new modes of organization (super-national, trans-geographical, "multitudinous", etc.) indicates an awareness that we have entered a distinctly new post-national and post-regional era, although, and probably also exactly because of this, the invocation of national values is growing. The recurrence of the national in a post-national age is an illustration of Hegel's observation that Minerva's owl is flying only at dusk. Indeed, the great trans- or multi- national corporations – entities which have no identifiable "home" or geographical locale, entities which offer services and information rather than produce products (such as the World Bank, but also in the likes Halliburton and Microsoft) and whose function is primarily to "transfer" signs from one part of the world-matrix to another, suggest the arrival of the post-national era. When the "social" as such ceases to matter, "history" as such has no object of study. If there are radically new modes of extra-social organization (or disorganization, as in the case of all of those many waves of displaced persons – growing millions of farm workers in China today are in constant migration within that country, without any permanent residence and completely detached from specifically "social" modes of being; millions of Africans are knocking at the doors of Europe in desperate attempts to escape poverty), the problem for the historian is how to grasp the origin of these new phenomena in a new conceptualization.[2]

---

2 | I am grateful to Hayden White for correspondence on this connection of history and the social in a globalized world.

It is exactly in a global perspective that is important that humanism avoids becoming escapism, where simplistic solutions are sought after to solve complex problems. Humanism must be more than a catchword. The question might be raised: what relevance the social as a concept has today after the communist failure and abuse of its name, but also after the collapse of Wall Street and its model of finance capitalism? This question in turn might be motivated by the fact that the Marxian utopia for the emancipation of the industrial proletariat from capitalist society does not provide any guidance for how to cope with social injustice within the information/ knowledge-based capitalist society of the twenty-first century, although the problem that Karl Marx dealt with has hardly become less relevant. However, like Dipesh Chakrabarty's discussion of Fanon and his utopia in this volume, one might argue that utopian images emerge in specific historical junctures, and that this is not the problem per se. The problem is rather how to de-escalate utopian over-reachings and transform them into pragmatic reform politics rather than making them the point of departure for unfruitful and potentially dangerous counter-utopias.

Part V: Towards the Future

Intercultural Competence:
A Humanistic Perspective

JÜRGEN STRAUB

"The men-eater in New Zeeland and *Fenelon*, the abject peschery and Newton are creatures of one and the same species" (Herder 1784/1989: 147).[1]

"Ah! others! That's all they have on their lips. Difference, alterity, multiculturalism. It's their dada. [...] Why all this cultural busyness, colloquia, interviews, seminars? Just so we can be sure we're all saying the same thing. About what, then? About alterity. Unanimity on the principel that unanimity is suspect. [...] What cultural capitalism has found is the marketplace of singularities." (Lyotard 1997: 6ff.)

Cultural Differences and Social Identity:
Pragmatic Basics of Intercultural Competence

As the scientific debates about the concept of globalisation have shown (Featherstone/Lash/Robertson 1995; Hannerz 1992; 1996; King 1998), the worldwide dissemination of knowledge and artefacts, of performative patterns and life styles does not in any way bring about an unfractured homogenisation of world views, forms of life; nor of language games, symbolic and material objects, or events and processes. Frequently things get mixed up in such a way as leads to an emergence of the new, or the so called "third way". Observers speak, in this case metaphorically, of "creolisation", "syncretisms" or "hybridisation" (e.g. Bhaba 1994; for further discussion in the context of "postcolonial studies" see Castro Varela/Dhawan 2005). Taking regional differences into consideration, it would be wise to take cultural differences into account for an indefinite future; For the Others have not disappeared into the epoch of globalisation, or, if you will, *"glocalisation"* (Robertson 1995), – *quite the contrary*!

---

1 | Own translation.

It is apparently not only the case that local particularities, established traditions included, sometimes simply persist, every now and then rather doggedly, in spite of the indisputable homogenising (or universalising) effects of globalisation. On top of that, in many cases one may observe that under the influence of globalizing homogeneity, such particularities and traditions are *preserved actively*, sometimes even *rediscovered and revived*. Now and then, the bygone past is retrieved from oblivion and revitalised in order to position and to assert the present and the future of a group, or a community in the face of the demanding globalised "world society". As is well known, one can speak in this respect of *identity politics* pursued in many places, which serves the aim of the *distinguishing* and *separating* of the collective Self from the Other. Insisting on traditional values and norms can also serve this purpose.

As psychology has evinced in numerous studies throughout the 20th century, this process of *social differentiation between groups* is much influenced by a virtually "natural" desire for a *positive social identity* (Tajfel 1981). No one wants to feel valueless as a member of a given group – and belonging to a group should strengthen, not weaken one's ego and self-confidence. Those affected see to that – depending upon their respective resources and opportunities – by drawing from the selected standpoints the so-called intergroup comparisons are arrived at. Such comparisons do not always lead to the desired result, that is, to the valorisation or appreciation of the self-group and therewith of the respective social identity. Through becoming utterly devaluated, discriminated against, marginalised, and then completely excluded, minority groups face a myriad of difficulties, often failing to provide their members a positive social identity which would effectively contrast with the one imposed from the outside. Nevertheless, as a rule, socio-cultural hierarchies leave enough manoeuvring room for diverse groups whose members are able to maintain a relatively positive self-perception. In social comparisons, they draw a distinction between themselves and others so that a positive self-identification is possible and no one must feel constrained to leave the natal group for another one of a higher status (which, of course, remains at all times an option). As a rule, however, intergroup comparisons tend to benefit one's own social identity.

It can happen that such processes of comparison result in parlous feelings of in-group superiority, especially distinguishing the Own, which do not allow for a dialogue with the Other, fruitful cooperation, and peaceful coexistence. Every identity politics coupled with social processes of comparison is in danger of fomenting competition and animosities between groups, drawing a polemical line between "us" and "you", and positioning "us" against these Others (for a conceptual analysis of the notion of [collective] identity see Straub 1999; 2004).

Regardless of this often risky, even dangerous outcome, which discriminates, stigmatises and devaluates Others (and possibly the Strange as well), the process of intergroup differentiation is an inextricable, elementary social fact. It generally applies to the comparison between people. Those who want to define who they are and want to be, must do so through a comparison with other people from whom they strive to distinguish themselves, or with whom they can identify. The *intra*-individual comparison can certainly play a role in this. Among other things, it yearns for a re-establishment of an autobiographical earlier Self, or devises wishful images of a future Self. The Others are and remain, however, of special importance. One inevitably compares oneself – particularly as a member of a group – with other groups and persons, with fellowmen just as with anonymous other people from one or another social category, a process which begins as soon as one wants to know *who he or she is and would like to be.*

Nevertheless, this empirically arrived at, thoroughly examined process of social comparison must not necessarily, unavoidably or automatically lead to the creation of hierarchies, aversions, aggressions and "polemogenous" conditions, that is, the circumstances pushing for repulsion, revulsion, and enmity (although due to the reasons just explicated, this is indeed often the case). "In principle", it can also remain at the level of more or less merely "neutral" articulations of experienced, perceived and negotiated – thus to a certain degree "constructed" – differences. We, who understand ourselves as contemporaries of the 21st century, have gained experience in this, to a certain degree neutral, preferably non-partisan, respectful observation of cultural differences as no society has done before. It is the objective of those programs of education and enlightenment – both old and new – which by and large take up the cause of *intercultural competence*. Subsequently, one can deal with the experienced, observed and discussed, or, actively constructed, differences with either a benign and tolerant attitude, or an adverse and aggressive one. All scientific attempts to analyse the patent difficulties of communicating, cooperating, and coexistence between cultures, as well as the ability to fathom (collaterally and complementarily), and to develop the yet unclaimed potential of intercultural competence revolve in this very space of alternative practical possibilities.

Those who accentuate and strive to preserve their own peculiar world picture, of familiar ways of life, and the practice of language games assert in this way their individuality and uniqueness. A group which acts in this way does not only say with it: "We are like this and like that, this is our qualitative identity!" but also: "We would like to be and to remain just like we are, to live and to act so! We also claim for the future the right to self-determination, and, if necessary, we shall assert ourselves in a fight for recognition!" (Taylor 1993; for the concept of identity see Straub 2004) The same is also true for individuals. As already mentioned, all this is often done out of anxiety in order to protect self-identity and distinctiveness. When individuals and groups mutually set themselves apart and draw a demarcation line between each other, they insist on the *sensibility towards differences* and the *psychosocial meaning* of experienced, perceived and articulated differences.

At present, those who also insist on *cultural* diversity, make reference to the essential nature of their experiences in multicultural societies and regard these experiences as a basic condition of interpersonal or intergroup communication, cooperation and coexistence, the violation of which would take a heavy toll in all aspects. This has already become a common place scenario: those who disregard, fail to recognise, and ignore such differences will get into trouble, perhaps utterly fail. They would block themselves off from "felicitous" communication, cooperation and coexistence from the very beginning. They would eschew all elementary practical requirements of culturally differentiated societies and therefore would very soon encounter problems and conflicts, which are "polemogenous" by virtue of their structure. Those who refuse to cognitively, emotionally, and practically acknowledge the fact of cultural plurality will get entangled in misunderstandings, defiance, and rejection, and therefore must fail in their own goals and objectives. Cultural diversity represents challenges of a specific kind – which, by the way, also occur in the sciences, and not actually only in the context of practical intercultural cooperation but also in the altercations concerning the validity of claims of indigenous forms of knowledge (with regard to psychology see e.g. Chakkarath 2007). Only an acting potential which is calibrated with regard to the respective peculiarities can do justice to such variations. It is what the concept of *intercultural competence* stands for.

It is, however, not very clear what this quite fashionable viewpoint implies exactly. Nevertheless, there are helpful clues and suggestions to guide us along. Among those disciplines which have been and are especially active in this field, are communication and language sciences; pre-eminently (socio-)linguistics, as well as psychology (for a survey of research see Lustig/Koester 2003; Straub/Weidemann/Weidemann 2007; Straub 2007b; for the ongoing debates see Thomas 2003; for introductory lecture see Bolten 2001 or Lüsebrink 2005). But before addressing the important aspects, it is indispensable to specify, at least briefly, what *culture* means in this context.

Culture as a Form of Life:
Notes on the Genesis of a Distinctive Concept

"Alles ist auf der Erde Veränderung: hier gilt kein Einschnitt, keine notdürftige Abteilung eines Globus oder einer Charte. Wie sich die Kugel dreht, drehen sich auch auf ihr die Köpfe, wie die Klimaten; Sitten und Religionen, wie die Herzen und Kleider. Es ist eine unsägliche Weisheit darin, nicht, daß alles so vielfach; sondern daß auf der runden Erde alles noch so ziemlich unison geschaffen und gestimmt ist. In diesem Gesetz: viel mit Einem zu tun und die größeste Mannigfaltigkeit an ein zwangloses Einerlei zu knüpfen, liegt eben der Apfel der Schönheit" (Herder 1784/1989: 34).

The notion of culture which is used here does not refer exclusively to national cultures or other, even chronologically and spatially larger construed cultures (such as western, European, Christian, Arab or Islamic culture, all sorts of advanced civilisations, etc.). On the contrary, one should regard such use of the concept with scepticism, as soon as one takes into account the fact of cultural differentiation and pluralisation of modern societies and of truly transnational spaces, as has often been stated of late.

The modern concept of culture, which was significantly influenced by Johann Gottfried Herder (1744-1803), has been subject to an emotional – also biased and unjust – criticism insofar as it often makes excessive claims as to the homogenous and unified nature of the above-mentioned advanced civilisations and national cultures. On top of it all, Herder has been faulted as sometimes described and "reified" cultures as largely static entities – as if cultures had been simply existing phenomena just like other "things". We are, on the contrary, already accustomed to be mindful of the ways in which cultures are made and unmade, constructed, symbolised and assert themselves, possibly in contrast to competing alternative "constructs"; that is, by continuous processes of reflection and negotiation, in somewhat occult discourses and subtle shifts in practices. Finally, in the present, it has become fashionable to take pot-shots at the concept, which on the one hand conceives of cultures as static, hermetically sealed-off "islands" (archipelagos) from the outside world, and on the other "essentialises" or "substantialises" them, withdrawing them from the stream of time or "de-historicising" them as if the properties of a culture could be established for good and all; impervious to any external influences, thus becoming virtually immortal. This standpoint becomes especially questionable in cases where belonging to a culture is regarded as a question of ethnological provenience and gets "naturalised" or "*biologised*".

This whole range of objections has long since been regarded as *bon ton*, and since decades past has brought us a more flexible concept of culture, which is also more adequate for present-day globalized living conditions (Hannerz 1992; Straub 2007a). According to this thesis, cultures are open, historically mutable, dynamic systems providing their members with culture-specific practical repertoires of cognitive orientation, which consolidate, organise and guide thought and emotion, desires ambition, and the experiences and actions of their fellow participants. The actions and the abstentions of those who share a cultural world picture, life-way, and the respective language games interwoven with the latter, are thus mutually coordinated and interrelated. Certain things can be expected from these fellowships, including the knowledge that they, for their part, act on the basis of their cultural "expectations of the expected". This creates trustworthy, reliable routines which save us from the necessity to preconceive and renegotiate everything each time anew. Cultures disencumber us from the intractable necessitation of having to constantly reflect upon everything and to forever contrive all proceedings over and over again. They embed our actions inside familiar narratives which we can share, invent aims and goals which we pursue together (employing for it culturally available means), and they suggest rules by which we can abide in daily routine or in particular domains of life and fields of action (Straub 1999). Frequently we *must* abide by them in order to avoid, for instance, negative sanctions, or even more disagreeable consequences. Cultures create more or less mandatory realities, but at the same time open up spaces for possibilities in which we can deploy our imagination and fantasy as well as our gumption, and by restraining our options and chances just as much as they afford us liberties. Culture provides us with the tools for separating the acceptable and utterable from the impossible and ineffable, and to determine our sense of the real and possible.

This usually happens in a barely perceptible, often totally inconspicuous way. Knowledge, with which cultures provide their members during the process of growing up, socialisation or enculturation, frequently remains unperceived and not directly accessible. It is only partially conscious or explicit, discursive knowledge. Predominantly it is unconscious, or implicit, practical, tacit knowledge which we possess more as physical beings rather than as rationally thinking, reflecting, and planning rational agents. It is more of a know-how rather than of a know that. It enables people to do things and to cooperate, to partake in life-ways and language games without giving it much thought and often without being able to say why and how they do what they do. As people who act on the basis of their cultural knowledge, we just simply speak and act as we do. And we just as simply leave other things be in the same natural, tacit way, – we would not even dream about them! – and we often become aware of this only upon meeting those Others, who are completely different and who for this may appear to us strange and alien. Only this disconcerting Strange confronts us with our well-practiced and familiar Own; only through this confrontation are we made to see ourselves and the manner of how we usually think, feel and act, which is determined by specific cultural imprints.

It is apparent that identities, as well as performative praxis and life experience of all human beings are inevitably culturally determined. Therefore they, at least partially, differ from identities, performative praxis and life experience of other people. All of it applies both to cultures of a large format *and* to "smaller", local or regional, particular as well as to fleeting (sub- or alternative) cultures. Last but not least it means that any person during his or her life span or at a certain point in time can belong to several and varying cultures. Cultural belonging is always an issue of plurality. It exists only in the form of *multiple belonging*. This plurality results in a complex and dynamic, internally differentiated structure of *transitory identity* (Straub/ Renn 2003). Therefore, both cultures and identities are far from being static, monolithic and uniform entities.

We distinguish between cultures in order to be able to capture and to consider *practically relevant* differences. In this, however, we significantly diverge from the advocates of the traditional, previously rejected *normative* concept of culture with regard to the following issue: cultures may well be different but it does not imply that one culture as a whole is of a greater or lesser value that another! We, the "contemporary" people, have become sensitised to and sceptical about the bigoted normative concept of culture, which views the natal culture as more advanced, superior, especially differentiated and evolved – all around better, and in addition to which excoriates alien cultures as primitive, underdeveloped and inferior.

The concept of culture which in the last couple of decades has become popular in the various sciences (as well as in public discourses) is distinctive, but not normative. It opens up opportunities for distinguishing between cultural aspects of life, language games and effective strategies without evaluating these with a jaundiced eye, a non-reflective benchmark created by, and biased in favour of one's own culture. It in no ways implies that one cannot critically reflect upon and argue about *peculiarities* of cultural mindsets and lives, – but moreover, one *must* occasionally. Controversies of a quite spirited nature are also possible (and sometimes inevitable) in this field. But in this case it can only concern certain *elements* within a culture – for instance, the attitude of men towards women and the role of the latter in society, the value of children, the treatment of animals or of nature at large, etc., – but not about the culture as a whole. Such elements or aspects are often highly debatable and a subject matter of serious intercultural altercations. Arbitrariness is out of place here. Those who avoid discussions about primarily practical – ethical, moral – all aesthetical questions – and want to allow for anything on an equal basis to demonstrate at most their indifference towards the Others and their claim to have something important to say. Such people simply do not take the Others seriously. Serious encounters neither take place where prejudices and half-baked notions of group superiority coupled with a dangerously narcissistic egomania, nor where socio/political notions of the "politically correct", announced with slogans, regarding the *unconditional* recognition of *all possible* cultural systems in conviction as well as practice, mindset and imperative. Dialogue and diapraxis can take place only when the participants are capable of communicating with each other and of reciprocally dealing with their convictions, their orientations, their knowledge and actions in a reasonably positive manner. Something totally alien – and psychologically far more demanding – than the uttering of a "yes" without hesitation to anything and anyone; in addition mixing up this despicable "generosity" with actual tolerance.

It is evident that the historical development of a flexible and neutral concept of culture represents some kind of lesson in, for the most part, unflattering history of Europe, or of the western world in general. Clifford Geertz makes his point when he writes:

Once upon a time, and not so long ago, as the Occident had a significantly higher self-certainty and was much surer about what it was and what it was not, the concept of culture had a fixed form and determined contours. To start with, it simply drew, globally and evolutionary, a demarcation line between the Occident – rational, historical, progressive, pious, – and the non-Occident – superstitious, static, archaic, magical. Later, as it appeared too crass and too arrant out of a number of ethical, political and deep scientific reasons, there emerged a need for a more refined, more appreciative representation of the rest of the world, and the concept shifted thus towards its form which we are familiar with today: the way of life of a people. Islands, tribes, communities, nations, civilisations [...], in the end also classes, regions, ethnical groups, minorities, youth [...] had cultures: ways and manners in which one did something, distinct and characteristic; and everyone had an own one (Geertz 1997: 53).

Obviously, this conception was also attacked, revised, differentiated (cf. ibid.). Further details can be left out from here on, for our aims it suffices that the idea of a so-called "meaning oriented" concept of culture, which in the outlined sense allows for distinguishing between cultural world pictures and life-ways, language games and techniques of collective interaction among groups of variable size. This concept prohibits an automatic alignment of cultures scarcely even gauged to ponder, to evaluate – in effect upholding the own positive social identity. Such a meaning-oriented concept of culture must turn out to be quite abstract. It can be determined in such way as it is done in the examples introduced here to illustrate our aims:

Culture is a field of action, whose contents range from the objects made and used by human beings to the institutions, ideas and myths. Being an action field, culture offers possibilities of, and by the same token stipulates conditions for, action; it circumscribes goals which can be reached by certain means, but establishes limits, too, for the correct, possible and also deviant actions. The relationship between the different material and ideational contents of the cultural field of action is a systemic one; therefore transformations in one part of the system can have an impact in any other part. As an action field, culture not only induces and controls action, but is also continuously transformed by it; therefore, culture is as much a process as a structure (Boesch 1991: 29).

Sometimes in a completely obvious, but more often, in a hardly perceptible way, culture provides large numbers of people with forms of order and patterns of meaning for rational and emotional identification, evaluation and structuring of events and things in the world, as well as with principles and paradigms of action-orientation and lifestyle. [...] Culture as an action-pragmatic, trans-individual system of knowledge transmission, signs, and symbols that consists of: collective *goals*, which individuals can put in concrete terms with regard to the situational specificity, and which they can assume and pursue as actors; culturally specific *rules* of action, especially concrete social norms (norms of request or evaluation, as well as values); a culturally specific reservoir of *narratives*, through which the affiliated members of a culture create, articulate and pass on their identity, their collective and individual understanding of the Self and the world. (cf. Straub 1999: 166).

These goals, rules, norms, and values, as well as the narratives which circulate in a culture and determine action, do not necessarily have to assume a linguistically symbolic or discursive guise. Often they are implied in actions and are at best present in a form of tracks or precursors. They can just as well be embodied by non-linguistic symbols; besides, they can be conceived of as precursors of something, or as a spoor leading to a cultural nexus of traditions, signification and meaning. When a [scientific] interpretation identifies, apprehends and explicates actions in a certain way, it foregrounds these precursors, or tracks, by striving to overcome the level of the individual actors in the construing of "cultural texts" and in correlating the latter with concrete actions (Straub 1999: 185).

With the above-outlined understanding of culture in hand, one can now analyse its relationship with *intercultural competence*, which is nowadays so often and willingly evoked. What can and should one picture to oneself by it? Intercultural competence is regarded by many as *the* key qualifier of the 21st century (Bertelsmann Foundation 2008). Along with leadership, organizational skills and teamwork capacity, or media competence and a general psychic flexibility and physical capacity to withstand stress, it belongs to the so-called *soft skills*, which complement and round out an educated person's subject-specific and professional knowledge, as indeed. its growing importance in numerous professional spheres is obvious. It is enough to think of the international human resources and organisational development (not only in economic enterprises); of multinational teams, international business communication and international marketing; of culture-specific technical communication, tourism or developmental cooperation, foreign culture and education politics (or other spheres of politics such as integration politics); of religious missions, of the international student exchange, of cooperation in science and research; of various training and further education institutions in which one daily comes across cultural differences; of administrative offices and bureaus (such as foreigners' registration office), to which the same statement is also applicable; of the legal system including the juridical practice in the law courts; of police forces – from the municipal to the international levels, – on up to military interventions; or of numerous caring institutions such as health care (medicine, psychiatry, psychosocial counselling, etc.) (for more details see Lustig/Koester 2003; Straub/Weidemann/Weidemann 2007).

In private day-to-day life, too, experiencing cultural difference, alterity and foreignness has become more frequent due to migration, ever-increasing mobility and new communication technologies. In this respect the daily, non-professional acting potential of countless people is nowadays also strongly emphasized, making intercultural competence a must for the world's citizens. It is indispensable in order to avoid the *demonstrably* frequent misunderstandings in the sphere of intercultural communication and cooperation, or to cope with these in a constructive way when their prevention cannot be avoided. Cultural differences in the patterns of thinking, feeling, will, and action should *by no means necessarily* end in crises of interaction and conflicts. There is no such universal mechanism that would inevitably lead to a struggle between cultures, a (e.g. religiously motivated) *Clash of civilisations* (Huntington 1997). Yet cultural differences on the level of personal conduct incorporate significant conflict potentials which must be taken into account, and that is exactly what we are doing in our present attempt to theoretically explicate intercultural competence and to promote its practical application. For this very reason, intercultural competence is indisputably regarded nowadays as desirable, as a *normatively* (ethically, morally, politically) particularly relevant aspect of human action potential. Some even go as far as to speak of a *value in itself*, or as an *ideal* of a contemporary person. It is also pertinent when intercultural competence is considered within the context of one of the numerous and even conflicting traditions of European or non-European humanism (see below). Generally it is given primary attention nowadays as the most important among the much-propagated and intensely promoted educational aims.

It is easy to notice that these respective debates are contributing to a gradual shift in the cultural semantics of the notion of competence. This notion is developing more and more into a valorative (value-laden) and normative concept which pertains equally to an *ideal objective* as it does to actual knowledge and potential, or available real world capabilities and skills of the "normal person". Evidently, this "ideal objective" (or ideal type) serves as a yardstick by which the knowledge inventory and acting potential of discrete, actual individuals can be measured. This becomes especially evident in the endeavours to develop reliable tests for diagnosing individually arrived-at degrees of intercultural competence; this research has already been undertaken in psychology (Deller/Albrecht 2007). In the first place, this would obviously require a clarification of what intercultural competence actually implies, since up to the present day, it has not yet been satisfactorily expounded upon. There are different reasons for that.

Intercultural Competence: Notes on the History of the Concept, Definitions and Models

The expressions "competence" and "competent", which are taken from Latin, have not been in use for very long (on that see Straub 2007b). They were introduced for the first time into German language in the 18th century, and the diffusion of these terms took root at a rather tenacious pace. First, they appeared in juridical contexts, and later also in other domains. Yet the notion of competence remained from the very beginning closely linked to two core concepts, namely, "responsibility, authority" on the one hand, and "potential, capability, skill", on the other. It is interesting that the concept from early on was used with reference to very different potentials, abilities and skills. The range comprised acting potential, which was rooted in scientific and specialised analytic expertise, as well as in multifarious experiences and the practical intelligence, which these furthered. In a very short period "competence" was deployed to describe *all* the possible potentials, capabilities and skills a person might possess, which in one or another respect would be perfectly able *to perceive and identify* the requirements in a given situation, *to think, sense, feel, want, decide and act* accordingly.

Furthermore, it is interesting that in the entry on "competent, competence" [German: *kompetent, Kompetenz*] some German reference books also introduce the obsolete expression for a competitor: *der Kompetent*. It reflects the *competitive* moment, which still reverberates in the notion of competence. It brings to the fore the competition between people, which is also important (although it is often ignored) for the semantic field in the notion of "intercultural competence", since in order to obtain a professional position or function, the competitors *vie for an attestation of a higher degree of competence*. One should bear in mind that the degree of intercultural competence functions today as a criterion of choice: those who would like to gain particular positions or to take over tasks must excel in intercultural competence, which has to be proved superior to that of other competitors. With regard to the collectives, cultures and cultural exchange, Cancik (1993) extrapolates the intercultural dialogue analogously to an *agonally* structured practice, in which groups compete with each other, and by virtue of being learning cultures, strive to profit from each other with the capacity of possibly surpassing one another. Comparably with individuals, the main aim of cultures in such apparently innocuous "intercultural dialogues" is often "to be the best and top the rest" – a Greek principle of life and action, which was absorbed by the Romans and is pertinent up to the present even in the most unexpected domains (and this principle was certainly not invented and passed on only in the Occident)!

"Intercultural competence" means, roughly speaking, that a person subjects him-or-herself to the anticipated experiencing of cultural difference, alterity and foreignness, accepts them, and is able to cope with them in a productive way. Such a person does not react in a fearful and defensive way in order to ingratiate him/herself within the presumably clearly defined, safeguarded and protected limits of the own (cultural) Self. An individual thinking along these lines will, moreover, regard the experiences of difference, alterity and foreignness as a challenge to which he or she should not react defensively. The openness of such an "ideal" person, which is interrelated with self-confidence and the strength of the own ego, makes it possible to experience self-transcendence as a positive, or of trespassing own identity boundaries, and even to further self-evolution in an active way. This openness does not issue from any outwardly imposed coercion but, rather, from autonomous desires and intrinsic personal motives. All this can be successful, but only to a certain extent. Also, in a restricted measure, the above-discussed openness, which is presumably the first and foremost fundamental aspect of intercultural competence, is anything but a given (as models and studies on intercultural learning show; see Weidemann 2004, 2007).

According to Thomas (2000), the initial, and often the only reactions demonstrated by people confronted with unfamiliar patterns of behaviour in the situations of so-called intercultural overlapping, are the following:

- at the emotional level: feelings of irritation, alienation, insecurity, repulsion, aversion, rejection, horror, and fear;
- at the cognitive level: personal attributions, especially in the form of an ascription of individual deficits, stereotypical perceptions and a stabilisation of prejudices and other (negatively charged) ideas on strangeness;
- at the practical level: avoidance, estrangement, flight, isolation, tensions or aggressions and other modes of acting, which hinder cooperative relations and collaboration, hamper peaceful forms of long-term coexistence, and in extreme cases lead to a subsequent escalation of violence.

Such negative consequences result from the problematic dynamics of interaction, which significantly impedes future encounters and at times sparks off undesirable escalation. But in the case of interculturally competent actors it will all be different! Why is it so? What components, exactly, does this competence consist of, and how can it be more precisely defined? One thing is clear: whereas *subject-specific* professional skills and capabilities are usually attested to by performance-related formal certification, such general key qualifications as "intercultural competence" embraces far more than professional knowledge and subject-specific mastery. There is more to it than the question of the potential and properties that would help to insure the success of rationally acting agents in a precisely demarcated, more or less technical metier.

If one takes a look at the popular definitions, interculturally competent praxis appears at first quite abstractly as an "effective and appropriate interaction between people who identify with particular physical and symbolic environments" (Chen/Starosta 1996: 358). By saying this, the authors embrace general rules of *interpersonal communicative competence* and simply apply these to a specific context – that is, to the situations of inter*cultural* overlapping. Nonetheless, the above-quoted definition is important inasmuch as it stresses two central criteria of interculturally competent, goal-oriented or successful action, namely *effectivity* and *adequateness*:

- Briefly speaking, "adequateness" means the following: "the actions of the communicators fit the expectations and demands of the situation. Appropriate communication means that people use the symbols they are expected to use in the given context" (Lustig/Koester 2003: 64);
- "Effectivity", on the other hand, can be assessed according to whether/in how far the "desired personal outcomes" can really be achieved: "Satisfaction in a relationship or the accomplishment of a specific task-related goal is an example of an outcome that people might want to achieve through their communication with others" (ibid.).

Both these criteria, either more or less overtly, surface in many definitions. Still, it does not bring us too far forward with our initial question, even though we know that interculturally competent actors in the above-explicated sense can act adequately and effectively. So, what distinguishes them further? Alexander Thomas gives the following definition:

Intercultural competence is manifest in the ability to comprehend, respect, honour and productively employ cultural conditions and factors in the perception, judgement, sensing and acting of oneself and other people in the sense of mutual adjustment, which ranges from the tolerance of incompatibilities to the development of the synergy-charged forms of collaboration, coexistence, and a viable pattern of orientation with regard to the interpretation and constitution of the world (Thomas 2003: 7).

It sounds both compact and complicated. This suggestion and similar definitions can be better grasped if one takes a closer look at each of their constituents and systematically arranges them, possibly explaining some things in detail and perhaps completing them with further examples. This is exactly what is done in the so-called *component, or constituent models* of intercultural competence. They itemise essential aspects of an evidently very complex theoretical construct within the frame of variable systematic orders in such a way that one gets a more concrete and differentiated idea of what such popular "magical formulas" have at their core, and what makes them consistent. Tables 1 and 2 represent two typical examples of such models. As you see, they align the components according to different dimensions. Not only the dimensions themselves, but also their number varies, and the same is true for the introduced components as well. All similar models instantly make evident that the theoretical construct of "intercultural competence" comprises and integrates a vast gamut of properties, capabilities and skills. By this token, this competence consists of numerous knowledge domains, psychic dispositions and potentials, and therefore cannot be described in brief.

Table 1: Chen's component model of intercultural competence (1987: 46)

Dimensions	Components
Personal Attributes:	Self-Disclosure, Self-Awareness, Self-Concept
Communication Skills:	Message Skills, Social Skills, Flexibility, Interaction Management
Psychological Adaption:	Frustration, Stress, Alienation, Ambiguity
Cultural Awareness:	Social Values, Social Customs, Social Norms, Social Systems

212 | Jürgen Straub

Table 2: Component model of intercultural competence after Lüsebrink
(2005: 77) and other examples, completed here with regard to language
competence

Affective/emotional dimension	Cognitive dimension	Conative/behaviour-oriented dimension
• tolerance of ambiguity • tolerance of frustration • capability to overcome stress and to reduce complexity • self-confidence • flexibility • empathy, role distance • freedom of judgement, openness, tolerance • lessened ethnocentrism • acceptance of / respect for other cultures • intercultural readiness to learn	• understanding of the phenomenon of culture with respect to the perception, thinking, mindsets, as well as the behavioural and performative patterns • understanding of the performative interconnections in foreign cultures • understanding of the performative interconnections in the own culture • understanding of cultural differences of the interaction partners • understanding of peculiarities of the processes of intercultural communication • capability of metacommunication (ability to see the own communication from a critical distance) • knowledge of foreign languages	• willingness and readiness to communicate in the sense of the initiating praxis of common attributes in the affective dimension • ability to communicate (also in foreign languages) • social competence (ability to establish relations with and confidence in interaction partners from foreign cultures) • consistency of acting: readiness to consistently employ mindsets in acting (both linguistically and extralinguistically)

Such models are in the end mere systematised lists, in which some allegedly important properties of interculturally competent people are collocated. Of course, in many cases there are good reasons for the inclusion of the objects appertaining to knowledge, capabilities or skills as common attributes of intercultural competence. Still, one should not speak in such cases of a well-elaborated theory, and besides that, many such lists are compiled with the aid of intuitive views on plausibility, and have not been properly founded theoretically or empirically. This remark is still legitimate in view of the current state of research, and does not contest or belittle either the value or use of such models. The strategy which they pursue is obvious: one would like to explicate the concept to any interested parties by listing what it should contain and presuppose, according to his or her own opinion or relevant recognitions. In one or another way such concept definitions make reference to the selected situations of cultural exchange, intercultural communication, cooperation and coexistence, = that is, the situations in which people reach the limits of their acting potential.

Decisive for the ensuing apprehension of the concept are the dimensionally aligned common attributes, constituents, or components. In such models everything depends upon the way in which individually mentioned components (and their correlation) are explicated. Often, but not always, (psychology) reference books can be of further help (which I should refer to here because not all the mentioned termini can be explained separately due to the problem of space; besides, in some cases they are self-evident). By this token, such models are helpful for the first approach to the concept. All in all, they indeed convey a relatively plausible idea of what acting in an interculturally competent way might mean and would require from a person.

It is clear that intercultural competence does not begin with the mastery of foreign languages, – although this can be and virtually always is a very important aspect, because competence in foreign languages and language games is closely connected with opportunities for partaking in a foreign praxis or form of life. (Those who underestimate this point, – and it is often the case that it does not even appear as a separate entry in models of intercultural competence, – probably do not themselves speak many foreign languages and "project" this limitation of their own acting potential onto the subject matter of their research. In such manner one may protect for some time his or her own Self and self-confidence, yet be unable to learn or say much about the prerequisites of successful intercultural communication, cooperation and coexistence. Good arguments are, on the contrary, supplied by those who stress the advantages of bi/multilingualism in intercultural constellations and who, with that view in mind, call for an appropriate educational protocol.) As was already shown by Wilhelm von Humboldt in his elaborate linguistic studies, languages are interwoven with specific "worldviews" and acting potentials. Those who speak a particular language see the world in a distinct manner and have a special approach towards it, – an approach, which they share with the fellow members of this linguistic group. This commonality encourages exchange, social inclusion and integration, and boosts likewise the chance to create personal proximity, to enter into engagements and to maintain them, not in the last place with the members of other, from the own viewpoint, relatively strange cultures.

Further aspects of an individual's acting potential become of course just as fundamental and important as soon as it is a question of mutual understanding in concrete situations, a short-term collaboration or the long-term coexistence of people belonging to different cultural groups. The above-described models apparently place great value on *affective* and *emotional* common attributes.

Intercultural communication, cooperation and coexistence are by no means just a question of common sense and reason, of conscience and accumulated knowledge, nor of an ability to think logically. One can dispose of education and always have at hand best arguments in discussions – and yet miserably fail as soon as it is the question of perceiving and accepting the Others and the Strange *as such*, and *treating them accordingly*. To address people with a sensibility and respect for their culturally determined peculiarities requires far more than classroom-based knowledge and academic excellence. This ability exceeds the *cognitive* dimension of intercultural competence as such. First of all, it has to do with deeply fundamental feelings and dispositions on the individual level, that is, with affective and emotional aspects of a person's relation to the Self and the world. It is not utterly decisive, what this person may know, say or explain, what he or she is capable of articulating, and it is at least of equal importance, *whether* and *in how far* a person is able to approach other people and to open up towards them on the basis of his or her affective-emotional temperament, his or her self-*apprehension*.

To be open for *the others'* practical knowledge and expectations, mindsets, ways of experiencing and acting, customs and wishes requires an affective colouring and emotional-motivational readiness of the own Self, which cannot be simply switched on by pressing a button. It also does not automatically appear when people are able to volunteer noble sentiments, socially desirable opinions or politically correct views (or simply to feign self-disclosure, that is, to stage-manage it strategically in a form of a nearly technical self-manipulation). This is the reason why someone is able to articulate expansively about intercultural competence and yet will not be able to behave *in compliance* with this concept. Conscious intentions and ideas often do not coincide with the unconscious motives and the actual capabilities of a person. Unconscious motives may often prevail and determine what one does or does not do to a far greater degree than announced intentions. Hardly anyone would concede that they favour ethnocentrism, intolerance or xenophobia – and nevertheless many behave exactly as an authentic ethnocentric, intolerant xenophobe would behave. They do it not because they want to but because, at the decisive moment, they cannot do otherwise (and often do not even notice what they are saying, doing and provoking). Most of us presume that they can very well master ambiguous, polyvalent or equivocal situations, empathise with others and accept their perspectives, – and yet they utterly fail when suddenly more patience and flexibility than is usual becomes necessary or when their ability to empathise proves not to be as expansive as they so vehemently assert.

Intercultural competence is not a concept that should be treated at the cognitive level of knowledge and comprehension. It concerns deeper layers of personality. It relates to personal "emotional household", which in part detracts from conscience. Incompetence in the field of intercultural communication has often more to do with individual psycho/emotional elements; unconscious fears, concrete worries, or unsavoury and repressed desires, rather than with knowledge deficits. This very fact, which is paid due attention to in all solid models of intercultural competence, is what makes intercultural learning so complicated, taxing and long-drawn-out (Weidemann 2004, 2007). Many learning processes that reside primarily in the affective, emotional, and conative dimensions, touch upon deep layers of personal psychosocial identity. Often we are not inclined to get involved with Others, especially the Strange. We are particularly unwilling to do it unless we have good reasons to believe that the impending learning pathway will eventually reward and enrich us. We usually derive these reasons from personal experience. The readiness required to learn largely depends upon previous or at least imaginable experience verifying that intercultural learning at some point would pay off and sooner or later lead to a desirable enhancement of one's own experiential and acting potential. Transcending the limits of the Self and changing thus a little one's own identity is often risky, and painful besides, even though later one would want not to have renounced on these experiences because they had opened important perspectives and new opportunities.

All of it is well evidenced by the models like the above-represented ones. In addition to which, these models articulate why "intercultural competence" should be conceived of as a normative, valorative *concept,* for, apparently, it is a question of objectives and ideal conditions, which no person can ever be expected to able to attain to the extent of completeness and perfection suggested by theoretical models. It is therefore quite comforting to realise that no one need achieve the perfectionist ideal of "fully interculturally competent person" in order to be able to experience enriching encounters and satisfying relations with people of one or another cultural origin. It also can be consolatory to know that all available models of intercultural competence are *themselves far from being "perfect".* They leave many questions open. A couple of these open questions shall be mentioned here. They indicate significant knowledge gaps and perhaps also compel us to reflect upon the theoretical limitations of such models:

1. The above-mentioned models have been labelled here somewhat dis-respectfully as *mere lists.* This does not just mean that their "constructors" simply, and sometimes quite deliberately, aligned those common attributes which they held up as relevant. What is more, such listings posit the question of precisely *which* theoretical and practical meaning, which *weight* and which *function* pertain to the adduced common attributes of intercultural competence. Are they strictly *necessary,* and, beside that, *principal and general* (that is, in all imaginable intercultural situations)? Are they necessary and *sufficient* for an adequate and successful handling of intercultural situations in their entirety or in specific – and then which – combinations? How do the common attributes listed *interact* with each other, how do they *mutually influence, strengthen or lessen their respective impact?* All these questions are open and some have barely even been touched upon.

2. Do such models legitimately raise *general* validity claims, are they customised to *all imaginable contexts and situations* in equal measure, and are these really practicable? Or, perhaps, some particular common attributes are more relevant in given domains of living and action than others? Should the latter be the case, then what we are implying by "intercultural competence" would change *according to circumstances*. There are good reasons for the adoption of these differential pragmatics and semantics of intercultural competence. One might ask oneself if intercultural competence, when applied to strategically led negotiations between managers in international business cooperation is and can be the same thing as an array of knowledge, capabilities and skills which make a bicultural marriage a successful and happy adventure in human togetherness. The same is true for policing missions and friendships, for the developmental cooperation, religious legations or intercultural psychosocial counselling or psychotherapy, as well as for many other contexts and situations. Isn't intercultural competence, in other words, more a *domain-specific* potential, rather than a general knowledge-centred capability and skill, which would be challenged always and equally in different fields of life and acting? This needs to be further elucidated on in comparative analyses which have been carried out so far only on a rudimentary level. Only then can one indeed speak freely of *truly general* aspects of intercultural competence.

3. Are the currently available models of intercultural competence really generally valid, *universal* models despite the fact that they quite obviously were devised, developed and made public by a small group of predominantly western, that is, US-American and European social scientists? (Although people from non-western cultures do sporadically participate, but then usually only as fellows socialised within western scientific institutions.) It is already a somewhat paradoxical situation, virtually an "irony of history": "we" have thus far talked about prevailing definitions, models and theories of intercultural competence without addressing directly those "Others" or "Strangers" which we have recently and often been appealing to. This is only a slight exaggeration: a real conversation in the sense of an intercultural dialogue about what it is exactly that we are doing and are going to do in different scientific disciplines, so as to analyse the questionable concept and reflect on it (also in its normative, political dimensions) has so far taken place only sporadically. The indigene's knowledge of so-called non-western cultures in this field also remains by far and large unclaimed (cf. Chakkarath 2007), which is highly noticeable in the models. It is enough to think about tacitly accepted references to psychological concepts and differentiations which are embedded rather arrantly throughout West European tradition. A Western bias has already become obvious in the self-evidence with which "we" regard and circulate the question of "intercultural competence" as an allegedly worldwide *equally interesting to all* and a *presumably quite new subject*. Only few ask whether this is really true.

Notwithstanding these deficits and further open questions (Straub 2007b), which shall certainly call for our attention in the future, one can still learn a few things from the above-quoted definitions and models. As it has already been said, it is the question of personal requisites, and of aspects of personal action potential which are equally important in intercultural constellations. It goes without saying that the success of intercultural communication, cooperation and coexistence does not solely depend upon personal factors but also upon given particular *situations* (Thomas 2003). These also include general institutional and political frameworks. What is more, just as is the case in all social (inter-)actions, the interculturally competent performance is not a "solo performance" enacted by isolated actors. It is, rather, woven into a *communication and interaction fabric,* in which present or imaginary Others have always something to communicate. What exactly *ego* does, and can accomplish in these situations of intercultural overlapping depends on *alter ego,* and therewith on will and capability, the doing and not doing of the opponent. This, too, can be regarded as an attribute of a "situation".

I will not plunge deeper into this subject, but shall instead proceed by resuming and finally asking one more important question: namely, what it all might have to do with humanism and a humanistic perspective. Are our theoretical and practical endeavours aimed at intercultural competence nowadays and in any way related to the numerous traditions of humanism? Can these traditions and perhaps the yet unexploited potentials of humanistic worldviews and ideas on humankind be revitalised and modernised with regard to the handling of intercultural differences in a "glocalised" world?

If we recall once again the above-made observations, the following premise can be sustained: intercultural competence represents for us, the contemporaries of this era, a *value in itself* and a *standards-determining norm.* We see in it an ideal and a counterbalance, which, as we hope, can back up our maxims and give orientation and guidance to our actions. We expect of it a successful, satisfactory, and to a certain extent, peaceful praxis, which would live up to those habits, wishes and needs of all involved parties in as far as it is possible in separate cases. Intercultural competence concerns our present-day ideas on legitimate moral and political theories, as well as a *desirable* social praxis. It constitutes an important aspect of our *ethical and moral self-image.*

Accordingly, every person as a typical representative of humankind, regarded as *pars pro toto,* should be or *become* (and is *willing* to be or become) interculturally competent. He or she must critically observe and judge, apprehend and conceive of themselves under this perspective. This sought-after "becoming" takes place inside a life-long, never-ending learning process; where all education and edification, from kindergarten for the youngest to continuing adult education for our elders, must be of a furthering and promoting nature. It is some kind of an imperative in the glocalised world of today, which can hardly remain unobserved. To ignore it would not be advisable; one should rather regard it as a far-reaching consensus, while not hushing up the fact that one should also critically proof this imperative (for instance, with regard to the implicit disciplinary measures to which modern individuals would then be subjected; or with regard to the danger of a shallow rhetoric growing up around "intercultural competence" which would remain without practical consequences, covering up and concealing psycho/social requirements rather than resolving them).

Intercultural competence then, is to be understood as broader than, and diverse from a nearly "technical" action potential that allows people to act in a goal-oriented rational way in order to achieve desired aims, or, in other words, to establish adequate and effective intercultural relations. This concept does not solely concern a configuration or "optimisation" of some given praxis which is otherwise in danger of failure or even engenders serious conflicts. Those who speak nowadays of "intercultural competence", as a rule lay claim to an over-arching consideration of the Others and the Strange as such, and by this token as an aim in itself, not just as a necessary constituting factor in the endeavours to stabilise and ameliorate intercultural communication, cooperation and coexistence. The pronounced deference for the Others and the Strange is required not simply for an outcome of a strategic calculation or of a generalized interest in successful communication, cooperation and coexistence: it leads us out of the *boundaries of instrumentalized thinking*. The Other and the Strange, whom we have cast as the Adversary in human shape, deserve more than a strategically calculated consideration of their cultural imprints and practices, habitus and dispositions.

At times in a scarcely perceptible and occasionally quite overt manner, this proposition reverberates in many public debates and scientific discourses on intercultural competence. These debates and discourses are directed against an instrumental conception of fellow human beings. The Others and the Strange are not mere (more or less suitable) means for achieving our personal or collective goals. They make far more "radical" demands of their deference, tolerance and recognition as *Others* and especially as *Strange*, whose thinking, feeling, willing and acting will forever remain partly *undisclosed* in spite of the successful attempts at translation and comprehension. This point of view, which is charged with socio- and cultural-psychological implications, is centrally important for the actual discourse. Our contemporary ideas on "intercultural competence" in a novel way *link* the categorical imperative of Immanuel Kant – in its version of the so-called "end-in-itself formula", which postulates that one must never regard, treat and use other people as a simple means, but on the contrary, must necessarily regard and perceive them as ends in themselves, – with an equally categorical commandment to conceive of the Others and the Strange *as such*, to respect and to accept them. This motto concerns those very dimensions of the Other and the Strange, which despite sensitive and thorough endeavours towards real empathy, the acceptance of different perspectives and understanding remain inaccessible, and even *must* remain sealed as phenomena of *radical* alterity and foreignness, which we can distinguish from the phenomena of a relative, merely gradual difference (Waldenfels 2006; Liebsch 1999).

In this sense the concept of "intercultural competence" is a constituent of a wide-spread contemporary self-and-world conception, in which the Other and the Strange play a totally new role. They are – just as any form of otherness and strangeness – significantly more valued, honoured and regarded as the antagonists of instrumental reason. In contemporary philosophy there are numerous testimonies of this strand of thinking which places all available knowledge in its boundaries and also makes the figure of the Other and the Strange a central point of reference to our ethical and moral self-and-world-relation. This stance has been for long related to *universalistic* validity claims. According to the opinion of many, it must become an obligatory way of thinking for the *whole of humankind,* which would not allow an emphasis on (radical) cultural difference to encumber or even to put an end to our search for universals out of which to produce commonality. This would not be only counterproductive, but would also an absurdity born in an effusive commitment to the (perennially elusive) Other and Strange.

To sum up the last observations, one can, for the sake of analytical purposes, distinguish between two concepts of intercultural competence. We come across both in scientific and public debates, and usually they are not kept strictly apart. On the one hand, there is a concept which should directly serve the purpose of *pragmatic bettering* of intercultural communication, cooperation and coexistence. It aims at a mutual understanding that would be satisfying for both parties, adequate with regard to the respective cultural peculiarities, not to mention efficient. Numerous empirical research studies and practical projects draw upon this concept. On the other hand, in the concept resonates a further-reaching claim, which makes intercultural competence a *value in itself.* It is then not only a question of perceiving, respecting and recognising the people, whose performative techniques, language games and lifestyles differ to some extent from the one's own, but also a question of considering the difference between people as a symptom of a possibly *radical* alterity and strangeness, and of "inscribing" this awareness of radical alterity and strangeness into the own self-and-world-relation.

This motive (which in a certain way could be defined as a "critique of reason", but by no means as a "rejection of reason") goes beyond the ethics and morals of, e.g., Kantian tradition. A concept of intercultural competence thus perceived makes reference to the ethics of alterity, which first took clear shape in the 20th century (in the first place in the essays of Emanuel Levinas). It gained special influence and attracted closer attention when in the history of progressive, "reason-bound" Europe, Others and Strangers had repeatedly become mass victims of sweeping, genocidal violence.

As soon as one speaks today about intercultural competence, it also concerns the question of what humans can aspire to become in future. It is the question of as yet unexplored potentials in experience and action, the strengthening of which is a primary ethical and moral challenge and a political and pedagogical task of the highest priority. Numerous scientific disciplines (for instance, psychology, ethnology, or sociology) assist in fulfilling it. One can perhaps say that this "strengthening" consists in the valorisation of a habitualised *psychic disposition coupled with practical attitude,* which in the history of human self-imaging was considered more as a "weakness" and at best elicited scornful pity. Those who *open up* towards the Other and the Strange in certain ways compromise their Self, creating a vulnerability to accusations and pillorying by their fellow humans. The charge: renouncing the hermetical enclosure and along with it the single-minded protection afforded by the established and familiar boundaries of collective and own Self; allowing the appearance of "weakness", of vulnerability and mutability to encourage fellow humans in a way scarcely controllable, to intrude upon, and interfere with that Self.

By this token, one can freely construe the concept of intercultural competence as one of the perhaps most impressive manifestations of the long-standing *decentring and communicative liquefaction* of the Self in modern humans. This is exactly what the (late-) modern socio-psychological concept of personal *identity* stands for. Personal identity has always been set against an idea of a totalised structured self-and-world-relation: "nothing from the outside must come inside; nothing from the inside must come out!" Identity, which constructs and re-constructs itself in intercultural constellations, has nothing to do with this obsolete motto backing an obstinate self-assertion (Straub 2004).

With this, we have arrived at the humanism of our own day, and can ask whether and how far the whole discourse on intercultural competence could be grasped and further developed in a humanistic perspective.

A Humanistic Perspective

As Hubert Cancik (1993) argues, there is no "humanism" – not even when one confines oneself to the territory and history of Europe without considering other world regions, in which different versions of humanism have long been established and have assumed new guises. Rather, we are dealing with a heterogeneous and vastly ramified, if inwardly contradictory tradition. Cancik holds exemplary, though in many respects, incompatible strands of humanistic thinking like the following: occidental, atheistic, Christian, dialectical, ethical, evolutionary, existentialist, Hebraic, classical, critical, socialist, and secular humanism (among some others: cf. Cancik 2003: 176). Humanism is apparently very heterogeneous and even today still spawns new versions.

As far as it concerns the history of the concept, it originated with the Roman *humanitas*, which connoted humanity or humankind; resurfacing later in different variants of meaning up to the 19th century, when Friedrich Niethammer (1766-1848) introduced the his theory of *humanism*. Niethammer's humanism was still aimed at reformist pedagogy and implied "general, not professionally oriented preparation for the study, and concern with 'the humanity of the pupil'" (Cancik 1993: 174). This so-called "classical humanism" was a primarily pedagogical innovation, a "modernisation" of overall edification targeting the general, encyclopaedic education of a person, which implied and integrated a study of antiquity. This innovative pedagogy craved a historically anchored self-conception as well as new endeavours for the *perfection* of the "complete person", which drew upon the most recent recognition of humanities, and up to the present day, has not become a homogeneous, clearly defined and compact system combining ethics and anthropology.

Only some decades after the declaration of the original reformist educational program, the concept was also introduced to denote the epoch of the Italian Renaissance (first employed by Georg Voigt and Jacob Burkhardt). It ended up being commonly used as a name for *all possible* spiritual currents with a practical ambition, which drew upon certain *anthropologies* and *images of humankind* and propagated corresponding worldviews and political goals, shunting further into the background the reference to Greco/Roman antiquity, then still central for the classical humanism. Therefore today we have a rich gamut of sometimes quite idiosyncratic humanisms on hand. This plurality and contradictoriness makes it difficult to connect intercultural competence to a humanistic perspective in an uncomplicated manner or to regard it as a humanistic project. One question is ineluctable: *which* humanistic perspective in particular should one assume? What does this adjective mean in this regard? What can one consider today as a humanistic perspective of intercultural competence that would make sense?

The inevitably dual meaning of humanity (*humanitas*), which has also influenced numerous humanistic projects and movements, provides the first helpful, albeit still quite general and abstract clue. As Cancik (2009) argues, humanity has always likewise implied "'education' (eruditio, litterae, scientia) and 'clemency' (mansetudo, comitas, benignitas)", as well as "(spiritual) scholarship" (eruditio), and "(active) charity" (philantropia)". Roughly speaking, this concept, and thus different humanistic programs and movements, unite

- endeavours for a universal (anthropological) identification of humankind as a particular species,
- ethical and moral reflections on the questions of equality and justice, which in modernity revolve about the universal dignity of humans and general human rights,
- pedagogically and politically motivated appeal to subject the humankind, that is, every individual, to a progressive education and edification, thus pursuing gradual (and evidently non-achievable) perfection of the "complete person",
- demand to orientate human life and acting practice in accordance with *humanitarian principles*, and to bestow special attention and support on those who are in extremity and need help.

Obviously, the concept of "intercultural competence" did not surface in any of the then existent humanisms. It has been born out of the epoch in which practical and politically motivated reflections on cultural differences has lead to unprecedented levels of awareness, and has likewise attained an untapped depth. Of course, people have always distinguished between cultural forms of life, language games and performative strategies: already in Greek antiquity Herodotus wrote about them with great care and a clear awareness of difficulties which the comparative contemplation of cultures entailed. But there were no comparative anthropological studies as such until in the 18th century when the discipline first appeared from the emerging humanities and cultural and social sciences, which focused on the systematic comparison between cultures. As the citation from Johann Gottfried Herder, which opens up this paper, shows, in the 18th century the relationship between separate cultures and universal commonalities of all human forms of life had to be stipulated anew due to the growth in sensibility towards difference and the radicalised awareness of strangeness. The deepened insights into the substantial differences between forms of cultural knowledge and practices, which were by and large a result of real problems of mutual understanding and serious conflicts, fomented the necessity to search for universal anthropological foundations. Only the latter made communication, cooperation and coexistence possible in spite of all incalculable, partly incomprehensible and irreconcilable cultural differences. This insight harbingered the advent of "intercultural competence", although this currently so-fashionable expression was first coined only in the latter third of the 20th century.

This concept has come into the humanistic heritage not only because it regarded the whole of humankind – that is – the totality of the species, against the background of the intensified and differentiated experience of cultural differences. With the insistent plea for intercultural competence, the unity of humankind has been declared *a practical, day-to-day task*. (By this token, it is no longer considered as already inherent by virtue of this or that anthropological constant!) This shining competence should establish, assert and thus to ensure the unity, intelligible relationship, and practical cohesion between people, as well as between their inevitably particular, culturally specific forms of life and language games, performative strategies, and identities.

Furthermore, humanistic legacy retains its relevance because this task is regarded as a challenge for our practical capabilities and skills, whose *development* is an imperative. Without this superordinate educational and edificatory goal, which refers to the principal possibility of amelioration and perfection of human beings, it would not be understandable why we have been speaking for so long of intercultural competence and have made it an objective of various psycho-pedagogical endeavours. As it has been stated above, the Other and the Strange have now become some kind of a "displaced entity", and a medium of perpetual learning. It is from all those other/alien cultures scattered worldwide that we can, should and *are* willing to learn. To a certain extent, we have to do it in order to find out who we are or have become ourselves, and would like to become in future. It is also important for our persistence in the fused world of "cultural competitors" (see above). The concept of "intercultural competence" encompasses all of this, although it concerns primarily the acting and learning potential of *individuals*.

The far-reaching ethical and moral claim of "intercultural competence" assimilates the so far untapped potentials of humanistic tradition and suggests their further exploration. As a concept, its share of dues must be claimed for sensitivity towards difference, respect for, and recognition of the Other and the Strange, which in the (European) history of "intercultural encounters" has often been drastically lacking for those who became victims of violence stemming from the very heart of Europe. In this respect, intercultural competence contains a self-reflective dimension and a self-critical stance, which is hard on the own past and present, and has spawned a very peculiar form of "*propriophobia*", representing some kind of fear and revulsion of the Self (especially notorious is the Nazi period in Germany, where the genocide of European Jewry, a crime against humankind, became a monument to inhumanity).

It is enough to take a brief glance at the above-cited examples in order to ascertain that the particular values and normative basic convictions, which in the course of the critical process of remembering, and reflecting on excessive collective violence have gained a noteworthy place in collective consciousness, are also intrinsically present in the concept of intercultural competence. In this respect, too, it proves to be a child of European, and in certain respects, global humanism, which takes up its principles. It is not least true for an appeal to connect the ethical and moral self-apprehension of each individual, and of humankind on the whole with the perception of the Other and the Strange so as to develop this perception to the point of a willed forbearance, strong enough for a necessary withdrawal of the own Self – for unobtrusive and stable relations of recognition, rather than for a violent overpowering of the opponent. In the readiness and possibility of experiencing cultural exchange, intercultural communication, cooperation and coexistence as a source of educating the "complete human", one should see both an important hallmark of those contemporary endeavours for intercultural competence *and* of some tradition and future of humanism.

I am concluding this paper with this statement: that the teaching of intercultural competence will eventually represent one further step in the painstaking process of education by which individuals, particular groups, and the whole of humankind are endeavouring to learn how one can encounter the Other and the Strange without perceiving them as enemies from the very beginning. Even in his own day, Herder was thought somewhat too optimistic (although by no means naïve), when he spoke of an end of the time of animosities and enmities marked by outbursts of excessive violence. Let us therefore quote him, or, rather, his question, which is perhaps not as "rhetorical" as its optimistic author meant it to be: "Where are the times when such tribes as troglodytes sat in their caves and behind their walls, and every stranger was an enemy?" (Herder 1784/1989: 659). We have to answer that these times have not ended up to the present day and, besides, are not likely to ever end. Yet they do signal an option for a future of humankind. Those with the courage to speak about intercultural competence and conceive of its achievement and furthering as a broad-spectrum "humanistic" project, must never lose sight of their goals.

Humanism yet Once More:
A View from the Other Side

Longxi Zhang

How could anyone as a human being have problems with humanism, the idea that human beings should take priority in considerations of a social or political nature? From a layman's point of view, it would be difficult to see how this could become a serious problem unless one is a committed misanthrope. In a different cultural context, this would not make sense, either. In ancient China, for example, as we learn from the Confucian *Analects*, once Confucius came back home and found the stable in his house burned down, he immediately asked: "Is anyone hurt?" But he did not ask about the horses. For him, the supreme virtue of *ren* 仁 or benevolence meant nothing but to "love human beings."[1] And yet, in Western academic or professional discourse, we do find a lot of problems with or challenges to humanism from a variety of positions. If we look back briefly at the historical process from the time when humanism as an idea or theory grew out of the European Renaissance through the Enlightenment to its later development in modern times, we may begin to understand the complexity of the problem.

Humanism started as the core idea of the Renaissance in putting emphasis on man rather than God at a time when the power of religion and the authority of the Church were still predominant. Therefore it had to walk cautiously under the huge shadow of religion and argue for the worth of man by evoking the biblical idea that man is made in the image of God and is free to develop. That is the argument Giovanni Pico della Mirandola presented in his famous *Oration on the Dignity of Man* (1486), in which he imagined God saying to Adam:

We have made you a creature neither of heaven nor of earth, neither mortal nor immortal, in order that you may, as the free and proud shaper of your own being, fashion yourself in the form you may prefer. It will be in your power to descend to

---

1 | Confucius, *The Analects*, x.17, xii.22; see Liu 1954: vol. 1, 228, 278.

the lower, brutish forms of life; you will be able, through your own decision, to rise again to the superior orders whose life is divine. (Pico della Mirandola 1956: 7-8)

According to Pico, then, man has the freedom and the capability to move in either direction, downward to "the lower, brutish forms of life," or upward to the divine, "superior orders." Pico argued of course for the upward movement, and the way up was through the study of philosophy and theology, by abandoning the sensual and bodily desires and living the contemplative life of a philosopher. In Pico's formulation, the idea of education is crucial. As an exceptionally erudite scholar of his time, Pico not only appealed to the authority of the Christian religion, but the teachings of the Hebrews, the Chaldeans, Arabic thinkers, Greek philosophers, and even some occult mystics. His *Oration on the Dignity of Man*, as Richard Norman observes, was "an explicit statement of the program of reconciling the literature and thought of the ancient world with Christian religious belief" (Norman 2004: 9). Renaissance humanism is thus closely related to the idea of liberal education, the disciplines of *humanitas*, i.e., the study of man or the cultivation of humanity as different from the study of divinity or theology, the study of nature or natural philosophy, and vocational studies like law and medicine.[2] From the very start, then, the humanities, particularly the study of the classics, was part of the idea of humanism.

In putting emphasis on man rather than God, even though with caution, humility, and profuse apologetics, Renaissance humanism did start a new tendency that eventually led to the secularization of Europe. "How marvelous and splendid a creature is man! This is the theme of Pico's oration," says Russell Kirk; but in that theme, he reminds us with Egon Friedell, "there lay a colossal *hybris* [sic] unknown to the Middle Ages, but also a tremendous spiritual impulse such as only modern times can show" (Kirk, introduction to Pico della Mirandola 1956: xiii-xiv). As much of European life was secularized during the Enlightenment or what used to be called the Age of Reason, humanism grew stronger and moved farther away from the kind of religious vision we find in Pico's plea for human dignity. Secular humanism has obviously developed in opposition to religion and it is not surprising that it has opponents from the religious establishment and from people who blame humanism for its faith not in God but in human rationality and capability. David Ehrenfeld criticized what he called the "arrogance of humanism." He clearly identified humanism with the rejection of God and religion, the hubris of science and technology, and he angrily denounced humanism, at one point in his book, as "this godless monster" (Ehrenfeld 1981: 8). The benefit of his critique of humanism, according to Ehrenfeld, is to "gain a better appreciation of what is going to happen," that is, to be

---

2 | For the concept of liberal education as cultivating humanity, see Nussbaum 1997. The idea of the humanities as the core of liberal education as distinct from the study of natural science and vocational training is much emphasized in Cardinal Newman's classic, see Newman 1996 [1873]).

better prepared for the doomsday disaster, "to live for a while at peace with ourselves, with the remaining fragments of the natural world, and with God." (Ehrenfeld 1981: 21, 22).

While Ehrenfeld castigates humanism for its blind faith in human rationality and the power of science, other critics, particularly the postmodern ones, go even further and exert a much greater influence in dissolving the very fabric of man or human subjectivity, thereby taking away the foundation of humanism. Toward the end of *The Order of Things*, Michel Foucault made a famous announcement, a kind of obituary of man himself. In an often-quoted passage in that book, Foucault claims that "man did not exist (any more than life, or language, or labor); and the human sciences did not appear" until the nineteenth century, when the modern *episteme* made an abrupt turn to man as the privileged object, with psychology, economics, and philology as the three basic models or paradigms. Thus Foucault's archaeology of knowledge reveals that "man is an invention of recent date. And one perhaps nearing its end." With a shift in the paradigm, says Foucault at the prophetic end of his book, "one can certainly wager that man would be erased, like a face drawn in sand at the edge of the sea." (Foucault 1973: 344, 387). Foucault's target is the human sciences, what in German is known as the *Geisteswissenschaften*, but it is certainly a bizarre overstatement to assert that man came into existence only in the nineteenth century in Europe, as if the idea of man was invented only in Europe and there were no human beings outside the West. In fact, that is just what Foucault thought. His definition of man is the Western man, as he has distinguished the West from the East, represented by China as an incomprehensible *heterotopia*, at the beginning of the *Order of Things*, where a bizarre classification of animals from a so-called "Chinese encyclopedia" supposedly represents a totally alien way of thinking that exemplifies the "exotic charm of another system of thinking," but a way of thinking that makes it impossible "for us [i.e., the Europeans] to name, speak, and think."[3] In any case, if the existence of man is prerequisite for the idea of humanism, Foucault's surreal dissolving of man as a figure drawn in sand would make humanism impossible to sustain.

Jacques Derrida's reflection on humanism gives another influential reading of man as the invention of the human sciences and also fading or drawing close to its end. For Derrida, the end of man is intricately involved with the *relève* of humanism and metaphysics, the fulfillment of man as his own end or telos. "Man is that which is in relation to his end, in the fundamentally equivocal sense of the word," says Derrida. "The transcendental end can appear to itself and be unfolded only on the condition of mortality, of a relation to finitude as the origin of ideality. The name of man has always been inscribed in metaphysics between these two ends. It has meaning only in this eschato-teleological situation" (Derrida 1982: 123.) Derrida's argument is typically couched in an obscure language, but whatever

---

3 | Foucault 1973: xv, xix. I have discussed in more detail Foucault's idea of China as *heterotopia*, see Zhang 1998: 19-24, 77-79.

the apparent complexity and sophistication of theoretical elaborations, such arguments have practical consequences that turn *la fin de l'homme* or the End of Man into a sort of postmodern slogan, a popular banner under which humanism and the humanities in higher education have come under serious challenge and deconstruction in the West.

In the various critiques of humanism, what is taken to be the problem is related to the problems of the entire modern times. The 18th century belief in reason, the 19th century optimism of progress, the confidence that modern science and technology can endlessly improve the quality of life, and the euphoric vision of an ideal society realized on earth through political organization and social programs that would maximize production and guarantee happiness to all – these were all shattered in 20th century through the experience of two devastating World Wars, by cruelty and destruction on a larger scale than ever before precisely because of the advancement of science and the refinement of weaponry, by the horror and atrocities of the Holocaust and genocide, by environmental disasters and damage to the world's ecosystem, and by scandal-ridden political regimes, bankrupt ideologies, and the widening gap between the obscenely rich and the hopelessly poor. Not only that, but Western nations with a supposedly humanistic tradition had invaded the other parts of the world and dehumanized both the other and the self in the barbaric brutality of racism, imperialism, and colonialism. The idea of the universal dignity of man and the confidence in the goodness of human nature are mocked by the political reality of oppression and the abuse of power. The dream is broken; hence the End of Man and the demise of humanism. In a melodramatic language, John Carroll declares that "We live amidst the ruins of the great, five-hundred-year epoch of Humanism. [...]. Our culture is past cruelty. It is wrecked. It is dead" (Carroll 1993: 1). Despite its original intended meaning, humanism is held responsible for failures in the modern world because it is perceived to be the ideology of the modern, indeed the foundation of modernity defined in terms of aggressive individual rights and human interests. The inference seems to be that man, or at least the Western man, has tried to play God but has only ended up making a big mess of it all.

The critique of humanism, particularly of the Eurocentric ideas of the West, is necessary and helpful, but to go from one extreme of the concept of man as almost angelic and divine to the other extreme of man as disappearing like a face drawn in sand is in itself symptomatic of a typical Manichaean binary opposition, the absolutist All or Nothing. Human beings and human affairs are rarely under such extreme conditions; they are, rather, located somewhere between the extremes. Temperance and moderation are true human virtues as we learn from philosophical wisdom in both East and West. If the problem of humanism, as the critics argue, lies in man's hubris or arrogance, his usurpation of the power of God, what do the critics propose to be a remedy or solution? Is it possible for the modern world to undo centuries of human history and revert back to the medieval world, which was hardly everybody's paradise, or to the medieval time when everyday life was, even as John Carroll describes it, "a miserable struggle to survive," "cursed by endemic warfare, famine, disease," and by horrible plagues that wiped out "entire cities" (Carroll 1993: 6)? No one would seriously entertain such a possibility, and here we may see the weakness of most critics of humanism, including the postmodern ones, who are quick to find the fissures and cracks in the wall and to demolish the entire modern building, but are short on plans to construct something positively better and more habitable. These critics are indeed confirmed dualists locked in either/or thinking, for whom there is no middle ground – either man is God or nothing at all.

The very Manichaean opposition, however, might be the problem. As someone from outside the West and informed by a different cultural heritage, I would suggest that the dichotomy between man and God is a false assumption. To give priority to human interest does not mean to oppose God or to damage everything else till it becomes detrimental to the interest of human beings themselves. In Chinese culture, the Confucian virtue of benevolence or maintaining loving and humane relationships with fellow human beings is not established in opposition to god or gods. It teaches that even though religion may play an important part in people's spiritual life, human beings must rely on themselves and their own effort to manage things in this world and in their lives. Not that there is no concept of god or deity in ancient China, but that the divine is not presumed to take care of everything in the human world. For Confucius, ritual is more formalistic and symbolic than substantial, for he said about rituals that one should "sacrifice as if ancestors were present, and sacrifice to the gods as if the gods were present."[4] Whatever religious or spiritual belief he might have, Confucius kept it to himself, for he "did not talk about uncanny things, violence, disorder, or deities."[5] Neither do the Taoist philosophers talk much about such things, as Zhuangzi says that "the sage acknowledges the existence of what is out there beyond this world, but does not discuss it" (Guo 1997: vol. 3, chapt. 2, 41). As Taoist philosophers, both Laozi and Zhuangzi advocate the leveling of all things under heaven, the non-differentiation of the human from the inanimate. That is to say, in the Taoist cosmos, man is not privileged above nature or other things. "Heaven and earth are not benevolent and treat all things as straw dogs," says Laozi (Wang 1959: chapt. 5, ibid., 3). "Not benevolent" here means that heaven and earth, or whatever is considered higher or divine, do not take a particular interest in the human world, nor do they particularly favor human beings. Such a naturalistic view is obviously different from the Christian concept of God who singles out man above all other earthly creatures for special treatment. The Confucians and the Taoists differ in their views about how best to live one's life, but they all present an outlook in which human beings must live their lives based on their own moral understanding of their relationships with the world, not counting on gods or a Savior to take the burden off their shoulders. That is to say, from the

---

4 | Confucius, *The Analects*, iii.12; Liu 1954: 53.
5 | Confucius, *The Analects*, vii.21; Liu 1954: 146.

Chinese point of view, humanism is not defined against religion and is not meant to replace the divine, but is understood as a human effort to manage the human world, as ethical, humane, and loving relationships, as the idea of a shared and common humanity, even a harmonious relationship with the inanimate nature. From such a point of view, then, it would be absurd to take humanism for man's hubris or arrogance, and it would be bizarre to dissolve the very concept of man because there are still problems in the human world. In reconstructing the idea of humanism in the West, then, it would be helpful to look at such different understanding of the human and humanism outside the West and to draw on such understandings from non-Western cultures and traditions.

Just as the Manichean opposition between man and God is a false one, the dichotomy between East and West is also dangerous and misleading. Today's world is rife with tension and conflict, and thus in urgent need of an encompassing idea of humanity to facilitate mutual understanding and communication among different nations. To understand man as only a Western construct is definitely not helpful in bringing different cultures and nations together, and to imagine the future of the world as an impending conflict of civilizations only aggravates the danger the world is already facing in reality. A new understanding of humanism must therefore acknowledge the different conceptualizations of humanity in both East and West and try to incorporate the insights of different ideas of the human in a truly global dialogue of civilizations. Cultural relativism or postmodern theories in the West tend to put too much emphasis on cultural differences, but it is crucial, given the tension and conflicts we now face in the world today, to go beyond differences – differences in religious beliefs, political systems, social customs, in language, culture, history, etc. – to achieve cross-cultural understanding and communication. Universalism has been discredited in Western academia because it is considered not truly universal, but tainted by colonialism and imperialism.[6] It is now time to differentiate universal humanism from its distortion or abuse, from colonialism and imperialism, and to incorporate non-Western understanding of humanity will help achieve that goal. That is to say, we need to go back to reexamine the different concepts of humanity in both East and West and study their original intended meanings, rather than their distortions in later time. In effect, that brings us back to the idea of humanistic studies in different traditions.

Similar to Renaissance humanism, of which the study of the humanities or a liberal education forms an integral part, learning and education also occupy a central position in the Chinese cultural tradition. Traditionally, Chinese learning consists first and foremost of study of the Confucian classics, just as traditional liberal education in the West put emphasis on Greek-Roman classics. In modern times, the content of study may have changed from strictly disciplined classical studies to a broader concept of the humanities, i.e., literature, history, philosophy, etc., but the cultural habit

---

6 | See, for example, Buck 1991: 29-30, editor's introduction.

of engaging in learning and the respect for learning persist in a new social environment. In our time, as I just mentioned above, it is very important to reexamine the cultural aspect of human life and reconfirm the value of the humanities. It is even more important, however, to conceptualize humanistic studies in a new way so that it will be not only studies of one's own culture, but of other cultures and traditions as well. In the early Renaissance, it might be enough for an Oxford scholar, as Geoffrey Chaucer described him in the *Canterbury Tales*, to have by his bed "Twenty bookes clad in blak or reed, / Of Aristotle and his philosophie."[7] Today, a good scholar probably should have at least two hundred books not only of Plato and Aristotle, Kant and Hegel, but Confucius and Mencius, Laozi and Zhuangzi, and many more works of both East and West. To reclaim humanistic values today cannot be a simple revival of the same traditional classics, but must expand humanistic studies beyond the boundaries of the East or the West, and must become fully human in the sense that humanism now encompasses both the European and the non-European, the West and the East, and takes the entire human cultural legacy into its scope and range. This is certainly ambitious and challenging, perhaps a goal hardly possible for most of us to accomplish, but that should at least be an ideal we all aspire to, the establishment of a new concept of humanity or humanism that may inspire us to make the world a more humane and more comfortable place to live in.

---

7 | This is Chaucer's description of an Oxford cleric in the *Canterbury Tales*, the General Prologue.

Logocentrism and beyond:

Some Concluding Remarks

HENNER LAASS

> Non so, se me spiego.[1]
> *Italian colloquialism*

> We feel that when all possible
> scientific questions have been
> answered, the problems of life
> remain completely untouched. Of
> course there are then no questions
> left, and this itself is the answer.
> *Wittgenstein,*
> *Tractatus Logico – Philosophicus 6.52*

1. Introduction

In one of his recent texts on historical consciousness, Jörn Rüsen explains
why Western historical thinking requires an intercultural orientation (2002).
This present volume is one of the various outcomes of his undertaking.[2]
Obviously, this task is immense and will call for huge efforts in research,
especially the attempt to reach "the goal of creating the means for an
intercultural comparison of its results" (Rüsen 2002: 10). Although in the
meantime Rüsen has produced an impressive series of proposals for coping
with the problem of "how to conceptualize intercultural comparison" (Rüsen

---

1 | I would like to express my gratitude to Jörn Rüsen for his generosity to
grant the honour of a concluding statement to a relative latecomer to his project of
Intercultural Humanism. I am also grateful to Sirka and Eva Laass, who have helped
me to translate this text. The translations of quoted authors, unless otherwise stated,
are mine. H.L.

2 | In an abbreviated form, his program is re-rendered in the introductory
chapter of this book.

2007a: 29), there seems to me a long way to go, since, as he has conceded, "the danger of such a theory of cultural differences lies in its tendency to substantiate or even reify the individual cultures concerned" (Rüsen 2002a: 29f). Agreeing to Rüsen's general thesis that "what used to be addressed as a simple-minded carelessness of an unconscious ethnocentrism, today must be critically reflected" (Rüsen 2002: 10), my argument will be that there is a subtle form of subliminal borderline, especially in academic discourse, that still prevails and yet is often overlooked. It is a specific form of logocentrism that has been called *scholastic habit* by Pierre Bourdieu (1990 and elsewhere). The question remains: what position must one occupy in order to be capable of comparing *all* transcultural documents and activities? Is the comparative historiographer not in danger of becoming a viewer from nowhere? As Waldenfels has pointed out,

there is no place beyond the cultures that would permit us an impartial and unrestricted overview. Being European we can escape neither from our own culture, nor our own bodies, nor from our own language. [...] Interculturality that is worth its name can only be conceived of, if we differenciate between *Eigenwelt* and *Fremdwelt*, similar to Husserl's differenciation of Home- and Foreign World. (Waldenfels 2006: 109)

If this insight is true, the consequence will be that any form of intercultural comparison that does not run the risk of being a view from too far outside will be kept in a mode of reflectively *transcending borders* of prior intracultural life forms.[3]

Since its established form as academic discipline, History has lost its imaginary moments and has increasingly become an intellectual construct. The concepts of "world history" or "global history" have multiplied the difficulties (cf. Stuchtey/Fuchs 2007a). Thus, the conceptualization of problems has gradually developed into an *actio per distans*. There is a tacit consensus among the professional historians and historiographers across the globe that the applications of their findings, that is the dissemination into daily routines, should be left to those in charge. Admittedly, this insight equally applies to what I am going to say. In contrast to common opinion I am not convinced, though, that this attitude may be overcome by even more elaborate forms of rationalization nor by further refinement of methodological strategy – the standard vocabulary being "reflexivity" or "historization". "Critical reflection" will be necessary, but not sufficient. Intercultural hermeneutics will have to be supplemented by intra-cultural hermeneutics (Holenstein 1998: 257). Both fields of activity will imply a focus on the ontogenetic respectively biographic origins of the historical consciousness in early childhoods. Since the generic origins of sense making do not take place in isolation but are the relatively late results of

---

3 | "In every history is buried a multiplicity of histories. The greater the scope of history, the greater the number of histories erased" (Dirlik 2007: 131).

the social construction of reality. Historical consciousness does not "work" in itself. It is a product of learning, interwoven with specific forms of labor, work, and action, it is the result of subjective embeddedness in particular social circumstances (cf. Rüsen 2002a: 71) Its pre-cognitive basis in infancy includes rootedness (dwelling, *Heimat*), nourishment, and self-awareness. Historical consciousness gradually develops out of specific life forms. Whereas the sociology of knowledge is concerned with the analysis of the social construction of realities (cf. Berger/Luckmann 1966), intra-cultural hermeneutics will also include its subjective origins as reconstructed by phenomenological research. Interculturality thus can be seen as a "sphere in between" (*Zwischensphäre*) (Waldenfels 2006: 109).

The following essay seeks to accomplish two related tasks: an exegetical and a programmatic one. In the first respect it attempts at highlighting some of the underlying assumptions of the concept of new Humanism as seen from a European point of view. Its second intention is to serve the aim of making a few proposals for its implementation by stressing the non-cognitive activities of human beings. My argument will be that the goal of intercultural humanism will be served best if the key term "historical consciousness" is regarded as embedded in the whole range of symbolic activities, including speech and action, the enactment of the arts, of myths and rituals.

To this end, a re-reading of some basic texts of Ernst Cassirer, Hannah Arendt, and George Steiner is suggested. Although the works of the former two were published more than six decades ago and Steiner's essay as early as 1989, they contain some insights that, in my view, are still valid and should be kept in mind amidst the sometimes somewhat blurring effects of postmodernist sophistication. Whereas Cassirer's conception of man as *animal symbolicum* stresses the principle that symbolizing activities philogenetically preceed conceptual work, Arendt's study on *The Human Condition* emphasizes the embeddedness of all theoretical endeavor in common speech and action. Both may yield a well suited framework of intra- and intercultural hermeneutics. Furthermore, both scholars permit an outlook on the importance of the arts for a deep cosmopolitan understanding, since they regard the latter – together with religion, myth and speech – as the all pervading media of man's self-positioning in the world. George Steiner's interpretative work may be regarded as mere "literary activity", if seen from the point of view of modern scientific poetics (cf. Todorov 1981: 3-12). However, its stimulating outcomes bear witness of the discreet charms of the transcultural and transdisciplinary formation of an individual mind. His insights are widely respected and regarded as key documents of modern criticism. Taken as examples, they may offer a further starting point for the ongoing effort of trancending the borders of logocentrism by what Schiller called *aesthetic education* (Schiller 1993).

My notes will be presented in three steps. No step in itself represents a novel insight, but it is their combination that – hopefully – will help to overcome some difficulties. Since, as Dirlik has reminded us, every history is buried in a multipicity of histories, it "is up to the historian to decide what histories to bring up to the surface of our consciousness and what histories to bury under different conceptualizations of space and time" (Dirlik 2007: 131). Being kept in a rather sceptical tone, my considerations may nevertheless serve as an incentive for further considerations on this subject.

2. Logocentrism and the Need for Intercultural Cooperation

A stimulating side effect of the concept of a new Humanism can be that it not only provides guidelines for international understanding but also serves to reassess the European past. Thus a re-establishing of the balance between "Prometheian shame" (Anders) and Eurocentric conceit seems possible (cf. Rorty 2004: 72).

The history of European humanism, as we know, is the history of a series of renaissances. It is essentially of Roman origin. For the first time the concept of *humanitas* comes up at the age of the Roman republic when *homo humanus* was opposed to *homo barbarus*, and *homo humanus* was the *civis Romanus*, who intensified his virtues by integrating *paidaia*. The latter he had taken from Hellenistic culture. (*Paidaia* was translated as *humanitas* which refers to *eruditio et institutio in bonas artes*). Thus, humanism was originally of Roman origin and the so called renaissance of the 14th and 15th centuries in Italy was essentially a *renascentia romanitatis*. This time, the inhumane was seen in the supposedly barbarian gothic and – as they were called afterwards – the Middle Ages. In the European context the study and revitalization of ancient Greek culture has always belonged to the history of humanism and it was reconsidered in specific ways. This is true also for the revival of humanism in late 18th century Germany as it was pursued by Winkelmann, Goethe, Schiller, Hölderlin and others. So we may conclude humanism is not a clear shaped entity, but when we speak of European humanism we speak of the conceptual result of retrospective hypotheses. They form the basis of a new intercultural humanism.

Europe is not just domination, not just hegemony, not just international capitalism. There is also the European *mission civilizatrice*. That term has been discredited by the behavior of the colonial powers, but it might be possible to be rehabilitated. (Rorty 2004: 72)

Reading Rorty's statement, one may ask if there is still a common source in the tradition of European thought that may justify the idea of its civilisatory mission.

Nine texts gathered in this volume are of non-European origin. Together with those written from a European viewpoint and despite variations in the authors' premises, all share the goal of developing concepts of a new form of transcultural discourse that does not turn a blind eye on their political impact. They are documents not only of impressive scholarly scrutiny and considerable sceptical enthusiasm. Also, the traces of intellectual and civic conflicts that their authors have been engaged in must not be overlooked. Their basic assumption is the necessity of anwering the conceptual and empirical challenges that the paradigm of a new Humanism has to face under the conditions of the imminent future.

The new Humanism should be considered as a moving cultural force in political, economic and social life. Its sense generating power cannot tolerate the limits of the real. It will not escape the constraints of practical life, but it will empower the human mind to transcend and make it more human (cf. Rüsen in this volume: 19).

In the Western tradition the list of such utopian views on mankind is very impressive. It ranges from the cosmopolitan idea underlying the philosophies of Lessing, Kant, Herder and Schiller that every citizen should be citizen of the world, and that cultures were not only to endure each other, but rather to acknowledge each other's intrinsic value, to modern statements as that by Levi-Strauss that "tolerance is not a contemplative attitude that views past and present events with leniency, but a dynamic one". It consists of the wish "to foretell, to promote and to understand what is about to happen" (Levi-Strauss 1972: 81). However, the somber voices must also not be overheard in this concert, as we know that the events of global history give evidence of severe drawbacks and even seem to prove that the hopes have been decisively deluded.

Looking back at the atrocities of the preceding century, Saul Friedländer expressed the need to ask the question "What is the nature of human nature?" (Friedländer 1988). And the traumatic experiences of the victims of genocidal actions in the first decade of the third millennium make us realize that the question is in fact unanswerable. Yet it is by no means obsolete since it can help us to become aware of the existential implications of Wittgenstein's statement which I chose as the motto of this essay. Both writers aim at that point of no return where the language of conceptual discourse falls silent.

The last decades, however, have led to an astonishing amount of global engagement. Encouraging efforts on all levels of activity have been initiated, nourished by the "solidarity of the disrupted" (*"solidarité des ébranlés"*) (Patocka 1990: 213). They are motivated by the conviction that the future history of mankind will be a common one or that there will be none.

The actual situation can be characterized as the global awareness of crisis together with the indication of an increasing willingness to change the situation to the better. During recent years, the urgency to act has become a driving force in our approaches to economic, social and political issues. But doubt may be permitted whether that impulse will prove strong enough in the contemporary economic and military contests and cultural warfare.[4] What will be needed, as Rüsen has suggested is the search for new normative

---

4 | Terry Eagleton speaks of "culture wars" which have also led to "oppositional cultures" (Eagleton 2000: 51ff.).

concepts of the "cultural nature of man", since there is no alternative, we have to accept the challenge and look for possibilities to strengthen the willingness and capacities of mutual understanding.

Following Francis Bacon's famous formula, we know that any form of scientific or scholarly knowledge is a potential source of power, as it is subject to social influences according to the forces that promote its conceptualization, utilization and administration. The "industrialization of sciences" (Plessner 1924: 17) has led to a certain loss of normative links in the twentieth century. But their institutionalization has helped to promote their stability and granted social security to its executors. The situation in Non-Western countries must be looked at separately and in a differentiated way. But what Western and Non-Western sciences have in common is the danger that all scientific activity, after certain problems have been conceptualized and found their proper principles of methodical procedure, tends to regard the treatment of these issues as an end in itself. "All research in the cultural sciences in an age of specialization", as Max Weber pointed out,

once it is oriented towards a given subject matter through particular settings of problems and has established its methodological principles, will consider the analysis of the data as an end in itself. It will discontinue assessing the value of the individual facts in terms of their relationships to ultimate value-ideas. Indeed, it will lose its awareness of its ultimate rootedness in the value-ideas in general. [...]. But there comes a moment when the atmosphere changes. The significance of the unreflectively utilized viewpoints becomes uncertain and the road is lost in the twilight.[5]

The global awareness of crisis is one of the loss of normative fundaments for global policies.

While the end of the Baconian Age keeps on being proclaimed (cf. Böhme 1993), the guiding principle of the political elites seems to be: Everything needs to be reformed, but nothing has to be fundamentally changed. *Business as usual.* In the meantime emancipation of the minds has reached a new stage of social impact. Social justice and human rights are being demanded by those who are no longer willing to accept their conceited suspension by those in office. The situation today indicates that Weber`s prediction has come true. Without undue exaggeration, the state of affairs may be characterized as one of elaborated discomfort. The strategic minds of all denominations claim to surpass each other in strategies to compensate for contingency (*Kontingenzbewältigungsstrategien*) and short term solutions. That makes the need for a long term perspective based on the conviction of the necessitude of intercultural exchange and co-operation even more urgent and – in case it can provide some guidelines – even more rewarding. It is the

---

5 | http://www.ne.jp/asahi/moriyuki/abukuma/weber/method/obje/objectivity_frame.html (05.07.09). See Weber 1973: 214.

plurality of perspectives, irrespective of conflicting views, that in itself may prove an incentive to mutual aid and understanding.

In this context, the principles valid for aesthetic judgment as elaborated by Kant can be of great help for further consideration. Since Kant did not write a conclusive political philosophy (he originally planned to write a *Critique of Moral Taste*), the best way to find out what he thought about this matter is to turn to the *Critique of Judgement* (1790/1987), where, in discussing the arts in relation to *taste* as the key category of aesthetic judgment, he was confronted with an analogous problem. The links of its two parts are closer connected with the political than with anything in the other *Critiques*. The most decisive difference between *The Critique of Practical Reason* and the *Critique of Judgement* is that "the moral laws of the former are valid for all intelligible beings whereas the rules of the latter are strictly limited in their validity to human beings on earth" (Arendt 1978: 256).

The "enlargement of the minds" of the latter is accomplished by their putting themselves in the place of any other person and by comparing their judgment with the *possible* rather than the *actual* judgment of others, Critical thinking is possible only where the positions of others are open to inspection. The faculty which allows for such consideration of inter- or intracultural diversity can be called "imagination". The force of imagination makes others present and thus moves potentially in a place which is "the public", open to all sides – in other words, it adopts the position of Kant's *world citizen*. This does not mean, however, that through paramount empathy we could gain knowledge of what actually goes on in the minds of others. Here the concept of *enlarged thought* (*erweiterte Denkungsart*) comes in. *Enlarged thought*, in Kantian terms, is the result of "abstracting from the limitations which contingently attach to our own judgment" and of "disregarding its private subjective conditions", in other words, of what we generally call self-interest. This still is, as far as I can see, the position held by most liberal intellectuals of all hemispheres. It does not tell, though, how to act. As Hannah Arendt has pointed out, there still remains "the clash between the principle according to which you act and the principle according to which you judge"(1978: 259). But this is not a topic of more and better reasoning but of volition.

In the Kantian perspective – contrary to widespread opinion – the position of the subject is not that of a sheer onlooker. Judgment, and especially aesthetic judgment of taste, always reflects on others and takes their possible judgments into account. In other words: "the non-subjective element in the non-objective senses is intersubjectivity" (Arendt 1978: 266). Or: "You must be alone in order to *think*; you need company to *enjoy* a meal" (ibid.).[6]

The following part will present a few notes on some facets of the widely branched works of three representative figures of European civilization in the twentieth century, Ernst Cassirer, Hannah Arendt and George

---

6 | Ibid; my italics, H. L. A growing number of those dining alone will no longer feel amused. A growing feeling of togetherness – as enacted for example in the big open air concerts – have become a source of global solidarity.

Steiner. Writers in exile and public intellectuals, all three have contributed considerably to the comparative study of cultures without being scientific in any strict sense. Far from being comprehensive, my notes will consider the three authors with regard to their possible contribution to a new humanism. However divergent their fields of activity and their philosophical backgrounds, they not only have become highly influential in the context of Western thinking but also their arguments have decisively been influenced by Kantian concepts, which also form one frame of reference for Rüsen's idea of Intercultural Humanism. According to Kant, the necessary "enlargement of the mind" (*Erweiterung der Denkungsart*) is based on moral "imagination" the operations of which prepare their objects for reflection.

3. Beyond Logocentrism: Three Western Voices

a) Ernst Cassirer – the Persistence of Mythical Thinking

Cassirer, exiled from Germany in 1933, published his two studies entitled *An Essay on Man* and *The Myth of the State* in 1944 and 1946 respectively. Cassirer's decisive step turning away from Kantian trancendentalism, though, was as early as 1923:

The task is to comprehend that, apart from the pure cognitive function, the functioning of the linguistic thought, the functioning of mythic-religious thought and the functioning of the artistic apprehension take place in such a way, that all of them may be regarded as a certain formations, not so much of the world but to the world, in order to yield an objective coherence of form and apprehension. Thus, the *critique of reason* becomes the *critique of culture* (1923/1994: 11).[7]

The *Essay on Man* starts with a chapter entitled *The Crisis in Man's Knowledge of Himself*, the main thesis of which in my view is still valid more than six decades later: In spite of the "astoundingly rich and constantly flowing body of facts", modern man, according to Cassirer, seems "not yet to have found a method for the mastery and organization of the material" (1944: 27).

For Cassirer, the clue to the nature of man is symbol. "Instead of defining man as animal rationale", he says, "we should define him as an animal symbolicum." By doing so we can understand the new way open to him – "the way to civilization" (ibid: 31). Long before man had discovered the state as form of social organization, he had organized and systematized his feelings, desires, and thoughts in language, in myth, in religion, and in art (ibid: 71). Language did and does not only express thought and ideas, but also affections and feelings. This relates it to myth. Myth cannot be separated from historical and political thought (cf. Blumenberg 1983).

---

7 | My italics, H. L.

Mythology itself is not simply a crude mass of superstitions or gross delusions. [...] It possesses a systematic or conceptual form [....]. Side by side with the conceptual language there is an emotional language, side by side with the logical and scientific language there is a language of poetic imagination (Cassirer 1944: 30).

For Cassirer, the latter need not be restated in terms of the former and vice versa. Their objects remain separate. At the same time, the sciences themselves have had to pass through a mythical age before they could reach their logical stage. Cognition as a specific feature of the human consciousness means that relational thought is dependant on symbolic thought, and any concept of philosophical or political writing remains imbedded into the history of symbolic meanings specific to its given culture.

Science strives to conceive the world *ex analogia universi,* not *ex analogia hominis.* Human culture taken as a whole may be described as the process of man's progressive self-liberation. Language, art, religion, science, are various phases in this process (Cassirer 1944: 244).

The term "phases" in this context has a somewhat ambiguous connotation. One should perhaps add that there is no teleology intended by Cassirer, but that the relation between subjectivity and objectivity is not the same in an artwork as it is in the works of scientists and scholars. *Kulturwissenschaften,* in other words, should not be confounded with *human sciences* (cf. Cassirer 1939).

Transposed to the agenda of a new Humanism, to conceive of man as an *animal symbolicum* can support strategies of sense making that are based on the totality of activities. They need not necessarily be re-stated in abstract vocabularies in order to be understood, since any notion inevitably makes us aware of "the absence of its object."[8]

Taking into account the date of publication during the Second War, the concluding lines of *The Essay on Man* cited above should be read not as a document of political naivité of a member of the ivory tower but as encouraging testimony of hope for the future of mankind The idea of history being a "process of progressive self liberation", published in 1944 (Cassirer died in 1945), makes it a document of confidence against the odds.

It must not be overlooked, though, that *The Myth of the State,* his following and last work finished, which was to be published posthumously in 1946, had a more somber ending, desillusioned by the persisting power of fascisms:

---

8 | "Der Begriff gilt als ein Produkt der Vernunft, wenn nicht sogar ihr Triumph, und ist es wohl auch. Das lässt aber nicht die Umkehrung zu, Vernunft sei nur dort, wo es gelungen oder wenigstens angestrebt sei, die Wirklichkeit, das Leben oder das Sein – wie immer man die Totalität nennen will – auf den Begriff zu bringen [...]. Der Begriff hat etwas zu tun mit der Abwesenheit seines Gegenstandes." Blumenberg 2007: 9. Cf. Konersmann 2007: 258f.

It is beyond the power of philosophy to destroy the political myths. A myth is in a sense invulnerable. It is impervious to rational arguments, it cannot be refuted by syllogisms [...] In order to fight the enemy you must know him. We should not commit the same error a second time (Cassirer 1946: 290f.).

This statement advises us not to forget that a new Humanism should not be confounded with global pacifism.[9]

b) Hannah Arendt – the Power to Forgive

Like that of Cassirer, Hannah Arendt's work on *The Human Condition* (1958) treats the foundations of logocentrism taking into perspective their longterm development. Whereas Cassirer focuses on the symbolizing activities of man in terms of language, myth, religion, and arts, Arendt concentrates on the embeddedness of thought and speech into human activities. She criticizes traditional investigations for not having differentiated sufficiently between labor, work and action. (Special attention is being given to Adam Smith and Karl Marx, the latter for his "confusion" between "labor" and "work"). Furthermore, she distinguishes two forms of living: the *vita contemplativa* and the *vita activa*. "With the term *vita activa*", as she puts it,

I propose to designate three fundamental human activities: labor, work, and action. They are fundamental because each corresponds to one of the basic conditions under which life on earth has been given to man. (ibid.: 7).

Labor is the activity by which the vital necessities are produced and fed into the life process. Work provides the "artificial" world of durable things. This world is meant to outlast human beings. It is the world of *homo faber*. "Action", the only activity that happens without the intermediary of things or matter, according to Arendt, corresponds to the human condition of plurality, to the "fact that men, not Man, live on the earth and inhabit the world" (ibid.: 7).

All three modes of activity and their corresponding conditions are intimately connected with the most vital aspects of human life: birth and death, natality and mortality. "The man-made world of things, the human artifice erected by *homo faber*, becomes a home for mortal men, whose stability will endure and outlast the ever-changing movement of their lives" (ibid.: 173).

The productivity of *homo faber*, in contrast, aims at the usage and the relative durability of fabricated objects. The relative stability of these objects gives them a certain independence from their origins and makes it possible to form identical objects of the same type. Because of their outstanding permanence, works of art, too, belong to this type of object.

Of central interest to our topic is the fifth chapter of *The Human Condition*,

---

9 | "The true enemy of peace is not war [...], but the belief in war as an political instrument worthy of mankind." Blankertz 1984: 23. Cf. Habermas 1996.

since it deals with the foundation of human speech and action in human difference.

If men were not equal, they could neither understand each other and those who came before them nor plan for the future and foresee the needs of those who come after them. If men were not different from each other they would need neither speech nor action (ibid: 175).

Signs and sounds to communicate common needs would be enough. Speech and action are the modes in which human beings appear to each other, they reveal their personal identities. A life without speech and action would be nearly dead to the world. It would have "ceased to be a human life", because it were "no longer lived among men" (ibid: 176). Action and speech remain unsurmountably interrelated and inseparable. Acting and speaking human beings become "parts of a whole" which had existed before and will transcend their lives. Acting and speaking, they insert themselves into the human world. This insertion is like a second birth not forced upon by necessity, like "labor", and is not prompted by utility, like "work".

To act, in its most general sense, means to take an initiative, to begin [...]. If action as beginning corresponds to the fact of birth, if it is the actualization of the human condition of natality, then speech corresponds to the fact of distinctness and is the actualization of the human condition of plurality, that is of living a distinct and unique being among equals (ibid: 178).

The essential feature of human beings thus is their capacity for moral intervention. The insistence on man's ability of volition, to begin afresh, to take an initiative, forms the core concept of Arendt's work. It is of utmost interest in our context, since it elucidates man's innate future directedness and its foundation in human action.

Two forms of action, according to Arendt, are fundamental to the humaneness of human beings: their power to forgive and their power to keep promises. The latter forms the basis of any legal contract and any political institution, the former is that force by which man enables himself to disrupt the irreversibility of fate. Without the ability to forgive there would be the vicious circles of bloodshed and revenge. Without confidence that treaties will be observed by the others ("*pacta sunt servanda*"), the negotiation of any trade contract or the operation of any international institution would be impossible. Both capacities are not essentially ones of intellectual calculation but they express the human faculty of willful activity. Without both, institutions would collapse and we would remain "rational fools" (Sen 1990). Progress in the history of political thinking will come about not by intellectual sophistication and its capacity to reformulate the issues by using new vocabularies, but by the power of human volition to change the agenda.

c) George Steiner – the Eminence of Art

> I am not interested in how people
> move, but what makes them move
> *Pina Bausch, choreographer (1940 – 2009)*

While the ongoing debates within studies on comparative literature are mostly concerned with the *state of the art* in their respective fields,[10] there has been, as far as I can see, a blatant negligence in recent discussions among intercultural historiographers of the contribution of the arts to a global understanding. The accomplishment of any work of art has been regarded by most scholars as an activity that needs conceptualization in order to leave the zones of aesthetic comfort. References to literature among historians have therefore remained somewhat marginal and restricted to those modes of expression that contain some form of "master narrative" of the past or some commentary on actual historical events. Whatever the outcomes have been, they were guided by the underlying assumption that the specimens of art should be taken as documents for the conceptualization and historiographical reconstruction and thus may help orientate individual recipients and organize collective memories. If it is true that "no source text contains that history which is constituted and formed into language by the textual source texts themselves" (Kosellek 1987: 117), history of art – like any other history – will have to acknowledge its status as a retrospective hypothesis.[11]

Referring to some of the insights of George Steiner's *Real Presences* (1989), the following notes suggest an approach which has been informed by Cassirer and keeps aware of the "mythic" dimensions of art that transcend conceptual language. However, this does not necessarily advocate its irrationality. Steiner's exegetic effort aims at the virtual contemporarity of their eminent specimens and their contribution to the enlightened minds of the *happy few*.

The first part of Steiner's book is a harsh criticism of academic discourse on art that he compares with Talmudic exegesis.[12] He notes a severe imbalance between the secondary and their objects, between the *texts* and their exegesis. The explicative-evaluative commentary they bring forth is regarded by him as "grotesque."

The mushrooming of semantic-critical jargon, the disputations between structuralists, post-structuralists, meta-structuralists and deconstrucionists, the attention accorded both in the academy and the media to theoreticians and

---

10 | A useful survey is given in Saussy 2004.

11 | "Kein Quellentext enthält jene Geschichte, die erst mit Hilfe textlicher Quellen konstituiert und zur Sprache gebracht wird" (Koselleck 1987: 117). Cf Kracauer 1968: 127

12 | "Hermeneutic unendingnesss and survival in exile are kindred [...]. In dispersion, the text is homeland" (ibid: 40).

publicists of the aesthetic [...] carry within their bustling pretence the germs of more or less rapid decay (Steiner 1989: 47f).

The aim of hermeneutics, according to Steiner, is the enactment of an active apprehension of the *texts* that, according to him, includes the art object, the musical composition, the dance, a.s.f. (Steiner 1989: 7). First of all, it is the performing artist who executes the work of representation (*Vergegenwärtigung*) when he or she rehearses its critical tradition. An actor interprets Agamemnon or Ophelia, a dancer interprets Balanchine's choreography, a violinist Bach's partita. Each of these interpretations is "understanding in action", it is "immediacy of translation." Such comprehension is "both analytical and critical" (ibid: 8). The intensity of the aesthetic re-enactment is regarded as being the rationale for the critic's business.[13] Aesthetic apprehension, conceived of as "the meeting with the other", signifies both "fear and perception" (ibid: 131). Serious painting, music, literature or sculpture make the audience aware, as no other means of communication can do, of the "unassuaged, unhoused instability and estrangement of our condition" (ibid: 139). Steiner emphasizes the fact that there is no major tradition of literature that is not focused on oral articulation. Literature, as art in general, is seen as body language

The meanings of poetry and the music, of those meanings that we call metrics, are also the human body. The echoes of sensibility they elicit are visceral and tactile. The erosion of such reading from most adult practices has subdued primary traditions in both poetry and prose (ibid: 9).

These issues are of utmost importance. They are "political and social in the strongest sense", since a cultivation of trained, shared rememberances sets a society in touch with its own past (ibid: 10).

Therefore, the adequate forms of reception, as Steiner puts it, would be "immediacy, of personal engagement and answerability" (ibid: 47). It is obvious that in this concept there is hardly any room for discursive reception. His emphasis on the autonomy of art and its essentials being indecipherable makes it difficult to integrate his insight into any form of theoretical conception and may even lead to a series of contradiction in terms if one would attempt at further qualifying the notion of "immediacy" and "answerability". Both rather suggest elaborate subjectivity.

There is always, there will always be, a sense in which we do not know what it is we are experiencing and talking about when we experience and talk about what

---

13 | "The readings, the interpretations and critical judgements of art, literature and music from within art, literature and music are of a penetrative authority rarely equalled by those affected from outside, [...] this is to say the reviewer, the critic, the academic" (ibid: 12).

it is. There is a sense in which no human discourse, however analytic, can make final sense of sense itself (ibid: 215).

This sense, according to Steiner, is the final paradox which defines the human being. It is the irreducible autonomy of art which denies both adequate paraphrase and unanimity of finding.

It points to that region where the awareness of man's essential 'otherness' becomes feasible. And it is but the personal encounter with the *text*, the act of reading, the act of hearing, the act of seeing, that gives sense to "material bodies":

In most cultures, in the witness borne to poetry and art until most recent modernity, the source of 'otherness' has been actualized or metaphorized as transcendent. It has been invoked as divine, as magical, as daimonic. It is a presence of radical opacity. That presence is the source of powers, of significations in the text, in the work, neither consciously willed nor consciously understood. (ibid: 211)

Poets and mythmakers of all cultures have given form to such moments of sudden epiphany and utopian salvation.

I have quoted in some length to give evidence of the critical verve of Steiner's suada which makes it a suggestive display not only of its rhetorics. It is the awareness of the spiritual dimension of art that makes his writing – in its best moments – transcend the limits of traditional criticism and enlarge the possibilities of discursive analysis.

4. Conclusion

Our re-reading of some basic texts of the European heritage may have shown that we need a concept of historical consciousness that is not restricted to the hermeneutic achievements of scholars but that integrates the concept of enactment of civil virtues. As has been noted, the underlying presupposition has been that the idea of a new Humanism is far too important to be left to the experts of cultural philosophy and the cultural sciences alone. Ironically speaking, it cannot be denied that this essay, too, has been drafting heavily on their results when applying some of their basic ideas. However, the argument that a new Humanism must leave its origins in the European republics of scholars (*Gelehrtenrepubliken*), if it aims to become of social and economic relevance, is still valid.

George Steiner's writing emphasizes human subjectivity as a constitutive element for rendering the world of human experience intelligible. His attempts at liberating the specimens of art from the cages of libraries, archives, and museums can be regarded as a series of encouragements of his audiences and readers to refine their sensibilities and to make them enact their aesthetic judgments. Thus, they exemplify the power of "cultural man" to transcend the limits of intellectual preconception.

Hannah Arendt was equally aware of the fragility of human life and the impact of suffering on human potential. Her emphasis on thought and cognition being inseparably interwoven with labor, work, and action underpins the multi-dimensionality of human activities and the importance of volition as a new category of historical interpretation. Thought must be seen in the context of those activities of the human species that help to transcend the borders of lifespan by durable works, including the arts. Arendt's humanism stresses the importance of developing the competencies of man as a political animal. She interweaves anthropological insights with both severe criticism on Marxian and any other form of teleological and deterministic thought – together with her respectful acknowledgement of Marx' contribution to human self-awareness.

Cassirer was seen to do justice to the immanent logic of myth, religion, and art, and thus to their stabilizing function with regard to the Gods and the human condition. A re-reading of his work can contribute to a concept of humanity that transcends the logic of sheer science and to write a new chapter in the history of *mythos* and *logos* (cf. Blumenberg 1971: 65ff). The scientist, since he acts into nature from the standpoint of the universe and not into the web of human relationships (cf. above, p. 241),"lacks the revelatory character of action as well as the abilities to produce stories and become historical, which together form the very source from which meaningfulness springs into and illuminates human existence" (Arendt 1958: 324). This is not irrelevant for the future of man.

The common denominator of the works in consideration can thus be seen in their emphasis on the human power to transcend. All three authors would agree on the importance of the arts being the one human activity by which the vanity of human life can be reconciled with the divine – in spite of whatever may have happened. They would consent to the view that we need a new respect fort the humanizing qualities of genuine art – as a counterbalance against the temptations of globalizing logocentrism. A piece of literature, or music, or painting will have to be conceived as a *residuum* of humanity, as a realm of the ineffable, as the seat of transcendental beauty:

The animate logic of congruent symmetries, of organic motifs in the human body, is of a designate wonder – a wonder of design as we see it in Leonardo's famous icon of frontal and cosmic man – such as to overwhelm understanding. And it is in this tensed caesura between analytic intelligibility and perception, when cognition holds is breath, that our sense of being is host to beauty (Steiner 1989: 200-201).

The dilemmata of Western rationalization referred to in the second part of this paper and its helplessness to come to terms with global justice will not be overcome by intellectual sophistication alone. What will be needed, too, is moral imagination to be developed in analogy to aesthetic judgment as initiated by Hannah Arendt, is its power to forgive, is the willingness to share, is the willingness for a new beginning.

As C. P. Snow phrased it half a century ago, the task does not need much erudition:

Changes in education are not going to produce miracles [...]. With good fortune however we can educate a large proportion of our better minds so that they are not ignorant of imaginative experience, both in the arts and in science, nor ignorant of [...] the remedial suffering of most of their fellow humans, and of the responsibilities, which, once they are seen, cannot be denied (Snow 1959: 63).

No, they cannot, can they?

Bibliography

Abu-Lughood, Janet L. (1989): *Before European Hegemony: The World System A.D. 1250-1350*, New York.

Acidalius, Valens (2006 [1595]): *Disputatio nova contra mulieres, qua probatur eas homines non esse*, Georg Burkard/Ralf G. Czapla (eds.), Heidelberg.

Ackermann, A./Müller, K.E. (ed.) (2002): *Patchwork: Dimensionen multikultureller Gesellschaften: Geschichte, Problematik und Chancen*, Bielefeld.

Adorno, Theodor W. (1997): *Aesthetic Theory*, London.

Adorno, Theodor W./Horkheimer, Max (1947 [1944]): *Dialektik der Aufklärung: philosophische Fragmente*, Amsterdam.

Agrippa, Henricus Cornelius (1996): *Declamation on the Nobility and Preminence of the Female sex*, tr. and ed. Albert Rabil, Jr., Chicago.

Algazi, Gadi (2003): "Scholars in Households: Refiguring the Learned Habitus." In: Science in Context 16.1 and 2, pp. 9-42.

Anders, Günther (1956): *Die Antiquiertheit des Menschen*, vol. 1: *Über die Seele im Zeitalter der zweiten industriellen Revolution*, Munich.

Appiah, Kwame A. (1992): *In My Father's House – Africa in the Philosophy of Culture*, London.

Arendt, Hannah (1958): *The Human Condition*, Chicago. Repr. 1974, 1998.

Arendt, Hannah (1977): "Thinking." In: *The Life of the Mind*. One volume edition, vol. 1, San Diego/New York/London, pp. 1-238.

Arendt, Hannah (1978): "Willing" In: *The Life of the Mind*. One volume edition, vol. 2, San Diego/New York/London, pp. 1-283.

Arkoun, Muhammad (1982): *Traité d'Ethique by Miskawayh*, 2nd ed., Damascus.

Arkoun, Muhammad (2005): *L' Humanisme arabe au 4e/10e siècle*, 3nd ed., Paris.

Arkoun, Muhammad (1988): "Algeria." In: Shireen T. Hunter (ed.), *The Politics of Islamic Revivalism*, Bloomington, pp. 171-86.

Assmann, J. (2001): *Moses der Ägypter: Entzifferung einer Gedächtnisspur*, Frankfurt/M.

Babu, Abdul R. (1981): *African Socialism or Socialist Africa?*, London.

Bacchelli, Franco (2004): "Medicina, morale e religione: il caso di Antonio Musa Brasavola." In: Annali di storia delle Università italiane 8, pp. 93-100.

Bachelard, Gaston (1988): La philosophie du non: Essai d'une philosophie du nouvel esprit scientifique, 2nd ed., Paris.

Badrinath, Chaturvedi (2006): Swami Vivekananda: The Living Vedanta, New Delhi.

Balibar, Etienne (2003): "Europe: An 'Unimagined Frontier of Democracy.'" In: Diacritics, Fall-Winter, pp. 37-44.

Balibar, Etienne (2005): "Europe: Provincial, Common, Universal" (unpublished paper presented at the Consortium of Humanities Centers and Institutes Annual Meeting, June 17-18, University of Utrecht, The Netherlands).

Balibar, Etienne (2006): Lecture given at the University of Chicago in Spring 2006.

Barthes, Roland (1978): Leçon, Paris.

Bauman, Zygmunt (1989): Modernity and the Holocaust, Cambridge.

Baumann, Zygmunt (2001): Modernité et Holocauste, La Fabrique.

Bediako, Kwame (1995): Christianity in Africa – The Renewal of a non-Western Religion, Edinburgh.

Belting, Hans (2005): Das echte Bild: Bildfragen als Glaubensfragen, Munich.

Benhabib, Seyla (1992): "Feminism and the Question of Postmodernism." In: idem, Situating the Self, Cambridge.

Berger, Peter L./Luckmann, Thomas (1966): The Social Construction of Reality, Garden City, New York.

Bertelsmann Foundation (2008): Intercultural Competence: The Key Competence for the 21st Century?, Gütersloh.

Bhaba, Homi K. (1994): The Location of Culture, London/New York.

Biale, David (2002): Cultures of the Jews, New York.

Biskupski, Mieczysław/Polonsky, Antony (eds.) (2007): Polish–Jewish Relations in North America. Polin: Studies in Polish Jewry, vol. 19, Oxford.

Blankertz, Herwig (1984): Kants Idee des ewigen Friedens und andere Vorträge, Wetzlar.

Blumenberg, Hans (1971): "Wirklichkeitsbegriff und Wirkungspotential des Mythos." In: Manfred Fuhrmann (ed.), Terror und Spiel: Probleme der Mythenrezeption, Munich, pp. 11-66.

Blumenberg, Hans (2007): Theorie der Unbegrifflichkeit, Frankfurt/M.

Boesch, Ernest E. (1991): Symbolic Action Theory and Cultural Psychology, Berlin.

Böhme, Hartmut/Böhme, Gernot (1983): Das Andere der Vernunft, Frankfurt/M.

Böhme, Gernot (1993): Am Ende des baconschen Zeitalters: Studien zur Wissenschaftsentwicklung, Frankfurt/M.

Böhme, Gernot (1999): Kants Kritik der Urteilskraft in neuer Sicht, Frankfurt/M.

Bolten, Jürgen (2001): Interkulturelle Kompetenz, Erfurt.

Bourdieu, Pierre (1990): "The Scholastic Point of View". In: Cultural Anthropology 5. 4, pp. 380-391.

Braidotti, Rosi (2002): "Identity, Subjectivity and Difference: A Critical Genealogy." In: Gabriele Griffin/Rosi Braidotti (eds.), *Thinking Differently: A Reader in European Women's Studies*, London, pp. 158-180.

Brasavola, Antonio Musa (1538): *Examen omnium syruporum*, Venice.

Breytenbach, Breyten (1984): *The True Confessions of an Albino Terrorist*, London.

Brezinski, Z. (1997): *The Grand Chessboard: American Primary and Its Geostrategic Imperatives*, New York.

Brunsdale, Mitzi M. (2005): "Dorothy L. Sayers (1893-1957), Medieval Mystery Maker." In: Jane Chance (ed.), *Women Medievalists and the Academy*, Madison, Wisconsin, pp. 423-439.

Buck, David D. (1991): "Forum on Universalism and Relativism in Asian Studies." In: The Journal of Asian Studies 50, pp. 29-30.

Budde, Gunilla-Friederike et. al. (eds.) (2006): *Transnationale Geschichte: Themen, Tendenzen und Theorien*, Göttingen.

Bunch, Charlotte (1990): "Women's Rights as Human Rights: Toward a Re-Vision of Human Rights." In: Human Rights Quarterly 12, pp. 486-498.

Butler, Judith (1990): *Gender Trouble: Feminism and the Subversion of Identity*, London.

Cancik, Hubert (1993): "Humanismus." In: Hubert Cancik/Burkhard Gladigow/Karl-Heinz Kohl (eds.), *Handbuch religionswissenschaftlicher Grundbegriffe*, vol. 3, Stuttgart, pp. 173-185.

Cancik, Hubert (2003): "Entrohung und Barmherzigkeit, Herrschaft und Würde: Antike Grundlagen von Humanismus." In: Richard Faber (ed.), *Streit um den Humanismus*, Würzburg, pp. 23-42.

Cancik, Hubert (2009): "Die Rezeption der Antike – Kleine Geschichte des europäischen Humanismus." In: Jörn Rüsen/Henner Laass (eds.), *Interkultureller Humanismus: Menschlichkeit in der Vielfalt der Kulturen*, Schwalbach/Ts.

Carroll, John (1993): *Humanism: The Wreck of Western Culture*, London.

Casanova, Pascale (1999): *La République mondiale des lettres*, Paris.

Cassirer, Ernst (1939): "Naturalistische und humanistische Begründung der Kulturphilosophie." In: idem, *Erkenntnis, Begriff, Kultur*, repr. Hamburg 1993, pp. 231-263.

Cassirer, Ernst (1944): *An Essay on Man: An Introduction to a Philosophy of Human Culture*, repr. Hamburg 2006 (ECW 23).

Cassirer, Ernst (1946): *The Myth of the State*, repr. Hamburg 2007 (ECW 25).

Cassirer, Ernst (1923): *Philosophie der symbolischen Formen*, vol. 1, ²1953, repr. Darmstadt 1994.

Castells, M. (2004): *The Power of Identity*, 2nd ed., Blackwell.

Castro Varela, Maria do/Dhawan, N. (2005): *Postkoloniale Theorie: Eine kritische Einführung*, Bielefeld.

Césaire, Aimé (1939): *"Cahier d'un retour au pays natal."* In: Wilder 2005, pp. 287-288.

Chakkarath, Pradeep (2007): "Kulturpsychologie und indigene Psychologie." In: Straub/Weidemann/Weidemann 2007, pp. 237-249.

Chakrabarty, Dipesh (2009): "The Climate of History: Four Theses." In: Critical Inquiry 35.2, pp. 197-222.

Chakrabarty, Dipesh/Majumdar, Rochona/Sartori, Andrew (eds.) (2007): *From the Colonial to the Postcolonial: India and Pakistan in Transition*, New Delhi.

Chatman, Seymour (1976): *Story and Discourse: Narrative Structure in Fiction and Film*, Ithaca, N.Y.

Chaucer, Geoffrey (2007): *Canterbury Tales*, London.

Chen, Duxiu (1984): *Science and Outlook on Life*, part I, Beijing.

Chen, Guo-Ming (1987): Dimensions of Intercultural Communication Competence, Ann Arbor.

Chen, G.-M/Starosta, W. J. (1996): "Intercultural Communication Competence: A Synthesis." In: Communication Yearbook 19, 353-383.

Colie, Rosalie (1966): *Paradoxia epidemica. The Renaissance Tradition of Paradox*, Princeton.

Comaroff, Jean/Comaroff, John (eds.) (1993): *Modernity and its Malcontents – Ritual and Power in Postcolonial Africa*, Chicago.

Confucius (2007): *The Analects*, New York.

Cooper, David E. (ed.) (1995): *A Companion to Aesthetics: Blackwell Companions to Philosophy*, Oxford.

Cornell, D. (2004): "A Call for a Nuanced Constitutional Jurisprudence: Ubuntu, Dignity, and Reconciliation." In: South African Public Law 19, pp. 661-670.

Coseriu, Eugenio (1974): *Synchronie, Diachronie und Geschichte*, Munich, pp. 245-246.

Cousins, A.D. (2004): "Humanism, Female Education and Myth: Erasmus, Vives and More's *To Candidus*." In: Journal of the History of Ideas 65.2, pp. 213-230.

Crystal, David (1987): *The Cambridge Encyclopedia of Language*, Cambridge.

Culler, Jonathan (1983): *On Deconstruction: Theory and Criticism after Structuralism*, London.

Danby, Herbert, transl. and ed. (1933): *The Mishnah*, London.

Davis, Gregson, transl. and intr. (1984): *Non-vicious Circle: Twenty Poems of Aimé Césaire*, Stanford, CA.

Deleuze, Gilles/Guattari, Félix (1980): *Mille Plateaux*, Paris.

Deller, Jürgen/Albrecht, Anne-Grit (2007): "Interkulturelle Eignungsdiagnostik." In: Straub/Weidemann/Weidemann 2007, pp. 741-754.

Derrida, Jacques (1977): *Limited Inc.*, Baltimore.

Derrida, Jacques (1982): "The Ends of Man." In: idem, *Margins of Philosophy*, transl. Alan Bass, Chicago.

Derrida, Jacques (2001), *L' Universite sans condition*, Paris.

Diawara, Manthia (1998): *In Search of Africa*, Cambridge, Mass.

Dirlik, Arif (2007): "Confounding Metaphors, Invention of the World: What is World History For?" In: Stuchtey/Fuchs 2007, pp. 91-133.

Du Bois, W.E. B. (1989 ['1903]): "Of the Dawn of Freedom." In: idem, *The Soul of the Black Folk*, New York.

Durkheim, Émile (1975): *Durkheim on Religion: A Selection of Readings with Bibliographies*, (ed.) William S. F. Pickering, London.

Durkheim, Émile (1975a): "Individualism and the Intellectuals." In: Durkheim 1975, pp. 59-73.

Durkheim, Émile (1978): *De la division du travail social*, Paris.

Dutta, Krishna/Robinson, Andrew (1997): *Rabindranath Tagore: The Myrid-Minded Man*, London.

Dux, Günter (2006): "How Meaning Came into the World and What Became of It." In: Jörn Rüsen (ed.), *Meaning and Representation in History*, New York, pp. 20-40.

Eagleton, Mary (ed.) (1996): *Feminist Literary Theory: A Reader*. 2nd ed., Oxford, pp. 373-378.

Eagleton, Terry (2000): *The Idea of Culture*, Oxford, repr. 2006.

Eco, Umberto (1972): *Einführung in die Semiotik*, Munich.

Eco, Umberto (1985): *Semiotik und die Philosophie der Sprache*, Munich.

Edmundson, Mark (1995): *Literature against Philosophy: Plato to Derrida. A Defence of Poetry*, Cambridge.

Ehrenfeld, David (1981): *The Arrogance of Humanism*, Oxford.

Elam, Keir (1980): *The Semiotics of Theatre and Drama*, London.

Elwert, Georg (1991): "Gabe, Reziprozität und Warentausch: Überlegungen zu einigen Ausdrücken und Begriffen." In: E. Berg/A. Wimmer (eds.), *Ethnologie im Widerstreit: Kontroverse über Macht, Geschäft und Geschäft in fremden Kulturen*, Munich, pp. 159-178.

Epstein, I. (ed.) (1961): *The Babylonian Talmud*. 18 vols., London.

Essbach, W. (ed.) (2000): *Wir – Ihr – Sie: Identität und Alterität in Theorie und Methode*, Würzburg.

Essen, Georg (2004): *Sinnstiftende Unruhe im System des Rechts: Religion im Beziehungsgeflecht von modernem Verfassungsstaat und säkularer Zivilgesellschaft*, Göttingen.

Essen, Georg (2006a): "'... allerlei unlautere Religionsideen'. Zur aktuellen Bedeutung der Religionsphilosophie Kants." In: Chr. Danz/Fr. Hermanni (eds.), *Wahrheitsansprüche der Weltreligionen: Konturen gegenwärtiger Religionstheologie*, Neukirchen-Vluyn, pp. 133-147.

Essen, Georg (2006b): "'Nature' as a Humanistic Principle of Universal Communication. A European Historical Case Study Regarding Natural Law." In: The Journal for Transdisciplinary Research in South Africa 2, pp. 277-288.

Essen, Georg (2007): "Ethical Monotheism and Human Freedom: Theological Convergences with the Pluralism of the Modern Age." In: N. Hintersteiner (ed.), *Naming and Thinking God in Europe Today: Theology in Global Dialogue (Currents of Encounter)*, Amsterdam/New York, pp. 265-283.

Fan, Shoukang/Liang, Qichao (1923): *Science and Outlook on Life*, Shanghai.

Fanon, Frantz (1968): *The Wretched of the Earth*, New York.

Fanon, Frantz (1970 [1952]): *Black Skin, White Masks*, transl. Charles Lam Markmann, London.

Featherstone, Mike/Lash, Scott/Robertson, Roland (eds.) (1995): *Global Modernities*, London.

Feng, Qi (ed.) (1989): *History of Chinese Modern Philosophy*, 2nd vol., Shanghai.

Feng, Youlan (1964): *A New History of China's Philosophy*, vol. I, Beijing.

Ferguson, James (1999): *Expectations of Modernity – Myths and Meanings of Urban Life on the Zambian Copperbelt*, Berkeley.

Forst, R. (2000): *Toleranz im Konflikt: Geschichte, Gehalt und Gegenwart eines umstrittenen Begriffs*, Frankfurt/M.

Forst, R. (2000a): *Toleranz: Philosophische Grundlagen und gesellschaftlichen Praxis einer umstrittenen Tugend*, Frankfurt/M.

Foucault, Michel (1973): *The Order of Things: An Archaeology of the Human Sciences*, English transl., New York.

Foucault, Michel (2003): *"Society Must be Defended": Lectures at Collège de France*, transl. David Macey, New York.

Frank, Manfred (1984): *Was ist Neostrukturalismus?*, Frankfurt/M.

Friedland, William H./Rosberg, Carl G. (eds.) (1967): *African Socialism*, Stanford.

Friedländer, Saul (1988): *Nazi Germany and the Jews*, New York.

Friedman, Thomas L. (2006): *The World is Flat: A Brief History of the Twenty-First Century*, New York.

Fry, Margery (1936): "Gilbert Murray at Somerville." In: idem, *Essays in Honour of GM*, London, pp. 49-61.

Fuchs, Eckhardt/Stuchtey, Benedikt (eds.) (2002): *Across Cultural Borders: Historiography in Global Perspective*, Oxford/ New York.

Fukuyama, F. (1992): *The End of History and the Last Man*, New York.

Geertz Clifford (1966): "Religion as a Cultural System." In: Michael Banton (ed.), *Anthropological Approaches to the Study of Religion*, London.

Geertz, Clifford (1997): *Spurenlesen: Der Ethnologe und das Entgleiten der Fakten*, Munich.

Genette, Gérard (1971): "Vraisemblance et motivation." In: Gérard Genette, *Figures II*, Paris, pp. 71-100.

Genette, Gérard (1991): *Fiction et diction*, Paris.

Geng, Yunzhi et al. (2003): *The Western Democracy in Modern China*, Beijing.

Gentile, Giovanni (1923): *I profeti del Risorgimento italiano*, Firenze.

Giddens, Anthony (1993): "Action, Subjectivity and the Constitution of Meaning." In: Murray Krieger (ed.), *The Aims of Representation: Subject, Text, History*, Stanford, pp. 159-174.

Gilmour, Sander L. (2006): *Multiculturalism and the Jews*, New York/ London.

Gombrich, Ernst H. (1972): *The Story of Art*, 12th ed., enlarged and redesigned, London, repr. 2002.

Goodman, Lenn E. (2003): *Islamic Humanism*, Oxford.

Graf, Friedrich Wilhelm (2008): *Missbrauchte Götter: Zum Menschenbilderstreit in der Moderne*, Munich.

Greimas, Algirdas Julien (1970): "Eléments d'une grammaire narrative." In: idem (ed.), *Du sens: Essays sémiotiças*, Paris, pp. 157-183.

Grunebaum, Gustave E. von (1962): *Modern Islam*, Berkeley.

Gumbrecht, Hans Ulrich (1986): "Über den Ort der Narration in narrativen Gattungen." In: Eberhard Lämmert (ed.), *Erzählforschung: Ein Symposion*, Stuttgart, pp. 202-217.

Gumbrecht, Hans Ulrich (2003): *Die Macht der Philologie*, Frankfurt/M.

Guo, Qingfan ([8]1997): "Zhuangzi jishi [The Variorum Edition of the Zhuangzi]." In: *Zhuzi jicheng*, vol. 3, chapt. 2. 41, Beijing.

Habermas, Jürgen (1996): "Kants Idee des ewigen Friedens: Aus dem historischen Abstand von 200 Jahren." In: idem, *Die Einbeziehung des Anderen*, Frankfurt/M., pp. 192-236.

Habermas, Jürgen (2001): *Glauben und Wissen: Friedenspreis des Deutschen Buchhandels 2001: Ansprachen aus Anlass der Verleihung*, Frankfurt/M., 37-56.

Hahn, Alois (1974): *Religion und der Verlust der Sinngebung: Identitätsprobleme in der modernen Gesellschaft*, Frankfurt/M.

Hannerz, Ulf (1992): *Cultural Complexity: Studies in the Social Organization of Meaning*, New York.

Hannerz, Ulf (1996): *Transnational Connections: Culture, People, Places*, London/New York.

Hastrup, Kirsten (2007): "Identity at Play: Individuals, Characters, and Theatres of Action." In: Deborah Fahy Bryceson et al. (eds.), *Identity and Networks: Fashioning Gender and Ethnicity across Cultures*, New York/ Oxford.

Heilman, Samuel C. (2006): *Sliding to the Right: The Contest for the Future of American Jewish Orthodoxy*, Berkeley, CA.

Helbing, Lothar (1932): *Der dritte Humanismus*, Berlin.

Held, Klaus (2007): "Lebenswelt und politische Urteilskraft." In: Giovanni Leghissa/Michael Staudig (eds.), *Lebenswelt und Politik. Perspektiven der Phänomenologie nach Husserl*, Würzburg, pp. 17-29.

Herder, Johann Gottfried (1989 [1784]): "Ideen zur Philosophie der Geschichte der Menschheit. Erster Teil. Vorrede." In: Johann Gottfried Herder, *Werke*, vol. 6: *Ideen zur Philosophie der Geschichte der Menschheit*, ed. by Martin Bollacher, Frankfurt/M.

Herder, Johann Gottfried (2002): *Ideen zur Philosophie der Geschichte der Menschheit. Werke*, ed. by Wolfgang Pross, vol. III/1, Darmstadt.

Hess, Ursula (1988): "Lateinischer Dialog und gelehrte Partnerschaft: Frauen als humanistische Leitbilder in Deutschland (1500-1550)." In: Gisela Brinker-Gabler (ed.), *Deutsche Literatur von Frauen*, Munich, pp. 113-148.

Holenstein, Elmar (1998): "Intra- und interkulturelle Hermeneutik." In: idem, *Kulturphilosophische Perspektiven: Schulbeispiel Schweiz; europäische Identität auf dem Prüfstand; globale Verständigungsmöglichkeiten*, Frankfurt/M., pp. 257-287.

Horton, Robin (1960): "African Traditional Religion and Western Science." In: Africa 37.1 and 2, pp. 50-71; pp. 155-187.

Hountondji, Paulin (1983): *African Philosophy – Myth and Reality*, Bloomington.

Huntington, Samuel F. (1997): *Clash of Civilisations and the Remaking of World Order*, London.

Irele, Abiola (ed.) (1975): *The Cambridge History of African and Caribbean Literature*, Cambridge.

Iser, Wolfgang (1991): *Das Fiktive und das Imaginäre: Perspektiven literarischer Anthropologie*, Frankfurt/M.

James, William (1982): *The Varieties of Religious Experience: A Study in Human Nature*, ed. and intr. Martin E. Marty, Harmondsworth/New York.

Jameson, Fredric (1972): *The Prison-House of Language: A Critical Account of Structuralism and Russian Formalism*, Princeton, N.J.

Jardine, Alice (1985): *Gynesis: Configurations of Woman and Modernity*, Ithaca, NY.

Jauss, Hans Robert (1984): *Ästhetische Erfahrung und literarische Hermeneutik*, Frankfurt/M.

Joas, Hans (2004): *Braucht der Mensch Religion? Über Erfahrungen der Selbsttranszendenz*.

Johnson, Pauline (1994): *Feminism as Radical Humanism*, Sydney.

Kant, Immanuael (1985): *On History*. Lewis White Beck (ed.), Indianopolis, Ind.

Kant, Immanuael (1987 [1790]): *Critique of Judgement*. Transl. Werner Pluhar, Indianapolis.

Kaufmann, F.X. (2001): "Globalisierung." In: *Lexikon für Theologie und Kirche*, vol. 11, pp. 98-113.

Kaul-Seidman, Lisa/Nielsen, Jorgen S./Vinzent, Markus (2003): *European Identity and Cultural Pluralism: Judaism, Christianity and Islam in European Curricula*. 2 vols., Bad Homburg v. d. Höhe.

Kaunda, Kenneth (1976): *A Humanist in Africa – Letters to Colin M. Morris*, Lusaka.

Kaye, James/Stråth, Bo (eds.) (2000): *Enlightenment and Genocide: Contradictions of Modernity*, Brussels.

King, Anthony D. (ed.) (1998): *Culture, Globalization and the World-System: Contemporary Conditions for the Representation of Identity*, Minneapolis.

King, Margaret L. (2005): *Humanism, Venice and Women: Essays on the Italian Renaissance*, Burlington.

King, Margaret L./Rabil, Jr., Albert (eds.) (1983): *Her Immaculate Hand: Selected Works By and About the Women Humanists of Quattrocento Italy*, Binghamton, N.Y.

Kobusch, Theo (²1997): *Die Entdeckung der Person: Metaphysik der Freiheit und modernes Menschenbild*, Darmstadt.

Konersmann, Ralf (2002): "Der 'cultural turn' in der Philosophie." In: Dirk Rustemeyer (ed.), *Symbolische Welten*, Würzburg, pp. 67-90.

Konersmann, Ralf (2006): *Kulturelle Tatsachen*, Frankfurt/M.

Koppe, Franz (1983): *Grundbegriffe der Ästhetik*, Frankfurt/M.

Koselleck, Reinhart (1979): *Historische Semantik und Begriffsgeschichte*, Stuttgart.

Koselleck Reinhart (1987): "Historik und Hermeneutik." In: idem, *Zeitschichten: Studien zur Historik*, Frankfurt/M., repr. 2003, pp. 97-118.

Koselleck, Reinhart (1988 [1954/1959]: *Critique and Crisis: Enlightenment and the Pathogenesis of Modern Society*, Oxford.

Kozlarek, Oliver (2000): *Universalien, Eurozentrismus, Logozentrismus: Kritik am disjunktiven Denken der Moderne*, Frankfurt/M.

Kracauer, Siegfried (1968): "General History and the Aesthetic Approach." In: H. R. Jauß (ed.), *Die nicht mehr schönen Künste: Grenzphänomene des Ästhetischen*, Munich, repr. 1983, pp. 111-127.

Kraemer, Joel (1986): *Humanism in the Renaissance of Islam: The Cultural Revival during the Buyid Age*, Leiden.

Krech, Volkhard (1998): *Georg Simmels Religionstheorie*, Tübingen.

Kroeze, I. J. (2002): "Doing Things with Values II: The Case of Ubuntu." In: Stellenbosch Law Review 2, p. 260.

Küng, Hans (ed.) (1995): *Ja zum Weltethos: Perspektiven für die Suche nach Orientierung*, Munich.

Lando, Ortensio (1544): *Paradossi cioe, sententie fuori del comun parere, novellamente venute in luce*, Venice.

Larrain, Jorge (1994): *Ideology and Cultural Identity: Modernity and the Third World Presence*, Oxford.

Larsen, Anne K. (1987): "Les Dames des Roches." In: Katharina M. Wilson (ed.), *Women Writers of the Renaissance and Reformation*, Athens, Georgia, pp. 250-256.

Lategan, B. (1999): "Kulturelle Diversität als strategische Chance." In: Jörn Rüsen/H. Leitgeb/Norbert Jegelka (eds.), *Zukunftsentwürfe: Ideen für eine Kultur der Veränderung*, Frankfurt/M., pp. 157-164.

Laurens, André du (1595): *Anatomica humani corporis historia*, Frankfurt/M.

Leclerc, Gérard (1972): *Anthropologie et colonialisme: Essai sur l'histoire de l'africanisme*, Paris.

Levinas, Emmanuel (1987): *Totalität und Unendlichkeit: Versuch über die Exteriorität*, transl. into German by Wolfgang Nikolaus Krewani, Freiburg/Munich.

Levi-Strauss, Claude (1972): *Rasse und Geschichte*, Frankfurt/M.

Li, Dazhao (1984): *Collection of Works of Li Dazhao*, vol. 2, Beijing.

Lichtenstein, Aaron (1981): *The Seven Laws of Noah*, New York.

Liebsch, Burkhard (1999): *Moralische Spielräume: Menschheit und Anderheit, Zugehörigkeit und Identität*, Essen.

Liu, Baonan (1954): "Lunyu zhengyi [The Correct Meaning of the Analects]." In: *Zhuzi jicheng [Collection of Distinguished Philosophical Works]*. 8 vols., Beijing.

Löwith, Karl 1949: *Meaning in History: The Theological Implications of the Philosophy of History*, Chicago.

Lübbe, Hermann (2004): *Religion nach der Aufklärung*, 3rd. ed., Munich.

Luhmann, Niklas (1986): "Das Kunstwerk und die Selbstreproduktion der Kunst." In: Hans Ulrich Gumbrecht/K. Ludwig Pfeiffer (eds.), *Stil: Geschichten und Funktionen eines kulturwissenschaftlichen Diskurselements*, Frankfurt/M., pp. 620-672.

Luhmann, Niklas (2000): *Die Religion der Gesellschaft*, Frankfurt/M..

Lüsebrink, Hans-Jürgen (2005): *Interkulturelle Kommunikation*, Stuttgart.

Lustig, M.W./Koester, J. (ed.) (2003): *Intercultural Competence: Interpersonal Communication Across Cultures*, Boston.

Lyotard, Jean-François (1993): *Moralités postmodernes*, Paris.

Lyotard, Jean-François (1997): *Postmodern Fables*, Mineapolis/London.

Maalouf, A. (2001), *On Identity*, London.

Macamo, Elísio (1999): *Was ist Afrika? Zur Soziologie und Kulturgeschichte eines modernen Konstrukts*, Berlin.

Macamo, Elísio (2005): *Negotiating Modernity: Africa's Ambivalent Experience*, London/Dakar.

Macamo, Elisio (2006): "Accounting for Disaster: Memories of War in Mozambique." In: Africa-Spectrum 41, pp. 199-219.

Macey, David (2000): *Frantz Fanon: A Biography*, New York.

Maclean, Ian (1980): *The Renaissance Notion of Woman: A Study in the Fortunes of Scholasticism and Medical Science in European Intellectual Life*, Cambridge. Republished as Maclean, I. (1999): "Medicine, Anatomy and Physiology." In: Lorna Hutson (ed.), *Feminism and Renaissance Studies*, Oxford.

Magnusson, Lars/Stråth, Bo (eds.) (2004): *A European Social Citizenship? Preconditions for Future Policies from a Historical Perspective*, Brussels.

Magonet, Jonathan (2003): *Talking to the Other: Jewish Interfaith Dialogue with Christians and Muslims*, London.

Makdisi, George (1990): *The Rule of Humanism in Classical Islam and the Christian West, with Special Reference to Scholasticism*, Edinburgh.

Mandela, Nelson (1994): *Long Walk to Freedom*, Randburg.

Mannheim, Karl (1936): *Ideology and Utopia*, transl. Louis Wirth and Edward Shils, New York; German original: Bonn 1929.

Mannheim, Karl (1985): *Ideologie und Utopie*, Frankfurt/M.

Mansbridge, Jane J. (ed.) (1990): *Beyond Self-Interest 1990*, Chicago.

Marinella, Lucrezia (1600): *Dell'eccellenza e nobiltà delle donne*. English transl. *The Nobility and Excellence of Women, and the Defects and Vices of Men*, ed. and transl. Anne Dunhill, Chicago 1999.

Marshall, T. H. (1992 [1950]: *Citizenship and Social Class*, London.

Marx, Karl/Engels, Friedrich (⁶1972): *Werke*, vol. 4, Berlin.

Mauss, Marcel (1992): *The Gift*, London.

Mauss-Copeaux, Claire (1999): *Appelés en Algérie: La parole confisquée*, Paris.

Max-Neef, M. (1991): *Human Scale Development: Conception, Application and further Reflections*, New York.

Mbeki, Thabo (1998): *Africa: The Time has Come*, Cape Town, pp. 31-36.

Mbembe, Achille (1992): "The Banality of Power and the Aesthetics of Vulgarity in the Postcolony." In: Public Culture 4, pp. 1-30.

McHale, Brian (1987): *Postmodernist Fiction*, London.

Mehta, Linn Cary (2004): *Poetry and Decolonization: Tagore, Yeats, Senghor, Césaire, and Neruda, 1914-1950*. Ph.D thesis, Columbia University.

Menasse, Robert (2001): *Die Vertreibung aus der Hölle*, Frankfurt/M.

Meredith, George (1968): *The Egoist*, Harmondsworth.

Miquel, André (1976): *La Géographie humaine du monde musulman jusqu'au milieu du 11e siècle*, 2nd ed., Paris.

Moi, Toril (1985): *Sexual/Textual Politics: Feminist Literary Theory*, London.

Mol, Hans (1976): *Identity and the Sacred: A Sketch for a new Social Scientific Theory of Religion*, Oxford.

Mottahedeh, Roy (1980): *Loyalty and Leadership in an Early Islamic Society*, Princeton.

Motzki, Harald (2004): *Hadith: Origins and Developments*, Aldershot.

Mudimbe, Valentin Y. (1988): *The Invention of Africa: Gnosis, Philosophy, and the Order of Knowledge*, London.

Müller, F. Max (ed.) (1995): "Upanishads." In: idem, *The Sacred Books of the East*, vol. 15. Delhi.

Müller, F. Max (ed.) (1996): "Hsiao King." In: idem, *The Sacred Books of the East*, vol. 3, Delhi.

Muthu, Sankar (2003): *Enlightenment against Empire*, Princeton, N.J.

Nagel, Thomas (1970): *The Possibility of Altruism*, Princeton, N.J.

Neusner, Jack (ed.) (1983): *Take Judaism, For Example: Studies toward the Comparison of Religions*, Chicago/ London.

Neville, Robert C. (ed.) (2001): *Ultimate Realities: A Volume in the Comparative Religious Ideas Project*, Albany.

Newman, John Henry (1996 [1873]): *The Idea of a University*, New Haven.

Niethammer, Friedrich Immanuel (1968 [1808]): "Der Streit des Philanthropinismus und Humanismus in der Theorie des Erziehungsunterrichts unserer Zeit." In: idem, *Philanthropinismus – Humanismus: Texte zur Schulreform*, Weinheim/Berlin/Basel, pp. 79-445.

Nkrumah, Kwame (1973): *Autobiography of Kwame Nkrumah*, London.

Noble, David (1992): *A World Without Women: The Christian Clerical Culture of Western Science*, Oxford.

Norman, Richard (2004): *On Humanism*, London.

Novak, David (1983): *The Image of the Non-Jew in Judaism: An Historical and Constructive Study of the Noahide Laws*, New York.

Nussbaum, Martha C. (1997): *Cultivating Humanity: A Classical Defense of Reform in Liberal Education*, Cambridge.

Nussbaum, Martha (2000): *Women and Human Development: The Capabilities Approach*, New York.

Nyerere, Julius (1968): *Ujamaa: Essays on Socialism*, Dar es Salaam.

Obeyesekere, Gananath (1992): *The Apotheosis of Captain Cook: European Mythmaking in the Pacific*, Princeton.

Old, W. Gorn (ed.) (1906): *Book of History*, s.l.

Olson, Niklas (2006): "Revising Historicism: Reinhart Koselleck's Search for a Historical Ontology in the Aftermath of World War." In: *Seminar paper in the framework of ongoing PhD Thesis work at the European University Institute*, Florence.

Paranjape, Makarand (ed.) (2005): *Swami Vivekananda Reader*, New Delhi.

Patocka, Jan (1990): *Essais hérétiques sur la philosophie de l'histoire*, repr. Paris.

Paulsen, Friedrich (1885): *Geschichte des gelehrten Unterrichts auf den deutschen Schulen und Universitäten vom Ausgang des Mittelalters bis zur Gegenwart*, Leipzig.

Peters, J./Wolper, A. (eds.) (1995): *Women's Rights, Human Rights: International Feminist Perspectives*, London.

Pfeiffer, G. K. Ludwig (1985): "Präsuppositionen kulturellen Schaffens. Studien zu einer Verarbeitungsgeschichte der englischen Literatur im 19. Jahrhundert." In: Hans Ulrich Gumbrecht/Ursula Lin-Heer (eds.), *Epochenschwellen und Epochenstrukturen im Diskurs der Literatur- und Sprachhistorie*, Frankfurt/M., pp. 265-282.

Pico della Mirandola, Giovanni (1953): *Oratio de hominis dignitate: Oration on the Dignity of Man*, transl. Elizabeth Livermore Forbes, Lexington.

Pico della Mirandola, Giovanni (1956): *Oration on the Dignity of Man*, transl. A. Robert Caponigri, Washington, D.C., pp. 7-8.

Pisan, Christine de (1959-1966): *Livre de la mutacion de Fortune*, (ed.) Suzanne Solente, Paris.

Plessner, Helmuth (1924): "Zur Soziologie der modernen Forschung und ihrer Organisation in der deutschen Universität." In: idem, *Gesammelte Schriften*, vol 10, Darmstadt, pp. 7-30.

Poullain de la Barre, François (1673): *De l'égalité des deux sexes*. English translation: idem (1677): *The Woman as Good as Man, or the Equality of Both Sexes*, London.

Poullain de la Barre, François (1674): *De l'éducation des dames pou la condite de l'esprit dans les sciences et dans les mœurs*, Paris.

Quirin, Michael (1994): "Kein Weg außerhalb der sechs Klassiker oder doch? Bemerkungen zum Verhältnis von gelehrter Tätigkeit und persönlicher Wertpraxis bei Cui Shu (1740-1816)." In: Monumenta Serica 42, pp. 361-395.

Radermacher, Franz Josef (2004): *Balance or Destruction: Eco-social Market Economy as the Key to Global Sustainable Development*, Vienna.

Radhakrishnan, Sarvapalli (1991): *Eastern Religions and Western Thought*, New Delhi.

Rawls, J. (1999): *The Law of Peoples: with "The Idea of Public Reason Revisited."* Cambridge, Mass.

Reckwitz, Erhard 1990: "Intertextualität postmodern: J. M. Coetzee, *Foe*; John Fowles, *A Maggot*; Julian Barnes, *Flaubert's Parrot*." In: Kunibert Behring/Werner L. Hohmann (eds.), *Wie postmodern ist die Postmoderne?*, Essen, pp. 121-156.

Rice, Philip/Waugh, Patricia (eds.) (1989): "Introduction." In: idem, *Modern Literary Theory: A Reader*, London, pp. 1-4.

Ricoeur, Paul (1985): *Temps et récit: Le temps raconté*, vol. 3, Paris.

Ricoeur, Paul (2006): *Wege der Anerkennung*, Frankfurt/M.

Rieks, Rudolf (1967): *Homo, humanus, humanitas: Zur Humanität in der lateinischen Literatur des ersten nachchristlichen Jahrhunderts*, Munich.

Robertson, Roland (1995): "Glocalization: Time-Space and Homogeneity-Heterogeneity." In: Mike Featherstone/Scott Lash/Roland Robertson (eds.), *Global Modernities*, London, pp. 25-44.

Roches, Madeleine/Roches, Catherine des (2006): *From Mother and Daughter: Poems, Dialogues and Letters by les Dames des Roches*, ed. and transl. Anne R. Larsen, Chicago.

Romus Devasahayam, J. (2007): *Human Dignity in Indian Secularism and Christianity: Christianity in Dialogue with Indian Secularism*, Barrackpore, Calcutta.

Rorty, Richard 1987: "Science as solidarity." In: John S. Nelson et al. (eds.), *The Rhetoric of the Human Sciences*, Madison, pp. 38-58

Rorty, Richard et al. (2004): "What Is Religion´s Future After Metaphysics?" In: Richard Rorty/Gianni Vattimo, *The Future of Religion*, New York, pp. 55-81.

Roseman, Mark (2002): *The Villa, the Lake, the Meeting*, London.

Rosset, Clément (1977): *Le réel: Traité de l'idiotie*, Paris.

Roudiez, Leon, trans. (1991): *Strangers to Ourselves*, New York.

Ruhloff, Jürgen (2001): "Bildung in Europa oder 'europäische Bildung' – Wieviel Einheitlichkeit verträgt die Vielfalt?" In: Klaus Held/ Franz Knipping (eds.), *Europa von innen und außen: Universalität und Partikularität*, Trier, pp. 15-25.

Rüsen, Jörn (2002): "Introduction: Historical Thinking as Intercultural Discourse." In: idem (ed.), *Western Historical Thinking*, New York/ Oxford, pp. 1-11.

Rüsen, Jörn (2002a): *Geschichte im Kulturprozeß*, Cologne.

Rüsen, Jörn (2002b): "Comparing Cultures in Intercultural Communication." In: Eckhardt Fuchs/Benedikt Stuchtey (eds.), *Across Cultural Borders. Historiography in Global Perspective*, Oxford/New York, pp. 335-347.

Rüsen, Jörn (2003): "Following Kant: European Idea for a Universal History with an Intercultural Intent." In: Groniek. Historisch Tijdschrift 36, pp. 359-368.

Rüsen, Jörn (2004): "How to Compare Cultures? The Case of Historical Thinking." In: Journal of the Interdisciplinary Crossroads 1.3, pp. 481-504.

Rüsen, Jörn (2007): "Ethnozentrismus und seine Überwindung: Ansätze einer Kultur der Anerkennung durch Geschichte im 20. Jahrhundert." In: Michael Kastner (ed.), *Kultursynergien oder Kulturkonflikte? Eine interdisziplinäre Fragestellung*, Lengerich.

Rüsen, Jörn (2007a): Towards a New Idea of Human Kind – Unity and Difference of Cultures in the Crossroads of Our Time: unpublished manuscript.

Rüsen, Jörn ([2]2008): *Historische Orientierung: Über die Arbeit des Geschichtsbewußtseins, sich in der Zeit zurechtzufinden*, Schwalbach/T.

Rüsen, Jörn (2008a): "Leidensverdrängung und Trostbedarf im historischen Denken." In: Tiemo Rainer Peters/Claus Urban (eds.), *Über den Trost: Für Johann Baptist Metz*, Ostfildern, pp. 76-84.

Rüsen, Jörn (2008b): "Humanism in Response to the Holocaust – Destruction or Innovation?" In: Postcolonial Studies 11.2, June, pp. 191-200.

Ryan, Marie-Laure (1991): *Possible Worlds, Artificial Intelligence and Narrative Theory*, Bloomington, Indiana.

Sacks, Jonathan (2003): *The Chief Rabbi's Haggadah*, London.

Sahlins, Marshall (1987): *Islands of History*, London.

Sartre, Jean Paul (1986): *L'imaginaire: Psychologie phénoménologique de l'imagination*, 2nd ed., Paris.

Sartre, Jean-Paul (1972): *Orphée noire*, Paris.

Saussy, Haun ed. (2004): *Comparative Literature in an Age of Globalization* Baltimore, Maryland.

Sayers, Dorothy (1971): *Are Women Human?* Intr. Mary McDermott Shideler, Grand Rapids, Mich.

Schiller, Friedrich (1993): "Über die ästhetische Erziehung des Menschen in einer Reihe von Briefen." In: idem, *Sämtliche Werke*, vol. 5, Darmstadt, pp. 570-669.

Schivelbusch, Wolfgang (2005): *Entfernte Verwandtschaft: Faschismus, Nationalsozialismus, New Deal 1933-1939*, Munich.

Schwartz, Benjamin I. (1975): "The Age of Transcendence." In: Benjamin I. Schwartz (ed.), *Wisdom, Revelation, and Doubt: Perspectives on the First Millennium B.C.* (Daedalus, Spring), Boston, pp. 3ff.

Sen, Amartya (1990): "Rational Fools: A Critique of the Behavioral Foundations of Economic Theory." In: Jane J. Mansbridge (ed.), *Beyond Self-Interest*, Chicago, pp. 25-43.

Senghaas, D. (1998): *Zivilisierung wider Willen: Der Konflikt der Kulturen mit sich selbst*, Frankfurt/M.

Sénghor, Leopold (1964): *On African Socialism*, New York.

Simmel, Georg (1992): *Soziologie: Untersuchungen über die Formen der Vergesellschaftung*, complete Works, vol. 11, (ed.) Otthein Rammstedt, Frankfurt/M.

Sloterdijk, Peter (2009): *Ändert Euren Sinn!*, Frankfurt/M.

Smith, Stephen 2003: *Négrologie – pourquoi l'Afrique meurt*, Paris.

Snow, C.P. (1963): *The Two Cultures and a second Look 1959*, New York.

Solomon, Norman (1991): *Judaism and World Religion*, Basingstoke.

Soper, Kate (1990): "Feminism, Humanism and Postmodernism." In: Radical Philosophy 55, pp. 11-16. Anthologized in Eagleton, Mary (ed.) (1996): *Feminist Literary Theory: A Reader*. 2nd ed., Oxford, pp. 364-366.

Sorabji, Cornelia (2006): "Managing Memories in Post-War Sarajevo: Individuals, Bad Memories, and New Wars." In: Journal of the Royal Anthropological Institute 12.1, pp. 1-18.

Southern, R. W. (1995): *Scholastic Humanism and the Unification of Europe*, vol. 1: *Foundations*, Oxford.

Stanton, Elizabeth Cady (2001): *The Solitude of Self*, Ashfield, Mass.

Steinem, Gloria (1987): "Humanism and the Second Wave of Feminism: a Four-Point Plan to Carry Feminism and Humanism into the Next Century." In: The Humanist 47, pp. 11-15.

Steiner, George (1989): *Real Presences*, Chicago. Repr. 1991.

Stierle, Karlheinz (1983): "Die Fiktion als Vorstellung, als Werk und als Schema – Eine Problemskizze." In: Dieter Henrich/ Wolfgang Iser (eds.), *Funktionen des Fiktiven: Poetik und Hermeneutik*, vol. 10, Munich, pp. 173-182.

Stora, Benjamin (1991): *La Gangrène et l' oubli: La mémoire de la guerre d' Algérie*, Paris.

Stråth, Bo (2000): *After Full Employment: European Discourses on Work and Flexibility*, Brussels.

Straub, Jürgen (1999): *Handlung, Interpretation, Kritik: Grundzüge einer textwissenschaftlichen Handlungs- und Kulturpsychologie*, Berlin/ New York.

Straub, Jürgen (2004): "Identität." In: Friedrich Jäger/Burkhard Liebsch (eds.), *Handbuch der Kulturwissenschaften: Grundlagen und Schlüsselbegriffe*. Stuttgart, pp. 277-303.

Straub, Jürgen (2007a): "Kultur." In: Straub/Weidemann/Weidemann 2007, pp. 7-24.

Straub, Jürgen (2007b): "Kompetenz." In: Straub/Weidemann/Weidemann 2007, pp. 35-46.

Straub, Jürgen/Renn, Joachim (eds.) (2003): *Transitorische Identität: Der Prozesscharakter des modernen Selbst*, Frankfurt/M., New York.

Straub, Jürgen/Weidemann, Arne/Weidemann, Doris (eds.) (2007): *Handbuch Interkulturelle Kommunikation und Kompetenz*, Stuttgart.

Strauss-Levi, Claude (1972): *Rasse und Geschichte*. Frankfurt/M.

Stuchtey, Benedikt/Fuchs, Eckhardt (eds.) (2007): *Writing world history 1800-2000*, Oxford.

Stuchtey, Benedikt/Fuchs, Eckhardt (2007a): "Introduction. Problems of Writing World History: Western and Non-Western Experiences, 1800-2000." In: Stuchtey/Fuchs 2007, pp.1-44.

Sturma, Dieter (ed.) (2006): *Philosophie und Neurowissenschaften*, Frankfurt/M.

Tagore, Rabindranath (1994): *The Religion of Man*, New Delhi.

Tagore, Rabindranath (transl.) (2002): *Poems of Kabir*, New Delhi.

Tajfel, Henri (ed.) (1981). *Human Groups and Social Categories: Studies in Social Psychology*, Cambridge/New York/Melbourne.

Tarabotti, Arcangela (1651): *Che le donne siano della spezie degli uomini*. English transl. in *Women are not Human: an anonymous treatise and responses*, ed. Th. M. Kenney, New York 1998.

Taylor, Charles (1993): "Politik der Anerkennung." In: Amy Gutman (ed.), *Multikulturalismus und die Politik der Anerkennung. Mit Kommentaren von Amy Gutman, Steven C. Rockefeller, Michael Walzer, Susan Wolf. Mit einem Beitrag von Jürgen Habermas*, Frankfurt/M., pp. 13-78.

Taylor, Charles (2002): *Varieties of Religion Today: William James Revisited*, Cambridge, Mass.

Tempels, Placide (1945): *La philosophie bantoue*, Elisabethville.

Thomas, Alexander (1993): "Psychologie interkulturellen Lernens und Handelns." In: idem (ed.), *Kulturvergleichende Psychologie: Eine Einführung*, Göttingen, pp. 377-424.

Thomas, Alexander (2000): "Forschungen zur Handlungswirksamkeit von Kulturstandards." In: Handlung, Kultur, Interpretation. Zeitschrift für Sozial- und Kulturwissenschaften 9.2, pp. 231-278.

Thomas, Alexander (2003): "Interkulturelle Kompetenz." In: Erwägen, Wissen, Ethik 14.1, pp. 137-150.

Tillich, Paul (1957): *Dynamics of Faith*, New York.

Todorov, Tzvetan (1981): *Introduction to Poetics*, Brighton.

Todorov, Tzvetan (1987): *La notion de littérature*, Paris.

Todorov, Tzvetan (1989): *Nous et les autres: La réflexion française sur la diversité humaine*, Paris.

Todorov, Tzvetan (1998): *Le jardin imparfait*, Grasset.

Tomasevski, Katarina (1993): *Women and Human Rights*, London.

Tönnies, Ferdinand (1963): *Gemeinschaft und Gesellschaft – Grundbegriffe der reinen Soziologie*, Darmstadt.

Tutu, D. (1999): *No future without forgiveness*, New York.

Ueding, Gert (1978): "Literatur ist Utopie." In: Gert Ueding (ed.), *Literatur ist Utopie*, Frankfurt/M., pp. 7-14.

UNESCO (2006): *Culture du dialogue en France et en Turquie: Quels projets pour aujourd'hui?*, Paris.

Van Binsbergen (2002): "Ubuntu and the globalization of South African thought and society." In: Quest. An African Journal of Philosophy 15, pp. 53-89.

Virt, G. (2002): *Der Globalisierungsprozess: Facetten einer Dynamik aus ethischer und theologischer Perspektive*, Freiburg.

Voigt, Georg (1859): *Die Wiederbelebung des classischen Alterthums oder das erste Jahrhundert des Humanismus*, Berlin.

Wagner Peter/Zimmermann, Bénédicte (2004): "Citizenship and Collective Responsibility: On the Political Philosophy of the Nation-Based Welfare State and Beyond." In: Magnusson/Stråth (2004)

Wagner, Peter (1990): *Sozialwissenschaften und Staat: Frankreich, Italien, Deutschland 1870-1980*, Frankfurt/M.

Waldenfels, Bernhard (2006): *Grundmotive einer Phänomenologie des Fremden*, Frankfurt/M.

Wang, Bi (1959): *Laozi zhu [Laozi with Annotations]*, Taipei.

Wattles, Jeffrey (1996): *The Golden Rule*, New York.

Waugh, Patricia (1992): *Practising Postmodernism, Reading Modernism*, London.

Webber, Jonathan (1994): *Jewish Identities in the New Europe*, London/ Washington.

Webber, Jonathan (1997): "Jews and Judaism in Contemporary Europe: Religion or Ethnic Group?" In: Ethnic and Racial Studies 20.2, pp. 257-79.

Weber, Max (1946): "Science as a Vocation." In: H. H. Gerth/C. Wright Mills (eds.), *From Max Weber: Essays in Sociology*, New York, pp.129-156

Weber, Max (1973): "Die 'Objektivität' sozialwissenschaftlicher und sozialpolitischer Erkenntnis." In idem, *Gesammelte Aufsätze zur Wissenschaftslehre*, (ed.) Johannes Winkelmann, 4th edn. Tübingen, pp. 146-214.

Weber, Max (2000): *Die protestantische Ethik I: Eine Aufsatzsammlung*. Ed. J. Winckelmann, 9th edition, Gütersloh.

Weidemann, Doris (2004): *Interkulturelles Lernen: Erfahrungen mit dem chinesischen 'Gesicht': Deutsche in Taiwan*, Bielefeld.

Weidemann, Doris (2007): "Akkulturation und interkulturelles Lernen." In: Straub/Weidemann/Weidemann 2007, pp. 488-498.

White, Louise (2000): *Speaking with Vampires – Rumour and History in Colonial Africa*, Berkeley.

Wilder, Gary (2005): *The French Imperial Nation-State: Negritude and Colonial Humanism*, Chicago.

Willard, Charity Cannon (1984): *Christine de Pizan: Her Life and Works*, New York.

Wils, J.P. (ed.) (2004): *Die Moral der Religion: Kritische Sichtungen und konstruktive Vorschläge*, Paderborn.

Wiredu, Kwasi (1984): "How not to Compare African Traditional Thought with Western Science." In: Richard Wright (ed.), *African Philosophy – An Introduction*, Lanham, pp. 166-184.

Wittgenstein, Ludwig (1961 [1921]): *Tractatus Logico-Philosophicus*. Transl. by D. S. Pears and B. F. McGuinness. With an Introduction by Bertrand Russell, London/New York repr. 2007.

Wittrock, Björn (2000): "Modernity: One, None, or Many? European Origins and Modernity as a Global Condition." In: Daedalus 20.2, pp. 31-36.

Wood, Diane S. (2000): *Hélisenne de Crenne: At the Crossroads of Renaissance Humanism. And Feminism*, London.

Woolf, Virginia (1929): *A Room of One's Own*, London.

Yates Frances (1964): *Bruno and the Hermetic Tradition*, London.

Yates Frances (1979): *The Occult Philosphy in the Elisabethan Age*, London.

Zammito, John H. (2002): *Kant, Herder, and the Birth of Anthropology*, Chicago.

Zhang, Longxi (1998): *Mighty Opposites: From Dichotomies to Differences in the Comparative Study of China*, Stanford.

Zimmerman, Joshua (ed.) (2003): *Contested Memories: Poles and Jews during the Holocaust and its Aftermath*, New Brunswick, NJ.

Zühlke, Bärbel (1994): *Christine de Pizan in Text und Bild: zur Selbstdarstellung einer frühhumanistischen Intellektuellen*, Stuttgart.

Index of Names

Notes on the Contributors

Arkoun, Muhammad born in Taourirt-Mimoun (Algeria), was professor of History of Islamic Thought at the Sorbonne up to 1992. He studied in Algiers and Paris (Sorbonne) and was Visiting Professor and Fellow at numerous universities in Europe, America, the Arab world, Africa and Asia. He is the director of ARABICA, *Journal of Arabic and Islamic Studies*. His main area of interest is the study of the history of Islamic thought. The periods of his research stretch from medieval philosophy and theology to contemporary thought, with a focus on Islamic thought in the Mediterranean. His works on the issue of humanism include *Humanisme et Islam: Combats et Propositions* (2006), *L'Humanisme arabe au 4e/10e siècle* (2005) and *The Unthought in Contemporary Islamic Thought* (2002).

Chakrabarty, Dipesh born in Calcutta, India, and educated in Calcutta and Canberra, is the Lawrence A. Kimpton Distinguished Service Professor of History and South Asian Studies at the University of Chicago. He is also a long-term Visiting Fellow of the Centre for Cross-Cultural Research, Australian National University, Canberra. He has held several visiting positions at universities in the USA, India and Germany. He is a founding editor of the series Subaltern Studies: Writings on Indian Society and History, and Postcolonial Studies. His publications include *Provincializing Europe: Postcolonial Thought and Historical Difference* (2000) and *Habitations of Modernity: Essays in the Wake of Subaltern Studies* (2002).

Chen, Yunqian born in 1935 in Shanghai, China, is senior fellow and professor at the Institute of Philosophy, Chinese Academy of Social Sciences (Beijing). He is former director of the institute (1991-1998) and former editor-in-chief of the journal *Philosophic Research* (1990-2003). His has published numerous books in the fields of philosophy and cultural studies, including *View on History, View on Truth, View on Value* (1995), *Philosophy and Culture* (1996), *Scientific and Technologic Revolution in the Contemporary World* (2001) (all in Chinese).

Essen, Georg born in 1961, is Chair of Dogmatic Theology, Faculty of Theology at the Radboud University of Nijmegen since 2001. Since 2006, he is also Chair of Theory of Religion and Culture, Faculty of Religious Studies in Nijmegen. He studied Catholic Theology and History in Münster and Freiburg (Germany). In 1994 he recevied his PhD (Dr. theol.), and 1999 the Habilitation (venia legendi for "Dogmatic Theology") at the Faculty of Catholic Theology Münster. His publications include *Sinnstiftende Unruhe im System des Rechts: Religion im Beziehungsgeflecht von modernem Verfassungsstaat und säkularer Zivilgesellschaft* (2004).

Graf, Friedrich Wilhelm born in 1948, is Chair of Systematic Theology and Ethics at the University of Munich. He studied Protestant Theology in Wuppertal, Tübingen and Munich. He taught at the University of Augsburg and the University of the Federal Armed Forces in Hamburg. He was Visiting Professor or Research Fellow at several universities, including Seigakuin University in Tokyo and the University of Pretoria. He is a member of numerous scientific associations and president of the Ernst-Troeltsch-Gesellschaft. His publications cover various topics of systematic theological studies (dogmatics, ethics and the philosophy of religion), with a focus on a contemporary perspective on a history of Christian thought.

Hanafi, Hassan born in 1935 in Cairo, has been professor of philosophy at Cairo University and Secretary General of the Egyptian Philosophical society since 1976. In 1966 he made his PhD in philosophy at Sorbonne University, Paris. Since 1983, he has been Vice-president of the Arab philosophical society. His many books were published in French, English and Arabic. He is the author of a major publication project on tradition and modernism based on three themes: first, the reconstruction of Islamic classical sciences: theology, philosophy, jurisprudence, mysticism and scriptural sciences; second, the foundation of the science of occidentalism to study the West and third, a theory of reality as hermeneutics.

Krech, Volkhard is professor for religious studies at Ruhr University Bochum. He studied Protestant Theology, Comparative Religious Studies, Sociology and Philosophy in Heidelberg and Bielefeld. His fields of research include the theory of religion with a social science approach, religious pluralism and globalization, religion and violence and history of the science of religion. His publications include *Götterdämmerung: Auf der Suche nach Religion* (2003) and *Wissenschaft und Religion:. Studien zur Geschichte der Religionsforschung in Deutschland 1871 bis 1933* (2002).

Laass, Henner Dr. phil, born in 1943, is co-editor of *Interkultureller Humanismus. Menschlichkeit in der Vielfalt der Kulturen* (2009) (with Jörn Rüsen). Publications of his include: *Samuel Beckett. Dramatische Form als Medium der Reflexion* (1978) and *Samuel Beckett* (1984) (with Wolfgang Schröder).

Lategan, Bernard C. born in 1938, was Director of the Stellenbosch Institute for Advanced Study (STIAS) (1999-2008) and Professor of Biblical Studies at the University of Stellenbosch (1977-2003). He taught at the Universities of Göttingen and Hamburg and was a research fellow at various universities in Europe and the USA. His special interests are the theory and practice of interpretation, intercultural communication, values studies and processes of social transformation and he has published extensively in this field, including *The Reader and Beyond* (1992) and *Focusing on the Message* (2009).

Macamo, Elisio is Professor of African Studies at the University of Basle in Switzerland. He holds a doctorate and a qualification to teach in higher education in Sociology from the University of Bayreuth. He was postdoctoral fellow at the graduate school on Intercultural Relations in Africa, research fellow at the Center for African Studies of the Instituto Superior de Ciências do Trabalho e de Empresa, Lisbon, as well as AGORA-Fellow at the Institute of Advanced Studies in Berlin and taught development sociology at the University of Bayreuth until September 2009. His publications include *Unraveling ties – From social cohesion to new practices of connectedness* (2002) (jointly edited with Yehuda Elkana, Ivan Krastev and Shalini Randeria) and *Negotiating Modernity. Africa's ambivalent experience* (2005).

Munshi, Surendra was Professor of Sociology at the Indian Institute of Management, Calcutta. He has researched and taught in India and abroad in the fields of classical sociological theory, sociology of culture, and industrial sociology. His current research interests include good governance and 'excellence' in individual and organisational domains. He led an international project on good governance with the support of the European Commission in which several European institutions of higher education took part, the outcome of which has appeared as a book under the title *Good Governance, Democratic Societies and Globalization*. His other publications cover topics such as *Ethics in the Era of Globalization,* and intercultural perspectives on Max Webers' sociology of religion.

Pomata, Gianna teaches women's history at the Johns Hopkins University in Baltimore. Her research interests include women's and gender history, the history of medicine and the history of historiography. She is the author of *Contracting a Cure: Patients, Healers, and the Law in Early Modern Bologna* (1998), and the co-editor of *The Faces of Nature in Enlightenment Europe* (2003) (with Lorraine Daston), *I monasteri femminili come centri di cultura fra Rinascimento e Barocco, Edizioni di Storia e Letteratura* (2005) (with Gabriella Zarri) and *Historia: Empiricism and Erudition in Early Modern Europe* (2005) (with Nancy Siraisi).

Reckwitz, Erhard is dean for the humanities at the University of Duisburg-Essen and holds a chair for English Language and Literature Studies. He is general editor of *African Literatures in English*. Publications of his include

Mfecane and Boer War. Versions of South African History (1991) (with Elmar Lehmann), *South African Literary History-Totality and/or Fragment* (1997) (with Karin Reitner and Lucia Vennarini) and *Constructing South African Literary History* (2000) (with Elmar Lehmann and Lucia Vennarini).

Rüsen, Jörn born in 1938, was president of the Institute for Advanced Study in the Humanities, Essen, and is professor for general history and historical culture at the University of Witten/Herdecke. He held chairs for modern history at the University of Bochum (1974-1989), and general history at the University of Bielefeld (1989-1997) before becoming president of the Institute of Advanced Study in the Humanities in 1997. His fields of research include theory of history and historiography, strategies of intercultural comparison, general issues of cultural orientation and intercultural communication in modern societies and last not least humanism in a globalizing world. His books are translated in many languages among them Bulgarian, Chinese and Russian. Recent publications are *History: Narration – Interpretation-Orientation* (2005) and *Kultur macht Sinn* (2006).

Stråth, Bo is professor of Contemporary History at the European University Institute, Florence. Before assuming his appointment at the EUI in 1997, he had been Professor of History at Gothenburg University since 1990. He has also been visiting professor in Aarhus, Berlin, Bielefeld, Frankfurt/ Main, Paris and Tokyo and has participated as expert member in a number of national and international evaluation committees. Stråth has published widely on political and economic processes. His current research focuses on the modernity of Europe and the images of Europe as well as the cultural construction of community. In recent years, he has widely published in the areas of national and European identities, namely on boundary construction of Europe, collective identity and collective memory in Europe, European discourses on work and unemployment and on enlightenment and genocide in European modernity. Recent publications include *Europe and the Other and Europe as the Other* (2000) and *The Meaning of Europe: Variety and Contention within and among Nations* (2002).

Straub, Jürgen is now professor of Social Theory and Social Psychology at the Ruhr-University Bochum. Before he was professor of Intercultural Communication at the Chemnitz University of Technology 2002-2008. In April 2004, he began leading the research group (Graduate School Intercultural) Communication – Intercultural Competence at the KWI and at the TU Chemnitz. Since 2008 he is co-leader of the project *Humanism in the Era of Globalization* at KWI.

Straub's general research topics are cultural psychology, intercultural communication and competence, methodology of qualitative research, identity theory, biography research, and historical consciousness. His recent book publications include *Pursuit of Meaning* (Bielefeld 2006, co-edited with Doris Weidemann, Carlos Koelbl, Barbara Zielke) and *Handbuch*

Interkulturelle Kommunikation und Kompetenz (Stuttgart 2007, co-edited with Arne and Doris Weidemann).

Thapar, Romila born in 1931, currently Professor Emeritus in History at the Jawaharlal Nehru University, New Delhi. She has had short term visiting appointments at universities such as London, Cornell, Pennsylvania, Columbia, the Library of Congress and the College de France in Paris. She was President of the Indian History Congress in 1983.

Her research interests are primarily in the social and cultural history of early South Asia and in aspects of historiography relating to this period. The titles of some of her books are: *Asoka and the Decline of the Mauryas* (1961), *History of India* (1966), *From Linege to State* (1984), *Cultural Pasts* (2000), *Early India* (2002), and *Somanatha* (2004).

Webber, Jonathan was trained as a social anthropologist at Oxford University, where he taught for twenty years, at the Oxford Centre for Hebrew and Jewish Studies and the Institute for Social and Cultural Anthropology. In 2002 he moved to the University of Birmingham, where he holds the UNESCO Chair in Jewish and Interfaith Studies. His principal research interests include the sociology of the contemporary Jewish diaspora, Holocaust studies, biblical studies, museum studies, and Polish–Jewish studies. He has been a member of the International Council of the Auschwitz Museum since 1990. Prof. Webber has held major research grants from the Economic and Research Council of the UK and from the European Commission; and he has held visiting fellowships in Germany and Hungary.

Zhang, Longxi, is professor of Comparative Literature and Translation at the City University of Hong Kong. He holds an MA from Peking University and a PhD from Harvard University. He has taught at Peking, Harvard, and the University of California, Riverside. He has many publications in both Chinese and English, and his major book publications include *The Tao and the Logos: Literary Hermeneutics, East and West* (1992); *Mighty Opposites: From Dichotomies to Differences in the Comparative Study of China* (1998); *Out of the Cultural Ghetto* (in Chinese) (2004) and *Ten Essays in Chinese-Western Cross-Cultural Studies* (in Chinese) (2005).